THE RISE AND FALL OF THE AUSTRALIAN DEMOCRATS

AN EYEWITNESS ACCOUNT

BEV FLOYD

Published by Watson Ferguson & Company
an imprint of Boolarong Press.

First published: July, 2013 as *Inside Story*

Revised edition: September, 2014 with the title *The Rise and Fall of the Australian Democrats*

National Library of Australia Cataloguing-in-Publication entry

Author:	Floyd, Bev, author.
Title:	The rise and fall of the Australian Democrats : an eyewitness account / Bev Floyd.
Edition:	Revised edition.
ISBN:	9781925046304 (paperback)
Notes:	Includes bibliographical references and index.
Subjects:	Floyd, Bev.
	Australian Democrats. Queensland Division--History.
	Australian Democrats--Officials and employees--Biography.
	Women--Queensland--Biography.
	Queensland--Politics and government--History.

Typeset in Minion Pro 11 pt.

Thanks are due to Matt Mawson for permission to use cartoons on pages 16 and 19. Thanks also to Lyn Allison (the editor of *30 years Australian Democrats*) for permission to use additional material from that publication.

Photos from author's collection.

Printed and bound by Watson Ferguson & Company, Brisbane.

Dedicated to
my good friend
Ron Cullen

CONTENTS

APPENDICES

FOREWORD BY CHERYL KERNOT

Being part of a new political party is an exciting thing. Being part of a progressive one based on participatory democracy was an extra attraction to me, and also an extra challenge for all of us. There's no doubt that in the first years of the Democrats we were energetic, ambitious and idealistic. And naïve.

There were, unsurprisingly, mistakes and personal rifts, but we forged a new way of doing politics … and today the Labor Party National President is elected by Labor members and electronic voting on policies via various sites is a reality as well.

This book is the account of a Democrat insider; one who was both a woman and a Queensland President. Its focus on Queensland makes very interesting reading for those of us who shared the experiences. The author, as did I, took part in the movement to abolish the gerrymander in Queensland. They were memorable times that galvanised a progressive collaboration.

From the historical vantage point of 36 years later, with our memories less acute and our friendships revived or having stood the test of time, this book serves the important role of recording the progress of Australia's significant third party in our political process.

I agree with the author that it's important to record history—what could be more challenging than actually starting a new political party seeking and gaining national representation. I left the Democrats in 1997 because I became increasingly uncomfortable at being required to negotiate with the starting points of Howard Government policies.

My whole experience up to that point had been to seek to improve upon Labor legislation. I thought that my move might contribute momentum to the possibility of defeating the Howard Government. Labor won the majority of votes in 1998, but not the majority of seats.

Existing within a male-dominated factional ALP culture made me appreciate the civility and democracy of the Democrats.

As we witness the current third party, The Greens, mount a Senate campaign using the *Keep the Bastards Honest* subtext, we should never lose sight of the mighty and enduring achievements of the Australian Democrats. It was a privilege to be a part of those times. I am happy to recommend this book. While it chronicles one person's journey, it is also a mirror to the achievements of thousands of Australians who played their role in shaping a fairer and more accountable Australia.

AUTHOR'S PREFACE

This is a book about politics—or at least my experience on the edges of it. In 1977 when the Australian Democrat phenomenon burst onto the political landscape, I found myself part of it. It was a tumultuous ride, but definitely worth the effort. This book endeavours to tell the story of that time.

Some of my friends ask 'Why anyone want to read about politics?' —with a hint more laughter than I appreciate! I reply seriously—one reason is to record what happened. If only a small number read this book, at least it is there. Recording history is a vital responsibility to those who come after us. As George Santayana said, 'Those who cannot remember the past are condemned to repeat it'.

Another reason is to encourage the next generation to 'have a go'; to have a vision of what can be achieved. Australians are fortunate to live in a peaceful and prosperous nation, but it didn't just 'happen'—it needed individuals to put their energy and their time into making Australia the great place it is.

Australian Parliaments *needed* a political party like the Australian Democrats and it *needs* decent, talented people—making decisions based on reason and ethics and doing it with civility. My hope is that some ordinary folk might read this book and think a career in politics a possibility. There are stories of attrition and misadventure in its pages, but don't let these be discouragements. This is a cautionary tale, and I would be happy to think that by reading this book, readers might manage to avoid some of the pitfalls I fell into. And fear not, those of us who took part in the game gained infinitely more than we lost in the struggle to achieve our goals.

ACKNOWLEDGEMENTS

I am very grateful to two writers who assisted with this book — **Patrick Holland** and **John Rumney**. We met on the Internet and our interaction has continued there. While the substance and views of *The Rise and Fall of the Australian Democrats* are mine, the editing and reorganising that my invisible friends contributed has added immeasurably to the outcome. Not only that, but their encouragement and support was invaluable. As this was my first major writing project, I was unsure of my ability to make *Inside Story* sufficiently interesting. Politics is not everyone's light reading. John and Patrick carried me along with their comments, and in John's case, a certain amount of entertaining detail. I think only John could make detail so fascinating.

John is a freelance journalist whose generosity of spirit and practical comments have given me an insight into my writing—how to make it compact; the pitfalls of libel and irrelevance. He was cheerful and mentoring in turn and I feel I have become a better writer because of him. Patrick Holland is a rising young novelist whose sensibility and imagination livened the descriptions and dialogue. He transformed *Inside Story* by his knowledge of narrative and structure and introduced me to several techniques that suited the story I was endeavouring to tell. However, I made all the final decisions, and if there are any errors they are mine alone. I feel deeply indebted to them both.

Thanks are also due to all of those who agreed to be interviewed and who were generous with their comments—Ron Cullen, Tony Walters, John Woodley, Cheryl Kernot, Meg Lees, Marjorie and George Blair-West, John Cherry, Andrew Bartlett, Aden Ridgeway, Michael Macklin, Lyn Allison, Sam Hudson, Patrick Weller, Bronwyn Stevens, Tracey Arklay, John Sinclair, Paul Reynolds, Terry White—the list goes on. There were also a number of folk who read portions of the manuscript and gave suggestions—among them Fay Lawrence, a founding Democrat member. Their feedback was invaluable.

I now know much more than I need to know … and much, much more than a book of this kind can tell.

1

JOH'S QUEENSLAND

It is 1977 and the longstanding Premier of Queensland, Sir Joh Bjelke-Petersen fronts the media on the stairs of Parliament to make a remarkable declaration: *'The day of street marches is over ... Don't bother applying for a march permit. You won't get one. That's government policy now!'* Liberal member Colin Lamont told a gathering at the University of Queensland that the Premier was *'engineering confrontation for electoral purposes'. 'Two hours later, he (Bjelke-Petersen) lunged at me across the floor of Parliament, waving a tape recorder and spluttered, "I've heard every word. You are a traitor to this Parliament".'* Lamont later learnt of a 'Special Branch' that kept files on Liberal rebels and reported, not to their commissioner, but directly to the Premier. *'The police state had arrived'*... and this was the political jungle, *'red in tooth and claw'*, into which the Queensland Democrats, the party I was later to become president of, were born and must stake out their territory.[1]

Colin Lamont and the author

I grew up in the 50's—the Menzies era—when the country seemed frozen in time. Nothing seemed to change. The war was over. It was a plentiful, balmy time. Jobs were available. Living standards were rising. As a child I would sit with my family around the radio listening to *Dad and Dave* or the chimes of the Westminster clock signalling the ABC news. Radio was king then, but TV was beginning to challenge its supremacy.

In the 50's we were schooled in the belief that prosperity would follow now that the war had been fought and won. Henceforth we could expect peace and prosperity. We weren't worried about drugs or terrorists or really much at all. We knew the outside world through cinema newsreels.

Mine was a family with ties in England. My great-grandfather, Arthur Howard, brought his whole family out from Cambridge to Queensland in 1907 to settle on a cane plantation near Bundaberg. In Cambridge my grandmother worked as a maid in a household and my grandfather was apprenticed as a chef in Quays College. As I grew my daydreams were of going to a university just like the one in Cambridge.

Our family admired the Queen and made sure we stood to attention in the cinema when 'God Save the Queen' was played. We didn't drink or smoke or gamble. We lived quiet family lives.

My mother's family were farmers and very generous. We always had produce—bananas, beans, pumpkins, watermelons, cheese, butter, meat. My dad loved to garden and he loved to fish so our spare fridge was always full to overfull. My grandmother regularly sent food parcels to her cousins still living in England. When I visited some of our English relatives in 1961, they repaid me a thousand times over as my grandmother's parcels had been a lifeline during the war. We were spared the full effects of the war. Neither my uncles nor my father went overseas as they were all in protected occupations.

My father's family were a mystery as he always claimed to be an orphan, and it was only years later that I found out more. He came of convict stock—all the way from Wales five generations beforehand. We didn't talk politics much in our home, although I knew my dad supported the unions. We lived in Mount Isa during the time of the 1964 Great Strike and dad was indignant about my comment 'Why don't they just talk it over and work it out?'

Years later after researching his family history I realised they had been in the gold-mining town of Waihi (New Zealand) during a similar Great Strike. It was an innocent comment but like all such childish understandings, it contained more than a gram of common sense and I like to think that my future interest in politics began then.

As a young adult I trained as a teacher and went to Papua New Guinea. When I came back a dozen years later, I found the world as I'd known it as a child and young woman had changed dramatically. In Papua New Guinea I'd missed most of that change. I missed the clamour over the Vietnam War. I missed the protest movements in the USA. I missed most of the music of the times and only caught up on it much later and it was shocking to return to my home State to find it in political and social turmoil.

****

By 1977, the then Premier of Queensland, Joh Bjelke-Petersen, had been returned to power year after year with a level of votes well below 50%. The Country Party managed this by maintaining electoral zones that gave an advantage to country voters. During the 1972 election the Country Party primary vote fell to 20% but, through a system of electoral malapportionment (locally called a gerrymander), the party managed to win sufficient seats to return them as the major coalition partner in government.

Bjelke-Petersen's long term saw the expansion of corruption within the police force and Parliament as well as in other public institutions, such as the media and local government. By 1975 he had been Premier for seven years. He was to stay in that position for another 12 years—long, frustrating and appalling years to those opposed to his type of governing and the problematic legitimacy of his rule.*

It is difficult for me to express my amazement at the behaviour of the Bjelke-Petersen Government. He had no appreciation of the traditions of Westminster Government. He was a law unto himself. But, despite opposition from Trade Unions and sections of the Church he continued to flourish.

I was drawn into the protest marches in 1977 when the declaration that began this chapter was made. The refusal of permits for public demonstration was a response to increasing ire against companies involved in uranium mining and the visit of the South African Rugby Union team.

South Africa's policy of apartheid meant sanctions were implemented in every state in Australia including the refusal to host South African sporting teams—every state, that is, except Joh's Queensland. This was a red rag to a bull for social activists who organised protest marches. When protesters were denied permits to march and the marches were declared illegal, police were called out in large numbers to enforce the orders and they used unwarranted violence to quell the marchers. Many of my friends and people I later met in the Australian Democrats were politically radicalised.

* Result of 1972 election, Country Party 20% and 26 seats; Liberals 22.23% and 21 seats; ALP 42.23% and 33 seats; 2 independents take the total seats up to 82.

The original issue—mining and the sale of uranium was lost in the street march furore. The Government wanted the transport of uranium oxide from the Mary Kathleen mine in North-West Queensland to continue. One hot and humid day I stood on the footpath in the centre of Brisbane city to observe a protest march. As I walked along I could see police massing in a side street while in the main street marchers had come to a halt and were sitting down.

At this point all was peaceful. Then the marchers were ordered to disperse. A Federal Parliamentarian, George Georges and other members of Parliament who were there as observers approached senior police and asked for some leeway in order to avoid trouble.*

While this was happening a large contingent of police had moved to the back of the marchers who were now surrounded and police began making arrests. It was a rough business—also dangerous. I was among onlookers who were being pushed back from the footpath and pressed into plate glass shop windows behind us.

Fearful but not wanting to leave, I watched as marchers linked arms and sat doggedly. One by one they were dragged across the bitumen and pushed unceremoniously into waiting vans. Police grabbed fistfuls of hair; put people in headlocks; man-handled limp bodies awkwardly into the vans.

The protesters were not just the young and rebellious but all ages and classes of Queenslanders who were united by their dislike of civil repression.

It was clear to those of us near the violence that the police force was in a state of generalised corruption. The Premier had knowledge through a cabinet minister, Don Lane, (former special branch policeman) about key players in the force. The Fitzgerald Inquiry later confirmed that from the police commissioner down, police were acting corruptly and carrying out violent and intimidating acts on anyone opposing them or the Government.

We all joked about our phones being tapped, but perhaps the joke was on us. Special Branch officers attended all the protest marches and photographed anyone and everyone. It was not uncommon for retribution to occur in the workplace. Many courageous people suffered when they endeavoured to speak out against the police or the Government.

John Sinclair, a public servant as well as president of the Fraser Island Defenders' Organisation (FIDO), was pursued by Joh for comments he had made about mining on the island. I knew John a little as he worked in Technical and Further Education (TAFE) as I did. His life was turned upside down by the pressure. He had suffered three unsolicited transfers in the

* However, the Parliamentarians were told to leave and when they declined, were arrested.

previous year and was 'one week's salary away from bankruptcy' as he was repaying $50,000 in court costs after losing a 1982 defamation action against Joh Bjelke-Petersen.

Police would turn on their own if there was a hint that someone might 'rat'. An officer, Inspector Basil Hicks, attended a meeting with the Premier who reportedly told him he was worried that another policeman, Tony Murphy, was about to become involved in prostitution again. The Premier wanted Hicks to replace Murphy as head of the Criminal Investigation Bureau (CIB). Hicks told the Premier that if he were to do so, he would be vilified by Murphy's mates. In due course a complaint was made claiming pictures had been taken of him with a well-known prostitute. He met the police commissioner, Terry Lewis, who told him that the statement by the prostitute 'had not been signed' by the attending detective.

Hicks and police woman Lorelle Saunders visited the prostitute in custody. She told Saunders there had been no sex and there were no photos. The next attack came on Saunders who spent several months in jail on the basis of tape-recorded evidence that may have been fabricated.

THE MESS BEGINS TO UNRAVEL

Phil Dickie, a young Courier Mail reporter, set himself the task of discovering everything he could about vice syndicates operating in Queensland. He and ex-policeman Nigel Powell roamed Fortitude Valley by day and night putting parts of the puzzle together—gathering licence plate numbers, observing patrons coming and going from 'casinos' and 'brothels'.

Eventually, he had sufficient information to write a series of articles. By the time the articles were ready for publication it was obvious that police were involved in protecting operators of these venues. Some time into their surveillance, Dickie and Powell were joined by Chris Masters and a team from ABC-TV who put together the images and text that became a stunning expose *The Moonlight State*. The program created anxiety among the perpetrators and stirred others to action. Politicians could no longer hide their heads in the sand or deny the allegations. The facts were out in the open.

I was still finding my feet in Queensland and played only a marginal part in politics during this time but was aware of the corruption and cover-ups. If I heard reports of Bjelke-Petersen's words (or those of others in the Country/National Party) in the newspaper or on radio I would tremble with rage and impotence. And the incidences were many and unabated through his time in office.

Joh spoke to the media in a blustering, illogical and muddled form that seemed to reassure his supporters and allowed him to avoid serious questioning. I thought his mannerisms were a cover for matters he just didn't want to discuss. 'Don't you worry about that' he would say and that was the end of the press conference or interview, although an ABC journalist, John Rumney, who attended many of Joh's press conferences, has a different take on this:

> 'I was present at such press conferences where the front-line political jounos grilled him to the point of their blue-faced frustration.
>
> His 'don't worry…' wave of the hand did not end the questioning—the grilling continued ad nauseam but he toughed it out without giving ground. Southern commentators and Joh's opponents generally seized on his 'feed my chooks' jibe as evidence of the Queensland media's failure to call him to account but the critics wouldn't have done any better. Whether Joh was simply so dumb he was smart, or vice versa, he was enigmatic.'[2]

Defenders of the Bjelke-Petersen Government point out that during this period, tremendous developments took place in terms of lands and buildings, ports and infrastructure.[3] They could point to the Wivenhoe and Burdekin Dam projects, electrification of the Queensland railway system, as well as airports, coal mines, power stations, and dams built throughout the state.

That was the Government's strength because Petersen had a flair for it. However, he didn't understand law, history or the Westminster tradition. Joh's questionable business dealings stretched the law to its limits, and sometimes beyond—his Government crossed many boundaries. He saw Queensland as his own fiefdom and cronies received preference for developments; egregious behaviour was overlooked; people around him gained powerful financial advantages.

In 1985 the Queensland Government passed special legislation, the Sanctuary Cove Act, to exempt a luxury development, Sanctuary Cove, from local government planning regulations.

The chief developer, Mike Gore, was a member of the 'white shoe brigade', a group of Gold Coast businessmen, backers and beneficiaries of Joh's reign; men who, in their own eyes, carried the flag for meritocracy and the virtues of the unrestricted marketplace. Perhaps no more evidence of Gore's elitism is needed than the fact that he established Queensland's first gated community at Sanctuary Cove. Bjelke-Petersen denied receiving money from Gore, though the developer's ability to transgress building regulations with impunity would continue to raise eyebrows.

Legislation, much like that which granted impunity to Gore, was passed to allow Japanese company, Iwasaki Sangyo, to develop a resort near Yeppoon in Central Queensland.

The *Morning Bulletin* newspaper would later reveal that Bjelke-Petersen's son-in-law, Lester Folker, had been appointed a director of the Australian division of the company. Indicative of the belligerent cronyism of the Bjelke-Petersen era was that the man responded to the public outing with a mix of defiance and bemusement, flatly denying a conflict of interest and declaring it was no more unethical than his children buying a Japanese car.

While developments took place in infrastructure, important social welfare issues were neglected. Civil liberties were trampled. Politics was corrupted. There was bribery; there was intimidation; there was a tamed media.

The Premier continued to wreak havoc on the state, on both its physical landscape and the integrity of its laws, whilst disregarding the majority of Queenslanders who had not voted for him.

I was in the crowd watching the demolition of the Bellevue Hotel in George Street but public protests could not save Brisbane heritage sites like Cloudlands, an iconic ballroom made famous during World War II, and the Bellevue Hotel, which was demolished. Indeed, 13 Liberal backbenchers supported Labor in Parliament, condemning the destruction of the State Government owned Bellevue. Then Liberal Parliamentarian Terry Gygar described the scene of the demolition; 'There was a cordon of police. They had thrown up a barbed ... a mesh wire fence around [the building]. And then the Deen Bros arrived, rolling through like an armoured division, straight through the crowd. People were knocked sideways. Police were dragging people out of the way. Parking meters were knocked over. Traffic signs were bent and twisted on the road. It looked like Stalingrad.'[4]

This was the final straw for a group of Liberal Parliamentarians who grew frustrated with the National Party's misbehaviour and in 1983 the new Liberal leader, Terry White, led them to the cross benches. But White and the Liberal Party had underestimated their wily opponent. Joh approached the Governor, had the Parliament adjourned for several weeks then called an election in which the Liberal Party was all but destroyed.

The Liberals lost 14 seats and after the election two Liberals, Don Lane and Brian Austin, (both former members of Joh's Cabinet) defected to the National Party. Bjelke-Petersen's Nationals then enjoyed a majority in their own right and the Liberals had just six members in the state Parliament.*

* See *A Prescription for Change—the Terry White Story* by Tony Koch

In my role as president of the Queensland division of the Australian Democrats, I phoned Don Lane and Brian Austin, to ask them not to defect. However, nothing I said could change their minds. My gesture was futile as ministerial positions beckoned and perhaps they realised their legal position would be 'chancy' if Bjelke-Petersen was not returned to power.

It is obvious Bjelke-Petersen had significant knowledge of what was happening in Queensland, and probably also much of what was happening within the police force. He was receiving reports directly from the Special Branch. I knew this from Rosemary Kyburz, a former state Liberal Parliamentarian and part of the White group of politicians who were opposed to Petersen. She told me how she was summoned to the Premier's office and reprimanded for her public comments. Then when she was not suitably repentant, the Premier pulled out a file and threatened her with the contents. Blackmail? Is it possible that certain members of the police also had power over the Premier? That might explain the rapid promotion of Terry Lewis to the position of police commissioner following the resignation of Ray Whitrod.

Rosemary Kyburz and her husband, fellow Parliamentarian, Rob Akers along with 12 other Liberals, lost their seats in the election. Terry White went to the back bench; and William Knox became the Liberal Party leader. Although White had been a Cabinet Minister, he had tried to secure accountable government. He was exonerated of wrong-doing by the enquiry but suffered significant financial disadvantage trying to preserve his reputation. At the next election he was returned handsomely with a majority in every booth. From my point of view, he was a hero. He didn't succeed but did what he thought was right and then had to wait until others completed the task of bringing the Bjelke-Petersen years to an ignominious end.

This came on December 1, 1987 after Joh's colleagues in the National Party insisted on his resignation. He was becoming increasingly autocratic. His foray into Federal politics was alarming but the main issue was the impending report of the enquiry into the police force which threatened to reveal some serious issues.

This was the Fitzgerald Committee of Enquiry which would bring the Joh era to an end.

****

2
EMERGENCE OF THE AUSTRALIAN DEMOCRATS

The parties seem to polarise on almost every issue, sometimes seemingly just for the sake of it, and I wonder whether the ordinary voter is not becoming sick and tired of the vested interests which unduly influence the present political patterns and yearn for the emergence of the third political force … it must come from those people who are disgusted with those politicians and political parties who indulge mainly in cheap political point scoring in the endless pursuit of votes at any price and from people who want their Parliament to identify the real and significant problems of the future and to take action now which will make the country a good, safe and sound place for future generations.[1]

Resignation speech of Don Chipp from the Liberal Party, 1977; see Appendix A

So much was happening in Queensland and in Federal politics in 1977 that I was readily attracted to the fledgling Australian Democrats when they came on to the scene. Along with the Petersen reign in Queensland, the Federal Parliamentary sphere was in turmoil—two Federal elections and a double dissolution of the Senate followed by scandals: the dismissal of five Federal ministers; and impropriety allegations that became known as the Jim Cairns/ Junie Morosi affair; the Khemlani loans scandal, where the Government was accused of attempting to bypass the Australian Treasury and borrow money from the Middle East without consent. All this culminated in the controversial dismissal on November 11, 1975 of the Whitlam Labor Government, an otherwise socially conscious government that had overseen the scrapping of military conscription and capital punishment and the introduction of the national health care system Australians take for granted today, free tertiary education and legal aid programs.

The time was ripe for change.

On March 24, 1977 Don Chipp (former Liberal minister for the navy and for Customs and Excise, and shadow minister for Health and Welfare) stood up in the Australian Parliament and delivered a speech of resignation from the Liberal Party. The speech was finely crafted, carefully worded and delivered and deeply felt, and it launched the Democrat phenomenon; the first shot in a series of volleys that would reverberate rapidly around Australia changing the direction of much of its politics.

Even prior to the establishment of the Australian Democrats, Don Chipp was well-liked by the Australian people. Born into a working-class home and initially attracted to the Labor Party, he did not entirely fit into the conservative mould and was never to receive the recognition from the party that he might have expected in terms of his capabilities. As a young man he was a star Australian Rules player and served in the RAAF. His public profile developed after he was appointed as chief executive officer of the Olympic Civic Committee which organised the successful 1956 Melbourne Olympics and in 1960 he won the seat of Hotham for the Liberal Party. In an era of censorship, he championed the right for people to read more or less what they wanted. He was forthright and spoke in a way that most Australians considered genuine.

It is accepted in the political accounts that before the 1975 election, Malcolm Fraser promised Chipp a ministry if the conservative parties won. After the election, he reneged on this promise and Chipp was cut adrift. Chipp was unimpressed both with Malcolm Fraser and with the role the Liberal Party had played in the dismissal of the Whitlam Government. His opinion on holding up 'Supply' in the Senate—blocking the bill of affirmation that would grant the government the money to implement its policies—would strongly influence him later in the Australian Democrats. By the time of his resignation speech, Chipp was unhappy with his treatment by colleagues in the Liberal Party.

Speculation was rife in Queensland as to whether he had intended to found an alternative party when he resigned. No doubt this crossed his mind many times and had certainly been put to him by the Liberal Movement in South Australia and by the Australia Party. A careful reading of his resignation speech shows that Chipp was fully aware of the possible outcome and worded his comments in a way that appealed to the widest area of support for 'the emergence of a third political force'. The speech also planted seeds of most of the future Democrat policies—his views on the role of small business in the economy, uranium, social welfare and the need for morality in government. Publicly, at least, Chipp kept his options open—but privately he was willing to be called to the task of forming an alternative party if he could be convinced the support was forthcoming.

He was not disappointed. Support for the stance he had taken against the Liberal Party was immediate. In the next few days, letters began to pour into his Parliamentary office. Within a few short weeks over 4000 were received including invitations to address public rallies in the capital cities.

Who could have thought I (TAFE teacher and ex-missionary) would help start a political party—but there I was, nothing more than an enthusiastic amateur, scrambling around trying to find out how it was done. It was June 1977. Don Chipp had been to Brisbane and spoken at a public meeting in the Brisbane City Hall. A follow-up meeting, to settle administrative issues, was held in the old Dendy theatre in Fortitude Valley. I went with a friend and we were soon caught up in the euphoric atmosphere. Who wouldn't have been? The hall was filled to capacity and the feeling was electric.

In the southern states thousands were rushing to join. It was the same in Queensland. After the meeting we both joined—and so, for me, began seven years of hard labour.

Starting a political party from scratch (should you be interested in doing so) is a lot harder than any of us could have imagined. The steering committee elected at the Dendy meeting was soon reeling not only from the complexity of the task, but also from the flood of people phoning day after day to inquire about the new party and wanting to join. It was a social phenomenon that none of us had ever witnessed, and one that is, perhaps, difficult to imagine in the political climate of today.

The first of the Chipp rallies took place in Perth, Western Australia on April 19. It was a resounding success with more than 1000 people attending and the new party was ready to be launched. On April 29, a meeting of centreline parties was held to discuss the possibility of forming a popularly based centre party. This was followed on May 9 by a public meeting at the Melbourne Town Hall to gauge public reaction. The response, once again was overwhelming. Thousands of people filled the hall while hundreds were turned away at the door. Enthusiastic and well-attended meetings followed in other capital cities—Sydney, Adelaide and then Brisbane on June 14 where the City Hall was packed and the atmosphere expectant.*

Most Australians spend very little time thinking about politics. They have more important matters to consider—the footy, the cricket, the beach, their job, their family and their social life—so when it comes to politics, they have only a hazy idea of what pollies get up to or indeed are supposed to be doing. Consequently, they judge the political class the way they judge their own lives. Most think politicians lie, but wish they wouldn't; think they are self-serving, but wish they weren't; think they are paid too much and do too little and also think they know too little about the people for whom they make laws.

In the world of ordinary people if you work you get paid; if you lie, you often get found out and if you promise something, someone will want you to honour your promise.

We Australians are a fairly easy-going lot. We don't tend to civil wars and mostly we just put up with stuff but there comes a point when even the most easy-going Aussie will have 'had enough'. 1977 was such a time. People were fed up with the political turmoil and ready for a better way of doing things—thrilled to think that the Australian Democrats might be a cure for the carping and unfriendly state of affairs that had been going on for years not only in the Federal Parliament but in Queensland as well.

From the first, the media spotlight was on Chipp. To many it must have seemed he *was* the Australian Democrats. From its inception and throughout 1977 he was its voice and spirit—and he drove himself relentlessly through gruelling feats of endurance to publicise its aims of bringing truth and civility to the Parliament; of putting the environment ahead of ruthless development and of treating people in a just and fair way.

It was as though his whole political career to that point had been preparing him for the role. His forthright and courageous stand to reform the

* In some states the Australia Party was still going; in Western Australia elements of the New Liberal Movement still existed and South Australia had the New Liberal Movement.

censorship laws; his ceaseless campaign to inform the public about a growing drug problem and his stand on the uranium issue had made his name and face well-known and, as man of the hour, Chipp did not disappoint. He gave the public a focus for their ill-defined but very real dissatisfaction with the political system. His constant refrain was the need to inject honesty, tolerance and compassion into political decision-making.* After successful public rallies in Perth, and in Melbourne where the decision to go full speed ahead was confirmed, a further meeting on May 15 in Caulfield town hall (Melbourne) established the Victorian division. At the Melbourne meetings Don Chipp predicted the party would win eight Senate seats and hold the balance of power. Further public meetings were held.

On May 29 thousands packed Sydney town hall. The hall overflowed; Chipp's speech was relayed on closed circuit television to about 1000 people waiting outside the hall. The party's 'future-oriented' outlook was reflected in the presence of Professor Charles Birch, author of *Confronting the Future* and lecturer in biology at the Sydney University. Colin Mason, who would become an Australian Democrat Senator for New South Wales after the Federal election, was also on the platform.

By mid-June the first issue of the national journal was printed. It contained an interim constitution, divisional contact addresses, policy formulation procedure and a message from Don Chipp which concluded:

'The problems ahead of Australia and of the world are of staggering dimensions. As Aurelio Peccei has said, they cannot be dealt with without chaos and destruction unless there is a change in the hearts and minds of men—*a quantum leap f*orward—in our culture. We have no illusions that a political party can itself make that change. But what it can do, and I believe that this purpose should underlie all our policies, is to set a legislative, social and economic framework in which kindness, generosity and wisdom can compete on better than equal terms with greed, materialism and mere cleverness which characterises so much of our present society.'

Possible names for the party were printed across the front of the journal. From the beginning the organisation was ultra-democratic, aiming for democratic procedures in all activities. The first ballot of all members was to choose the name. 'Australian Democrats' won by a clear majority.

Queensland waited until June 14 for Don Chipp's visit. After his March 24 resignation, a number of Queenslanders had written asking him to consider forming a third force in the Federal Parliament. They included Michael

* For biographical detail see 'Don Chipp' by Tim Hewatt and David Wilson. A visa book, published by Widescope International Publishers. Camberwell. Vic. 1978. ISBN 0 86932-041-6

Macklin, a lecturer in education at the University of Queensland. Macklin later became the Queensland Democrats' first Parliamentarian when he won a Senate seat in 1980.

Michael told me what happened prior to the public meeting in Queensland:

'Friends of Don Chipp helped organise the party in Queensland. One had been Don Chipp's personal secretary.

'There were two or three others and they flew up. They took a three bedroom unit in Dutton Park for about a week. We went every night and talked. Then they all flew off and said 'Good Luck'. This was after the Perth meeting. Chipp knew after that meeting that something would go ahead. The people who invited Chipp to Brisbane gave personal guarantees for the costs, about $4000. The newly established Victorian and New South Wales divisions assisted with funds.'

The Queensland section of the Australia Party posed an early problem. In southern states, the Australia Party had, with the New Liberal Movement, been instrumental in nudging a 'centre party' into being and subsequent agreements aimed to weld their groups together. Few Queenslanders had heard of this. The Australia Party in Queensland was no longer a viable political force. Michael Macklin told me that after the Perth public meeting an interim National Executive was established for the Australian Democrats and he had been appointed the Queensland representative.

The remainder of the Australia Party in Queensland decided they would set up as the Australian Democrats in Queensland and began to appoint a President and other officers. Macklin had been invited to their meeting and they told him about their intentions. 'No', he said, 'I am the only Australian Democrat in Queensland to this point. You must wait until the public meeting.' They disagreed so Macklin said 'If you go ahead, I will expel you', and he did, so very few of them joined up. Well, it's a moot point if they could be expelled from a party they weren't actually members of, however the Macklin move was successful and so started the stormy history of arguments within the Australian Democrats. On the whole these arguments were the result of absolute conviction about the need to protect the new party and its ideals. In only a few cases were the arguments a result of personal selfishness.

So, eventually, the Democrats in Queensland began as a completely new group and when Australia Party members came to early meetings expecting a special role they were probably disappointed to have to start on the same footing as other members.

The Public meeting in Brisbane was just as enthusiastic as elsewhere and the meeting at the Dendy Theatre, Fortitude Valley on June 19 set up branches and an organisational framework. By this date throughout Australia there were 5000 paid-up members and 110 branches.

A Gallop Poll estimated that the Democrats could win about 4% of the national vote and support was growing beyond the wildest expectations of even the most optimistic. The Queensland division began in a burst of euphoria.

I asked Michael. 'Why do you think the Australian Democrats took off so well?' and he said 'It was 1977, just two years on from the [Whitlam] Dismissal. Hatred between two parties was strong, you had not just a division—a chasm. It was really quite nasty. What people were looking for was what we used in the Parliament 'Get Australia together'.

'There was a lot of movement going on at that time, a lot of ferment within the social structure. [Members of] our group were in a sense, small l liberals and there's always some of those in every community—people who tend to be at the forefront of social change. 'Just because something has happened in the past is no reason for it to happen in the future'. We've ignored indigenous rights for 200 years so let's go on ignoring them. In Queensland the sentence for gay sexual activities was 14 years hard labour, more than first degree murder. So we were saying No, what's this got to do with government?'

A state steering committee met for the first time on June 21 with Michael Macklin as chairman and called nominations for a Queensland divisional executive to comprise a chairperson, secretary, treasurer, policy development co-ordinator and six other members.

If the executive members had foreseen the hours of struggle and difficulty ahead in Queensland it is likely none would have had the heart to continue. Optimism ruled and committee members set about shaping an organisational structure suitable for the needs of a highly democratic group.

The generosity of Australian Democrat members was apparent from the start and they were as forthcoming with their thoughts and ideas as with their money. Early meetings resembled an assembly of noisy kookaburras, but from the hub-hub of meetings came consensus on most issues. Everyone was heard, and contributions, no matter how seemingly small were accepted. Fundraising proceeded slowly and while the division existed hand to mouth it managed to stay just above starvation level because of members' generous financial donations. Many volunteers worked full time for five days a week, and without their assistance the party could not have functioned.

"In the early days, Democrat meetings resembled an assembly of noisy kookaburras in a local tree."

A divisional newsletter to keep members informed soon became a respectable little publication. Membership rose steadily. State executive meetings were open to rank-and-file members and as branches were established they sent representatives.

In Queensland, nominations were called for the Senate ticket as soon as the division formed. A membership ballot soon approved the Democrats contesting the State election (due later in 1977). A first major test stemmed from selection procedures for state candidates.

The interim constitution gave little assistance in this regard and procedures had to be hammered out meeting by meeting.

Some candidates who missed the Democrat endorsement ran on a ticket describing themselves as 'independent democrats'. This highlighted the need for an ombudsman to arbitrate in such matters. Until the organisation could establish this position, the role fell to Michael Macklin as the division chairman.

Don Chipp visited Queensland late in July and then returned in September to launch the State election campaign and introduce the candidates. The meeting at Lone Pine Koala Sanctuary issued a statement of intent. Radio, TV and the papers gave the event good coverage. Twelve candidates nominated.

During this period painful mistakes were made in relation to internal ballots. For fairness some ballots were declared void and the issue again put to the vote. This was time-consuming, but experience with the ballot system eventually lessened such problems.*

An offset printing machine was purchased. During the campaign it would print more than one million how-to-vote cards along with a great deal of the literature needed for letterbox drops and information pamphlets, describing our new ideas and policies. Although this was eventually a saving, at the time the decision to buy strained finances. There were also occasions when our patience with the temperamental machine would come to an end. For those so inclined, a stream of unsavoury swear words would fly its way.

Members worked feverishly, expecting Queensland to be the first State to test the newly-established Democrats with voters. Polls showed rising support. The first electoral test had to be successful. Branches were active with fundraising events such as wine-bottling, second-hand stalls, socials and barbecues. It was truly a grassroots people's movement. Funds trickled in slowly but steadily in preparation for the double test of State and Federal elections.

South Australian Premier Don Dunstan announced a snap poll and that State went to the polls on September 17, so the Australian Democrats faced their first electoral test when the Democrats were just 14 weeks old. Membership had grown nationally to 7000, but a great deal rested on the 500-strong South Australian division.

With one week to campaign, Robin Millhouse, leading the Australian Democrats in South Australia, gained 32% of the primary vote in the Mitcham electorate to retain his State seat and become the first Democrat in an Australian Parliament. The Democrat vote in the 12 seats contested was 13%. In September 1979, Millhouse would gain sufficient primary votes to win the seat outright.

The Queensland State executive called a special meeting on the 18th of the month to present nominees for endorsement as Senate candidates. Tape-recordings of their presentations were sent to all branches before the membership ballot. The ticket chosen was Paul Griffin, a popular TV newscaster; Michael Macklin; and Maureen Burton, part-owner of a small business in Toowoomba. Nominees were also sought for Queensland's 19 Federal electorates.

Speculation about whether the State or Federal election would be first had ceased a week earlier on October 10 when the Queensland Premier announced November 12 as polling day.

* A system of optional preferential voting was used. A 'none of the above' category was later inserted on ballot forms so members could reject all options.

On November 5, one week before the Queensland elections, a by-election was held for the Victorian State seat of Greensborough. The Democrat candidate was David Ross, a barrister who had helped set up a local free legal service in his home town. Ross won 17% of the primary vote. Following Millhouse's victory in South Australia, this result was excellent and it was clear the party was gaining momentum.

The focus shifted quickly to the State where change was most vitally needed, Queensland, where Joh stood defiant.

The Government had rejected calls for inquiries into several police matters, in particular the Cedar Bay raid where police burnt dwellings and personal belongings of members of a hippie commune.

Democrats opposed the mining and processing of uranium until proper safeguards were established, but they did not publicly support civil liberties groups on the 'right-to-march' issue. They were concerned not to alienate the many Queenslanders who believed violence in the streets was solely the fault of the marchers. Don Chipp believed the only way to restore civil liberties in Queensland was through the ballot box.

The stumbling block for Chipp's view was the gerrymander which favoured country voters. Without proportional representation, minorities and small parties had almost no chance to win seats in the State Parliament, and even less to gain power to govern.

Parliamentary seats are calculated on the basis of population and when populations change or there are shifts, electorate boundaries must be recalculated. This should be done in a fair and above-board manner.

Soon after the Democrats formed there were redistributions affecting both State and Federal electoral boundaries. Branches were set up on Federal electoral boundaries and membership allotted on the basis of where people lived, only to have everything change when the boundaries changed.

The changes created confusion as we struggled to get branches operational. The changes to State boundaries didn't affect our organisation, but we were planning to run candidates and were uncertain of electorate boundaries.

Christian clergymen were attacked under Parliamentary privilege as the march issue dragged on. Indeed, the issue continued after the Federal election and well into 1978.

A cartoon in *The Financial Review* editorial of April 26, 1978 depicted a wizard pouring destructive chemicals into a ballot box and ran with the tag line, cropped from the larger article:

'What is happening in Queensland at the moment is the most corrosive alchemy that has ever been applied to the Australian political system.'

"What is happening in Queensland at the moment is the most corrosive alchemy that has ever been applied to the Australian political system."

Courtesy of Matt Mawson

I was assigned to the Ryan branch. The electorate of Ryan, in the western suburbs of Brisbane, was home to the typical Democrat member—usually well-educated and politically aware; financially secure; often from the professional classes and possibly self-employed. The first Ryan branch meeting took place in Kenmore in the middle of winter. Not long back from Papua New Guinea, I had yet to acclimatise to the colder weather and, although wrapped about with a warm over-coat, shivered uncontrollably in the 14° temperature. There was a good turnout at the meeting so we simply called for nominations and elected ourselves a chairperson, a secretary and a treasurer. We were under way.

The State election was due by the end of the year so at the following meeting we agreed to contest the Toowong electorate. 'It's the easiest to do letterbox drops.' said a young lawyer who had constituted himself our adviser, and that was the basis of our first campaign.

The suburb of St. Lucia lay within the Toowong electorate and the university sits on the attractive St. Lucia reach of the Brisbane River. I was familiar with St. Lucia as I had recently finished a Bachelor of Education degree on the University of Queensland campus. Playing fields occupy low-lying land, but the buildings creep up a rising hill. The rest of the St. Lucia suburb and Toowong consists of the foothills of the Brisbane Forest Park across to Mt. Coot-tha, 'one-tree-hill', the highest vantage point in the city. For our ignorance we were condemned to campaign up and down some of Brisbane's steepest hills.

In many ways, though, Toowong was a good choice. It included an area around the university that had an informed population—the kind of voters receptive to the Democrat message. Also, its long-term Liberal Party incumbent, Charles Porter, had made inflammatory statements about Aboriginal people and about the environment, and his comments did little to impress well-educated voters living in the electorate.

The November 12 State election resulted, as expected, in a return of the Liberal/National coalition, but with a reduced majority. The Democrat results were sound, with across-the-board support at 11%, a highly significant figure for a minor party so recently established.

The swing against the coalition was most pronounced in the south-east corner of Queensland where it affected Liberals more than the National Party. Liberal support fell by 8% where most of the Democrat candidates stood.

In December, South Australian Labor Premier, Don Dunstan, stirred up a sudden constitutional and political controversy with the announcement that he planned to appoint Democrat Janine Haines to the Senate to fill the vacancy left by Steele Hall's decision to stand for the House of Representatives.

Haines had been the third candidate on the Liberal Movement's Senate ticket in 1975 after Hall and Michael Wilson.

For Queensland Democrats, the State election had been a handy experience in conducting a campaign, but the Federal election, due on December 10, would be the real thing. Hopes were high that an Australian Democrat from Queensland would be elected to the Senate.*

Across Queensland we fielded 12 candidates. The lowest vote received was 5.6% in Toowoomba North (a conservative area) and the highest was for

* State election statistics from 'Details of polling at general election' 58503 A4 1978 Queensland Government Printer.

Mike West, our candidate in Toowong, who attracted 18.6% of the vote. Six of the candidates got double figures.

Across Queensland the Democrats' average vote in the electorates contested was just under 11%. Translated to the Proportional Representation system of voting used for Senate elections it could be just enough to win a Senate seat. We didn't win Toowong, but our candidate received the most Democrat votes in Australia to that point. Enough to make up for the effort of toiling up those wretched hills? Almost.

Qld election shows Chipp support rising

From PETER BOWERS

Courier-Mail Political Correspondent[2]

BRISBANE.-The Australian Democrats, continuing their drive as a new political force, have polled strongly in the Queensland election.

They averaged 10.9 per cent of the vote in the 12 seats they contested, polling as high as 19 per-cent in one electorate. Saturday's election returned the Bjelke-Petersen Government to power with a reduced but still overwhelming majority.

In terms of the Federal election to be held on December 10, the Queensland result presents problems for the Prime Minister, Mr. Fraser, and the Leader of the Federal opposition, Mr. Whitlam.

Both Labor and Liberal officials do not give Labor much chance of winning more than four more seats in Queensland on December 10. Labor now holds only one.

Mr. Fraser has been warned by senior Queensland Liberal Party officials that the drift against the Liberal Party was most severe in the metropolitan area and in provincial cities.

In the south-east region, which includes Brisbane, the Liberal vote slipped 8.2 percent. Mr. Fraser is coming under increasing pressure from Queensland Liberals to announce a vote-catching scheme for Brisbane such as a new and longer runway for Brisbane Airport.

Serious policy formation began at a national level. In the rush to get ready for electoral challenges, policy had consisted of items Don Chipp covered in his resignation speech and policy objectives set out in the national constitution. Now the work of formulating detailed policies began in earnest.

Letterbox dropping and doorknocking are essential campaign elements. Once you get into the swing, there are compensations. A keen garden-lover, I admired the electorate's gardens. I also enjoyed chatting with people I might never otherwise have met. Of course, the aim was to win Democrat votes, but sometimes I felt like a social worker as I gave a listening ear.

Tony Walters told me that once when doorknocking with Cheryl Kernot they came upon a household with a destitute young woman and her children. The husband had left and one of the children was autistic. They spent the rest of their day contacting aid agencies to ensure that the young woman had the assistance she needed.

Occasionally I met a curmudgeon. I knocked firmly. The door opened and a mild-looking gentleman appeared. 'Hello,' I said. 'I'm from the Australian Democrats. Could I offer you some of our literature?' The 'gentleman' in question snatched the pamphlet from my hand, scrunched it up and, without a word, threw it in the bin. 'OK,' I said politely backing away. Appearances *can be* deceptive, but I guessed he wouldn't be voting for us.

I went to the Sunshine Coast one weekend—first stopping at the Nambour police station to get a permit to distribute election materials—and then heading to Eumundi's country market where I parked my van and handed out Democrat leaflets. Eumundi in the 1970s was a sleepy town looking like it was still in the pre-war era and a centre for sun-cooked fruit and vegie growers, but its flourishing market was popular and the town was filled with visitors looking for produce or a novel experience. The matriarch of the town, wife of the local councillor, descended upon me. 'You can't do this,' she said. 'I have a permit,' I replied. She marched off to find a policeman. In a dyed-in-the-wool, National Party electorate, how dare another party canvas for votes.

The constable duly came and found himself caught between the devil and the deep blue sea. He would have to live in the town when I had gone so he tried to persuade me to leave. 'What harm am I doing?' I asked. 'Well,' he replied in a nice manly policeman voice. 'First there is just one person. Then a few more gather around and soon there is a riot.' 'Oops! I think I missed something in the middle.' 'Say that again, please.' He did, but I stayed and there was no riot. What a surprise.

Country justice, like its city cousin's, could be partisan. An acquaintance whose husband inspected and weighed trucks near Gympie told me he simply stopped issuing tickets as few of the drivers he wrote tickets for were ever charged or came to court.

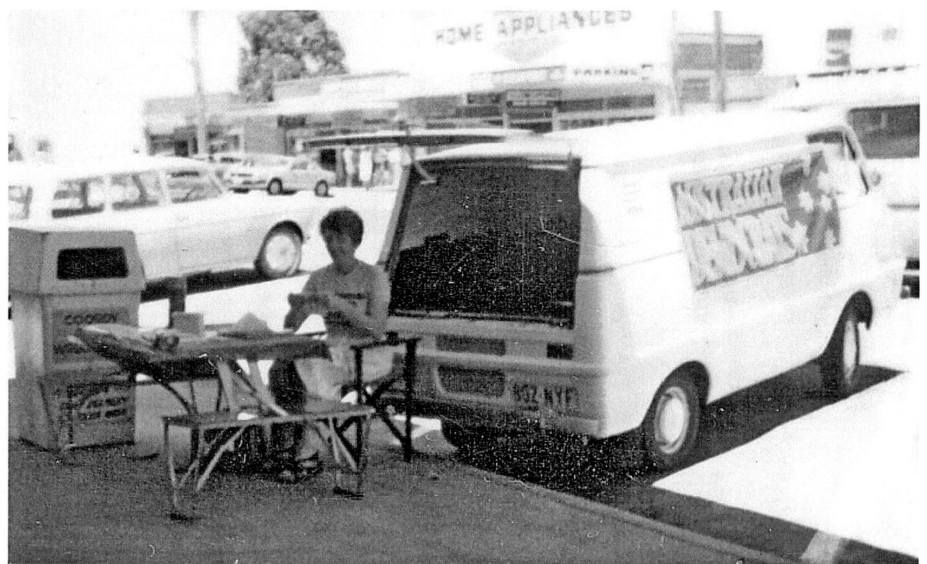

Author campaigning in Eumundi

While handing out how to vote cards during the State election I received a choice piece of wisdom from a youthful party member: ‘Nice guys don’t win’; a lesson learnt from his National Party elders. After hearing his comment I wasn’t feeling too nice, so he was probably lucky to escape intact.

****

3
CARRYING ON THE FIGHT

On October 29, 1941, U.K. Prime Minister Winston Churchill visited Harrow school. When he was invited to give a speech, Churchill stood before the students and said:

> 'Never give in, never give in, never; never; never
> in nothing, great or small, large or petty
> never give in except to convictions
> of honour and good sense.'

The State election had been a practice run for the Federal election, which was approaching rapidly. Party headquarters, on the third floor of a vacant retail store, was in Fortitude Valley. We used just one corner and the vast, empty space we weren't using gave an eerie feeling of being in the garage with Deep Throat. Anyone could wander in and around. There was no security. By day, volunteers toiled to answer constantly ringing phones, register new members, file mounting piles of letters and other paperwork, write campaign material, select candidates and devise ways to raise money. Work continued in the evening with a new batch of volunteers to take the place of the daytime workers.

Fortitude Valley in the late 1970s was in decline, run-down and gloomy, the haunt of drunkards, prostitutes, criminals—and Democrats. We worked there because it was cheap. It was central as well as being close to restaurants and pubs—nothing like a take-away and a beer to help with the chores. There was very little furniture so we sat cross-legged on the floor to conduct our business. Outside, people walked back and forth, with no inkling of what was taking place in this seemingly empty building.

Queensland politicians denied knowing about police corruption. They mocked any talk of police protection of gambling and prostitution. This was amazing, as anyone who visited the area could have discovered the truth. In 1973, the Whiskey Au Go Go, a nightclub in Fortitude Valley, was firebombed.

We heard rumors of police involvement and the possibility that men arrested for the crime were verballed by police after being incited to commit the crime.*

Nowadays Fortitude Valley is a flourishing retail and entertainment area.

Chinatown stretches along the street where the Australian Democrats experienced their early exhilarating days. Maybe in future someone will put up a plaque to commemorate our beginnings. Memories slip away so easily.

The theme of our increasingly maddened lives was money. Indulging in politics takes quite a lot of it. Most of that came, in the first years, from the pockets of members and friends. We had parties, barbecues, more parties and more barbecues. We collected for trash and treasure sales. We bottled wine. I think we also had a few raffles. After all we were novices. We sent begging letters. We looked for sponsors and finally we dipped into pockets

* The Whiskey Au Go Go affair was a fire, in the Whiskey Au Go Go nightclub in Fortitude Valley in 1973. The building was firebombed, resulting in the deaths of 15 patrons and staff. James Finch and John Stuart were arrested soon afterwards. Both loudly protested innocence at their first court appearance and continued to do so for many years.

and paid the bills ourselves. Several budding fortunes were squandered in that manner. We were offered money, but with strings attached. Like good little Vegemiters, we refused such offers. We would not be bought like old-fashioned politicians.

Malcolm Fraser called an early Federal election. Many thought this was an effort to strike before the party could get well-established. Both the Liberal Party and the ALP were doing whatever they could to diminish our chances of success.

Nothing, however, could have stemmed the tide of energy unleashed by a multitude of people with a vision of 'how things could be'. Members were out to change the world, *now*. Perhaps they had taken on board the street marchers' slogan. 'What do we want? When do we want it? NOW.'

At the Fortitude Valley headquarters the famous off-set printer ran hot, spitting out campaign literature for the election we poor deluded fools were going to win—the one we felt sure would give the Australian Democrats the balance of power in the Senate. Sometimes the printer didn't spit out campaign literature, it just spat, full-stop. Then the volunteers would spend valuable time trying to persuade it into action. Ink-splattered and desperate, we would finally get it back on track

Chipp vote critical in Senate
By DON CHIPP, M.P.

Leader of the Australian Democrats[1]

In six short months the Australian Democrats have emerged as a credible alternative in Australian politics. Our growing public support at the polls has confounded the pundits and shattered our political opponents — South Australia, 12 per cent; Greensborough 18.3 per cent; Queensland, up to 20 per cent.

Last week's Gallup Poll found that 33 per cent of Australians are seriously considering voting for us on December 10.

To what may this phenomenal progress be attributed? Not to a high-powered, well-oiled party machine. We rely totally on a few unpaid and inexperienced part-time volunteers.

Not to money, for we are stone, motherless broke.

> Not simply to public disenchantment with the tired faces, lacklustre policies, broken promises and pathetic performances of the two old parties.
>
> Our support is due to ...

Four years after the infamous Whisky Au Go Go fire we were heading home as the night-life sprang into action. The party HQ was not quite the Labor movement establishment at Breakfast Creek; nor the heritage-soaked setting of the Trades Hall, nor the crispness of the National Party engine room in Leichhardt Street.

I was an underling in those days—welcome to help, share coffee and to chat. It was fascinating. I had been in Papua New Guinea during the move to independence. We had talked endlessly about the process, breathlessly interested that a country was deciding, by referendum, and from scratch, the form of its future political structure. Would it be the Westminster system, the American presidential system or some hybrid?

In PNG, patrol officers trudged over the country's ridges and roads to allow a democratic vote for each citizen.

Most Papua New Guineans could not read or write, but they would be entitled to their say on the country's future. As interested as we expatriates were, we always come back to the bottom line: it was their country, not ours. But now, not long back from PNG and finished with university study, I was participating in 'real' politics. My efforts might help change the Australian political scene.

Our branch selected a candidate for the Federal electorate of Ryan. Imagine our horror when the candidate wasn't nominated on time. What a blunder. Other electorates had candidates, but the election would go ahead without ours. Not only that, the lack of a candidate in a potentially good area might reduce the vote for our Senate candidates.

Red faces poll slip-up[2]

> The party's Queensland campaign director, Mr. Graham Maskiel, said human error was responsible for the failure to nominate for Ryan, Darling Downs and Dawson. 'We are so young, so few and our money is so short. We had our back to the wall,' he said. 'It is most unfortunate and we are very disappointed at missing the three seats….'

The election came and went in a daze of activity. Two Democrats were elected—Don Chipp in Victoria and Colin Mason in New South Wales. 'What shall I do?' Mason asked Chipp. 'Watch my back' was the response.

The Australian Democrats now had three senators, as six months earlier South Australian Premier Don Dunstan, had appointed Janine Haines to a vacancy, but none from Queensland. The Democrat percentage of the vote across Australia was 11.3%.

PICKING UP THE PIECES

What do people do after they give their all and it isn't good enough? In Queensland, some left. Others dug in for the long haul to the next Federal election. Arguments broke out about the debt the Queensland division had incurred. Tiredness and disappointment fuelled the arguments, but several facts were indisputable. The division was in debt. In retrospect, the debt was minor—about $10,000—not much in today's terms, but a fair amount then and it seemed enormous to the amateurs involved. Some members in north Queensland felt neglected in the decision-making and wanted more say. John Galvin, originally from Bundaberg but later living at Mt. Tamborine, was asked to stand as treasurer. He was elected handsomely and was the Queensland division treasurer for several years. During his tenure Democrats' finances were on a sound footing. John was not only treasurer, but a treasure as well—a good man to have around.

Eventually, when the clouds cleared and sense returned, the organisation picked itself up and took practical steps to get back into shape for round two. Several members stood guarantors against the debt and it was no longer a problem. Candidate selection began. Colin Mason and Janine Haines attended the first convention in Queensland where an important task was to discuss a new constitution to give members more say in decision-making. I spent many hours in committee working on that constitution. A useful technique we learnt as we went along was, 'If in doubt, leave it out'. After much painful discussion, we eventually finalised a document that served us well over the years. The task helped educate me on the various pitfalls that could be lying in wait.

The activities of our Parliamentarians in Canberra kept hopes alive. We avidly followed the debates. The southern media gave considerable coverage to Don Chipp, but in Queensland, following the Federal election, a curtain of silence had fallen.

Across Australia, Democrats began winning State seats. In South Australia Robin Millhouse, retained his seat in the House of Assembly, but as an Australian Democrat. Millhouse had been a member of the breakaway Liberal Movement and was well-known and respected. In 1979 Lance Milne won a seat for the Democrats in the South Australian Legislative Council. Gordon Walsh was elected to the ACT House of Assembly in 1979 and Ivor Vivian the ACT House of Assembly the same year.

In Tasmania, the progressive system of proportional representation made winning easier for a candidate from a small party with limited means. Norm Sanders was a member of the Tasmanian House of Assembly from 1980 to 1982.

Over the years Democrats would win many seats in State Parliaments. They were most successful in South Australia where the Liberal Movement had been strong and least successful in Queensland where the Parliament consisted of just one house, the Legislative Council having been abolished in 1922 by the Labor Government. This, many think, was one of their poorer political decisions because over the years it facilitated attempts to rush through legislation without the review process that an upper house makes possible.

Local government seats were also won, although usually incognito. Council elections in Queensland were relatively free of party politicking, with the exception of a few major cities like Brisbane and Townsville. The sympathies of candidates may have been known, but party machinery did not operate overtly to elect a ticket. This approach seemed to have public support throughout the State. Only a foolhardy party would have extended the bickerings and squabbles of its politics into local government.

Democrat philosophy was based firmly on grass roots involvement and participation in decision-making and found a common ground with the aspirations of those at the local level.

In March 1979 three Democrat candidates were endorsed in the Brisbane City Council election and gained reasonable returns. Outside Brisbane our candidate, Bill Elson-Green, was elected mayor of the Hervey Bay Council. Australian Democrat members or sympathisers won seats on councils, but without party affiliation.

Later, Elson-Green would contest the Senate nomination against Michael Macklin. The contest was fierce. Elson-Green was the proprietor of a local newspaper; he was wealthy and his wealth could have been available to the Queensland Democrats. There was an absolute furore at the meeting to decide on the candidate, but eventually the party in Queensland chose Michael Macklin. To this point Macklin had guided the party in Queensland through significant hazards. He had earned the right to stand as the prime

Senate candidate. It was a case of doing the right thing and letting the pieces fall as they would.

Several by-elections and much effort later, it was time for the 1980 Federal election. We had hung on grimly for this and, much wiser and warier, would give it our best shot. We were ready!

The official draw for positions on the Senate ballot paper took place in downtown Brisbane two or three weeks before polling day. Almost half those present were Democrat members and were overjoyed when first place went to our Senate team. This position on the ballot paper generally meant a bonus of 'the donkey vote', the 1 to 2 per-cent who marked across the ticket from left to right. In a close contest it would be a critical advantage.*

Behind the scenes the campaign committee contacted all candidates to establish the correct wording for how-to-vote cards. Early on it was decided not to direct preferences to either major party, so when the design was ready, two separate cards had to be prepared. Then the copy had to be delivered to the printer, printed, and finally parcelled for consignment across the State.

A power strike delayed the start of printing and then halfway through the second print run an error was found. Pandemonium!

This threw the timetable and finances into disarray. Many of the cards had to be stamped by hand. The second print run had to be over-printed to eliminate the error.

In Ryan we selected our candidate carefully. Gilruth Rees was articulate and well-informed, a good candidate. No mistake about nominating. She was probably reminded a dozen times beforehand by some very nervous nellies.

In the Ryan electorate campaign, my task was to gather sufficient people to attend to the booths on polling day. They would hand out how-to-vote cards and be the beaming face of our new party. We could win! I have since thought that starting a new party is like having a baby. There has to be excitement and hope, but the work is hard. Ryan stretched from well past Ipswich to the western side of Brisbane. It was huge and had dozens of polling booths. We would need hundreds of people. Some could come for a few hours or to certain places. Some had no transport. I had never before tried such an organising task.

Part of that wretched Toowong electorate, with all its hills, was in Ryan. I was pretty dark about our first experience of running a candidate there. I also considered myself by now a seasoned political operator. No-one would ever sell me a pup like that again.

* This no longer happens in Tasmania and the ACT where candidate positions are rotated on the ballot papers.

Many filing cards and a million phone calls later (all paid for by me) we had the hundreds of volunteers. The printer had delivered the how-to-vote cards. We had posters (bought by the candidate) and several weeks before the election woke at the ungodly hour of 3 am to nail them into the ground with steel stakes.

Election Day is usually mild in contrast to the efforts that precede it, but this time machinations of the 'old' parties tested our organisation to its limits. A spurious complaint was laid about our how-to-vote cards and inexperienced volunteers were targeted. For several hours, before head office could control the situation, helpers in several key electorates were unsure if they should hand out the cards. Communication was difficult in those days; mobile phones were not available until 1983. How did we manage? The all-clear came though by mid-morning, but the setback had diminished our chance of winning a seat.

During the afternoon we ran out of cards. Fully committed to recycling, we rescued the still perfectly good cards from litter-bins. This caused some merriment from members of the other parties and voters. But what is a new party for if not to challenge the old ways.

We would later consider cards a stupid waste of paper and ink and suggest that the Electoral Commission simply put party names on the ballot papers or place large sample ballot papers at each booth, but for now it was necessary to rummage in the bins.

Staffing polling booths has its place. Unlike the lad who gave me the advice about 'nice guys not winning', most of those on the booths were friendly. Conversations were interesting, if cautious. Sometimes booth helpers would hand out cards for one another during a toilet visit or some emergency. In a democratic country, the right to contest elections freely and in a secure environment is basic.

The acceptance and friendliness shown by most booth-workers confirmed the underlying Aussie attitude of a fair go. It was impressive.

The counting was our next challenge. It is customary for candidates to have scrutineers at each booth. In Federal elections, voting stopped at 8pm* and soon after 8pm the counting began and carried on until 9 or 10pm. Some booths with fewer votes to count finished earlier, but for party workers and electoral officials alike, it is a long and tiring day. Having been totally absorbed in getting people for the day sessions, I had more or less forgotten (or pushed to one side) this important task. I was sunburnt and weary, but we had to get scrutineers for as many of the booths as we could. What the

* In 1984 this changed to 6pm to align with state elections.

human frame is capable of doing in an emergency is surprising. Somehow we scratched up enough scrutineers.

Scrutineers must be wily. Established parties know the tricks of the trade. Our scrutineers looked and learnt as quickly as possible. They enthusiastically queried any decisions if they looked like going the 'wrong' way. Oops! It's really a bit embarrassing to talk about it now, but as a prominent Labor Party politician was much later heard to comment 'It seemed like a good thing (to do) at the time'.

Throughout Queensland the campaign had been vigorous. Several caravanserais had visited northern Queensland and regional areas. The public, in the guise of country newspaper editors, shopkeepers, pensioners, farmers and other 'ordinary' folk, were willing to give us a fair go, and most Queenslanders were friendly and helpful.

While Brisbane's major media outlets still gave limited coverage, regional newspapers and radio and TV stations were more obliging.

However, as results trickled in on election night, they were less than we had hoped. The community's initial excitement had receded and with this, and a lack of major media coverage, our vote had fallen. The gibe that we 'had no policies' had taken hold.

In a tour of the State's north, the campaign team reported that the university had banned the sale of our policy documents in its bookshop. But one had to understand this was 'deepest, darkest' Queensland at the height of the gerrymander and a degree of political wariness.

During election-night counting, Don Chipp welcomed another Victorian, John Siddons, as our fourth win, while also dismissing the chances of a Queensland seat. Was that it? Were all our efforts for nothing?

The day after election night is devastating for losing candidates and their parties. The tiredness, the removal of the campaign pressure and the emptiness are hard to ignore. We felt disorientated and disillusioned. Why couldn't the voters see what we had to offer?

Ours was a new view of politics, more compassionate and honest. Why? We were like tired children whingeing about something they wanted and couldn't have. After three years of struggling to keep the party afloat, many regular workers were exhausted. They had experienced tensions when their dedication to the cause conflicted with personal or family commitments. These were the hidden, but nonetheless real, costs of such an unequal struggle. Candidates were sometimes poorly equipped in terms of the usual qualifications required of public officials. Some developed new skills and confidence in their own abilities; others fell by the wayside, casualties of the battle.

Was this the final skirmish for the Queensland division?

Senate results are never clear-cut or immediately available. Because of the sophisticated voting system for Senate ballots, counting takes a long time. On election night, counting for the House of Representatives has priority.

After all, the 'Reps' decides who will form the government. Only first preferences are counted for the Senate. Then on Sunday everybody stays home, has a good sleep, reads the results and either commiserates or celebrates.

We were in limbo. Although Chipp conceded for Queensland early on election night, some members still thought a win might be possible. Conservative parties in Queensland had been in considerable disarray and lost ground prior to the election. A popular northern candidate was displaced on the National Party ticket to make way for Florence Bjelke-Petersen, the wife of the Premier.

At work and at home, I could think of nothing except the outcome of the election. I walked about in a dream. My thoughts constantly went one way and then the other. Could we win? Perhaps that was too much to hope. There was the possibility of a preference drift and no-one was too sure where the preferences would go; probably not to the other coalition party because relations were strained at the State level; certainly not to the socialists. Our campaign strategy of focusing on northern and regional areas might just be enough to win us the seat.

****

4
WE FINALLY HAVE A PARTY!

Dr Michael Macklin (soon to be Senator Macklin) with the cartoon printed in *The Courier Mail* on November 11, 1980.

We waited. Four weeks after the election the fifth seat in Queensland was still undecided. A recount was in progress. Then on November 11, 1980, the announcement came. Dr Michael Macklin had won the seat, beating his nearest rival by almost 16,000 votes after preferences were distributed. In the northern electorate of Kennedy, 32.2% of Macklin's preferences came from conservative voters. In effect, more than 200,000 Queenslanders had put our candidate in the Senate. We were jubilant.

In Queensland, unlike at Federal level, the National Party was the dominant partner in the coalition. The Liberal Party existed predominantly along the coastal regions where most of the population lived. Consequently, they experienced the same disadvantage as the Labor Party with respect to the gerrymander. In the northern parts of Queensland, the Nationals had significant support, however, this was impacted by a decision made in Brisbane to select Florence Bjelke-Petersen (wife of the Premier) to the number one position on the ticket. In the event, she won a Senate seat, but a high proportion of preferences leaked away from the Liberal/National coalition as a result of a local candidate being pushed aside.

November 11 is an historic day for Australia. It marks WWI Armistice Day, the centenary of Ned Kelly's hanging, the anniversary of the Whitlam Government's sacking and the death of former Queensland Labor Premier Vince Gair. Now we had another milestone—Democrats shared with Brian Harradine the balance of power (or balance of reason) in the Senate. For 40 years conservatives had dominated Queensland's Senate contingent. In 1980 the tide turned at last.

We did have a party! The word went out and people from near and far gathered at Macklin's home. Chipp arrived. Drinks were drunk. There was a lot of noise. Babies were kissed. Utter joy and exhilaration were abroad. It went late into the night. This was our reward for three years of back-breaking labour and unremitting toil. The party took place at Michael and Jenny Macklin's stylish but modest home in Brisbane. People crammed into every nook and cranny. The kitchen overflowed and revelry spilled out on to the lawn under a pale moon and some lights that had been strung hastily for the celebration. We brought red wine and chips—all we could afford after spending most of our spare cash on the election campaign.

Jenny had prepared food for a multitude and we fell upon it like a horde of hungry grasshoppers. Don Chipp made a speech but, in the hub-hub, it's doubtful if anyone really heard much of it. Michael Macklin thanked everyone for their efforts and speculated about the future while waving a cartoon that *The Courier-Mail* had published that day. The morning afterwards we went back to work again as, despite our encouraging success, we couldn't afford to let our guard down.

Dr Michael Macklin and the author

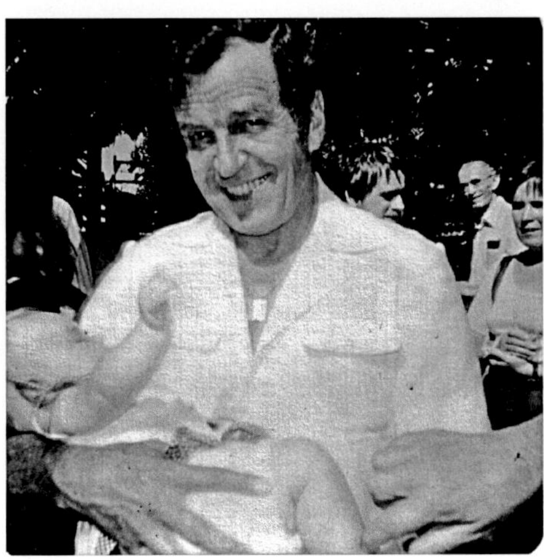

Don Chipp with baby

When not raising money or attending meetings, members completed ballots on policy. Some of us toiled night after night, faithfully trying to record our opinions about the multitude of policy items. The organisation strove to be ultra-democratic. A ballot of the membership decided every policy—transport, the environment, taxation—what had we let ourselves in for?

Policy formation proceeded slowly. The era of computers had not yet arrived, so everything was done by snail mail. The TAFE College where I worked was in the first stages of trying out Tandy computers and a few adventurous university lecturers were using a form of the Internet, but it was an awkward and unwieldy tool. The task of participatory policy-making was really too advanced for the available technology and began to bog down. By 1978 the *Journal of the Australian Democrats* was published with a number of draft policies, but the participatory process continued with fewer participants than would have been ideal.

Re-reading some of the Democrat policies, I am astonished. They are still, 30 years later, a model for progress. Far-sighted? Yes. Sensible? On the whole. Idealistic? Perhaps, but certainly food for thought. I say to myself 'What would Australia be like if most of these policies had been introduced?' and my answer is 'wonderfully advanced'.

An example from the Aboriginal Affairs draft policy paper: 'acceptance of the idea that Aboriginal people do have a valid claim to the land they occupy'. Remember this was 1977, before the late 1980s Mabo decision and decades before the Keating Native Titles legislation in the 1990s.

From the Parliamentary, Electoral and Constitutional Reform draft policy paper:

> 'if laws are to be honest and just, it is essential that both Parliament and the public be given ample time to examine and discuss all proposed legislation.'

This was of particular importance to the Democrats as they had the almost impossible task of keeping up to date on all the issues, and when bills were pushed rapidly through both houses of Parliament there was no chance to review them properly.

I took policy formation seriously. Perhaps that is why I had been so outraged when major parties and the media claimed the Democrats had no policies. No policies, I complained. What was I doing up at midnight for weeks filling in answers to policy questions?

One of the major parties was circulating a 'cheat sheet' describing terms for their press releases, interviews and conversations. The list included, 'The Democrats have no policies'. It awakened me to the cynicism in politics and the lengths some would go to win. The person who said 'Nice guys don't win' really believed it. I did not share the belief, but the list reminded me how innocent some of us were in trying to formulate a better, more honest method of doing politics.

WHAT WOULD THE AUSTRALIAN DEMOCRATS BECOME?

The 1981 Parliament looked set for some lively debates. The new senators would take their place in July 1981—six months in the future. The five would then boldly tackle the policy agenda put together during the lean years. They would vote according to their consciences without the tight bonds foisted on others by their own parties.

The Democrats, however, would commit to not voting against Supply to bring down a legitimate government; the lessons of the 1975 Dismissal were still fresh. They would use their influence to establish committees of review so shoddy legislation was not raced through mindlessly. Between the five, they would cover all the government portfolios.

The workload was enormous, but somehow they managed it. They stimulated debate on the environment, nuclear disarmament and education. They were fresh, intelligent and challenging.

Janine Haines was back in the Senate and speaking out strongly on economics as well as women's issues. She worked closely with the women's movement, amending legislation and making proposals. Haines was a forceful public speaker who had come to politics and feminism simultaneously by seeing the gender imbalance and lack of women's voices in the Parliament. Janine had a great sense of humour; it livened her speeches and kept reporters on the hop, but she didn't put up readily with 'fools' and could easily ruffle feathers.

I can imagine the tenor of discussions in the Democrat Senate party-room with Macklin, Siddons, Chipp and Haines in full flight. There was conflict in a few State divisions when some male Democrats thought Haines was going to extremes with her feminist message, but Haines swept ahead regardless.

It is interesting to consider the role of women in the Australian Democrats. Because the party was new and progressive we didn't have the baggage or the necessities of the older parties. Women played a significant role. There were tasks aplenty for everyone so they chaired meetings, ran as candidates and worked on everything and anything. On the other hand, from the beginning men occupied the leadership positions on the management committee. This was the pattern across most of the State divisions at the beginning—Macklin in Queensland, Siddons in Victoria, Gilfillan in South Australia. They had walked in and declared themselves prepared to lead, whereas in the 1970s women held back.

Was it a lack of confidence? Was it simply going along with the way things had always been? Our lack of understanding on the topic of women's inequality was stunning.

However, strong, capable and intelligent women—Haines, Powell, Kernot, Lees and many others who had grown wings following the women's movement were preparing themselves and they moved steadily and surely into positions where their capabilities could be recognised and expressed. It helped that the new party valued participatory democracy and that women made up a considerable proportion of the membership.

For Queensland women, the 1970s was a time of awakening. Propelled by American women, the consciousness-raising movement was in full swing. There was a plethora of books opening our eyes. It was also a time of personal awakening. I joined a professional women's group that met each week to discuss opportunities and pitfalls for women. I read all of the feminist literature I could find—*The Second Sex* by Simone de Beauvoir; *The Feminine Mystique* by Betty Friedan; Germaine Greer's *Female Eunuch*, Marilyn French's book *The Women's Room.*

Our own, home-grown Dale Spender wrote *Man made language.* Her book revealed the inequalities in language and made a significant impression on me. Being interested in words, I immersed myself in the particulars of this book.

We discussed the use of language (mostly with men, who were resisting), for example the relative use of 'he' when a protagonist was clearly 'she' and the use of 'chair-man' instead of 'chair-woman' or 'chair' where appropriate. These discussions took place everywhere—over coffee, in meetings and no doubt in bedrooms, too, as women discovered the power language had to shape their lives.

That topic has now been dealt with. Our language is fairer, but even in 2013 full equality for women is yet to be achieved—in business, in Parliament, in wages and in social mores.

This is not a moment for feminist propaganda, but one point of inequality stands out vividly for me. As a young teacher in the early 1960s, I was appalled at the notion of having to resign from teaching if I married. My 'husband' was supposed to provide for me! Meg Lees told me that she moved to New South Wales because there was equal pay for women and that Janine Haines was obliged to resign from the public service when she married. Women were told 'Don't expect to be promoted, you're a woman'.

By 1984 when dealing with the aftermath of a serious struggle within the Democrats I came upon a book by Anne Wilson Schaef which clarified my ideas and brought the pieces of the puzzle together. It was *Women's Reality—an emerging female system in the white male society.*

Schaef was a psychotherapist and wrote: 'As more and more women came to see me, it became clear that I did not know what to do with them. As I reviewed my training, I began to realise that what I had been taught was useful in working with men, but at best useless and at worst harmful in working with women.'[1]

She went on to describe two systems—a white male system and a female system. Her hope was that these concepts would help women in particular (but also men) conceptualise and understand what it means to be female in our culture.

I could not bring myself to be a militant feminist. I still believed in equality for both men and women and thought when women were truly equal, men would benefit. I reckoned it would take a long time to undo what had taken millennia to bring about and we needed to understand the significant transition men would face to make room for us, in the workplace, the boardroom and the bedroom. It wouldn't come easily or soon.*

In 1979, while living in Toowong, I ran for the first time as a Democrat candidate in the Brisbane City Council elections and garnered a vote of 12.5%. I gathered a team of friends and Democrats to help with the campaign and asked for donations. The campaign team produced a business and community directory; we designed campaign posters and distributed them around the electorate. We wrote a policy booklet. After work and at the weekends I door-knocked most of the electorate. I was back sweating on those hills again and facing the same curmudgeon or two with new confidence. Early mornings I would be up to speak on radio talk-back. I wrote press releases, went to meetings and occasionally slept. The result was encouraging at the time, although considering all the hard work I thought it could have been a bit higher.

In following years I was to run again twice for Brisbane City Council: in 1982 again for the Democrats and in 1986 as an independent with support from Citizens for Democracy the movement to end the Queensland gerrymander.

I found political activities incredibly interesting. I met a wide range of people, learnt to use the media and had opportunities for public speaking. My research for our campaign platforms brought me more awareness of the issues. While a Democrat member I attended the Australian Democrats National Council, meeting senators and organisers and members from other Divisions. It was a time of fast growth and huge activity.

* See appendix L: *Not just a dream*

I WRITE A BOOK

In August 1981 I had published a small, happy-go-lucky book about the formation of the Democrats in Queensland. It was called *Let's have a party*. No computers in those days, so the book was composed on a typewriter and as each page emerged I pegged it on a line to keep my ideas in order. If I wanted to change anything, it could sometimes mean retyping two or more pages. What an effort.

Friends and Democrat members went through the pages with a fine tooth comb until we were sure it was ready for publication.

We sent it off to the typesetter. When it returned, the gremlins had thrown in dozens of spelling errors and a few very suspicious (possibly politically influenced) gaffs. Once again we went over the manuscript carefully before returning it to the typesetters for the corrections. These were made by painstakingly gluing a small piece of paper over the word or letter that was incorrect. We proofread it a third time and then sent it to our printer.

I was frustrated when the book came from the printer, still with many errors. Some corrections apparently had fallen off. Such were the problems with a book of that kind. Nevertheless, I pressed on and the book was distributed to many of the newer members.

In July 1981 my mother and I drove down to Canberra for the Democrat national conference, which was held at the original Parliament House. We also attended the swearing in of the new senators. It was my first visit to the Australian Parliament and I was excited by the prospect of watching our senators sworn in. However, our seats in the gallery were up steep stairs and as my mother had angina I was afraid every step could be her last.

By 1982 my involvement in Democrat activities had increased, and after publishing *Let's have a party*, I felt more confident in my knowledge of the party, the members and the current issues, so my mind turned to problems I had noticed. I disliked the tone of some of our media statements as they reminded me of gung-ho, old-style politics. I believed the Democrats could, and should, do things differently.

I decided to challenge the ruling clique for the Queensland presidency. I had done my apprenticeship and was well informed. I got along fairly well with most members so started campaigning by letter and word of mouth. I don't take things lightly. Someone once wrote in my autograph book when I was a kid, 'Whatever you do, do with all your might. Things done by halves are never done right'. Following that dictum, I put in a 100% effort and in 1983 the membership recognised my years of hard work, electing me president of the Democrats in Queensland.

****

5
PRESIDENT OF THE QUEENSLAND DIVISION

Australian of the Year Ita Buttrose is in two minds about how far women have come since the early **Cleo** days. Sure, women are better educated, she says, but she's concerned at how they remain under-represented in boardrooms, and believes misogyny is alive and well in Australian "old boys' networks".

'My father always believed Australian men didn't really like Australian women,' she says. 'You can't say that about every Australian man you've ever met, but there are a lot of places where men still rule.

'I remember Marilyn French writing in her book **The Women's Room** that after a while men become more marginal to your concerns. I'll probably frighten men off again, but it's true. I love the company of men—I am not a man-hater—but the only thing that hasn't changed in 40 years is the Australian male ego.'

Ita Buttrose on sexism and misogyny from interview with Alex Sloane, ABC local radio, 2013.

The year of my presidency was a challenge as I had accumulated adversaries in the party. My election annoyed some men who had been in at the beginning and thought they were fixtures. Their games were annoying and hurtful. One or two had little respect for women and actively discouraged any who wanted to be candidates and committee members.

Michael Macklin was well prepared for the 1980 election and had accumulated a campaign fund, although we knew little about it then or the inner workings of the campaign committee.

The committee was established early—a good idea—but its members became an 'in-group' and it was hard to challenge their ideas or to know what they were doing. The committee included Stan Stanley, then a timber sales representative; Mike West, a cork tiler with a small business; and Les Loynes, an importer/exporter.

Mike West, a rough-hewn fellow with a decidedly colloquial manner of speech, was in the Ryan branch with me. Mike and I didn't see eye-to-eye on many issues. He had followed Macklin into the Queensland leadership and been State president from July 1978 to mid-1980. While president he cultivated TV and newspaper journalists and then continued in the media role.

Although his tone in media statements did not align with my view of how Democrats should be portrayed, it was difficult to suggest anyone else as media spokesperson. In Mike's favour, possibly because of his 'colloquial manner', he appealed to ordinary folk. Reporters got good copy and Mike got us media coverage. He was also a committed environmental warrior and used his media role to highlight environmental issues.

Results of the ballot for president were announced at a social gathering and I won by a significant margin. Stan Stanley, the losing candidate, was livid, soon coming up to me and saying he would ensure my term was short. Someone more confident than I was at the time may have responded to his anger calmly; might even have managed to win his trust, but I was stunned by the angry tone of voice and lost the opportunity. While capable and confident in many ways, I'd previously led a relatively sheltered life with little exposure to male aggression.

So started my time as president.

In the same election, Ray Hollis was elected to the State management committee as treasurer.* After the election, we settled down to see what shape

* Ray later was selected as the number two candidate on the Democrat Senate ticket for Queensland. Some years later he left the Australian Democrats to join the ALP; ran for the seat of Redcliffe and went on to become Speaker of the Queensland State House of Parliament.

everything was in, but found no account books. Appeals to the previous treasurer, Les Loynes, did not help us. Ray took several months to get on top of the situation we had inherited. Ron Cullen, the Queensland president from 1981 to early 1982, told us he had faced a problem with the accounting. However, Ron eventually resigned (exhausted and frustrated) part-way through his second year as president.

I visited Michael Macklin in his Brisbane office. He was now a Queensland Senator with standing to match that of the other Democrat Senators—Don Chipp, Colin Mason, John Siddons and Janine Haines. The Democrats held the balance of power in the Senate. Much of the day-to-day running of the organisation in Queensland went through Macklin's office and the management committee had a secondary role. I went to his Brisbane office and told him we had difficulties getting records. Michael flew into a rage, during which I wondered whether my words offended him or the request to use his influence with the 'old guard' had caused the outburst. He was so angry I felt I could be thrown out physically, which in hindsight I came to realise was only a remote possibility. Nevertheless, although rather shaken, I was still determined to do the best I could with the resources at my disposal. Michael has since admitted that he has never been a very patient person. Given all the issues he had to face at that time, it is understandable that his temper would be uncertain. He was a man driven by a high purpose and on a roll. He wanted nothing to stop him from achieving what he had set out to achieve.

However, the encounter should have taught me to always have someone with me when tackling delicate subjects. From then, it appeared to me that Macklin, Stanley and West were not my best mates. Les was always polite, but very reserved, so I never knew what he was thinking. Soon, David Dalgarno, who had incorporated a form of industrial democracy in his small business, became part of the group. In the 1980 State election, Dalgarno had achieved 20.75% in the electorate of Mt Coot-tha. That had been our best result to date.

David was a successful businessman with money to donate. He was fairly pleasant, affable and easy to talk to, but on the whole, I thought, quite malleable.

A key task was finding potential Democrat candidates and supporters. I invited a young woman member who showed a lot of potential to run for the management committee. She said she would like to but had a small child. I said, 'Don't worry about that. We'll do anything we can to make it possible'. She came on to the committee and later became Queensland branch president, then won a Senate seat. The political career of Cheryl Kernot, who would become one of the most significant Australian Democrat leaders, finished on a sad note, but Australians should always be grateful for the Democrats' watching brief while she was at the helm.

Cheryl, and her husband, Gavin, were recently back from the USA where Gavin had been teaching and Cheryl completing studies on the indigenous people of North America and Canada. They were a pleasant young couple, friendly and engaging, and absolutely devoted to their new baby. Cheryl had experienced severe medical problems during her pregnancy and there was no possibility of further children. Before heading to America they were active Democrat members, but were not planning to be active again until I came on the scene.

When we first met they were involved on a committee to start a new school. Gavin, a physical education teacher, was working on plans for a confidence-building ropes course; Cheryl was fascinated by curriculum and the possibilities of a new approach in a new school. I saw qualities that just screamed 'potential'.

Membership inquiries and renewals slowed down by 1983. Like previous leaders, we tried to revive interest, but the initial enthusiasm of 1977 had ebbed. During that year, however, at every meeting and in every possible manner my adversaries raised the topic and blamed me. The membership officer, Tony Walters, explained that national membership lists were in disarray and he spent much time working with the national membership officer to sort out the problems. Macklin had more resources than the management committee to tackle the issue, but it remained.

However, between 1985 and 1987 under Cheryl Kernot's leadership, the Queensland division flourished and membership grew significantly.

I watched and listened carefully to everything Senator Macklin said and was hugely impressed. His speeches and activities in the Senate more than satisfied my expectations of an Australian Democrat. It was a mystery to me that his political skills were less evident at a personal level. His attitude towards me was aggressively dismissive and confrontational, even when I made the mildest comment.

My aim for managing the Queensland division was to ensure everything ran efficiently; we adhered to the party's standards and were open about what we were doing while responsible for its progress. It has been pointed out to me that I was 'keen on process while the [old guard] was not too interested in the minutiae of rules and regulations'. It is interesting to speculate how much this difference in approach added to the tension in the situation.

The enthusiastic members of the party in Queensland carried on their crusade to elect a Democrat to the Senate. I, of course, noticed the criticism and stone-walling, but it was in the background for most party members. I had to negotiate a careful path. I did not want to indulge in the same kind of behaviour, but needed constantly to affirm our work and fend off criticisms. I thought, 'Why bother starting a new party with a motto of "honesty, tolerance and compassion" if we do not make an effort to live up to it?'

At the Queensland election in 1983, poet, educator and political activist Kath Walker (who later used her Aboriginal name, Oodgeroo Nunuccal) stood as Australian Democrat candidate in Redlands, a Bay-side seat near Brisbane. The electorate included Kath's family home on North Stradbroke Island. She focused on the environment and Aboriginal rights. As both were important in Democrat policies she was welcomed as a candidate. I was with her for much of the campaigning and we talked about poetry (I was a fan of her work), her educational program on Stradbroke to increase understanding of Aboriginal history and culture, and the way she dealt with men who thought they had the right to run things. She disliked direct confrontation, but nevertheless was really feisty. I should have listened more as hers was a voice of reason.

My view at the time was that if something needed to be said, someone should say it. Tony Walters told me: 'You were blunt (if not prickly).' Later, with increased self-confidence and experience, I learnt to measure my statements in terms of whom I spoke with. It isn't just a matter of speaking to men differently. In fact, everyone has a different way of receiving and acting on information.

Don Chipp came to Brisbane in 1983. Queensland party members formed a rough semi-circle as Chipp walked around greeting people. He knew I was president and I waited for him to greet me, but he deliberately walked right past—greeting first the person on my left, then the one on my right. I was taken aback. My friend Ron describes me as 'very sensitive and fairly easily hurt'. What does one do about such a slight? Despite his obvious talents and commitment to the party cause, Chipp behaved that day like a totally unreconstructed chauvinist and he had been briefed by the lads beforehand. Their game was to rattle me. Unfortunately, in the old models of politics, this is common. Some would say politics is just another field of battle and, if the goal is to win, anything goes.

I had trusted colleagues who understood my difficulties. Ron Cullen became a close friend and was very supportive. George and Marjorie Blair-West were always on hand and helpful. John Woodley, who later became a senator, was thoughtful and kind. Cheryl Kernot was ropeable about what was going on. Her good friend Tony Walters was supportive. Cheryl told me recently, 'While we decided we couldn't save you, we certainly weren't going to let them win. Tony and I were deeply upset by what had happened and I think that the blokes were upset that I [later] won [the position of president.] Ironic isn't it, we were a participatory democratic party.'[1]

The Bundaberg branch hosted the 1983 annual state executive meeting. Thirty or 40 people came to the meeting from all parts of Queensland. The Bundaberg branch had done an excellent organisational job; arrangements were working out well and we settled down to the meeting agenda. I wondered why Michael, Stan and the others hadn't arrived, but was enlightened when they came fresh from the airport with Les and Clive, secretary of the management committee. They had flown up with David Dalgarno. Difficulties as soon as they arrived made it hard for me to chair the meeting. They talked among themselves and frivolously opposed motions. One thing followed another. They showed no respect for me either as a person or as chair of the meeting. To battle with this attitude without losing my cool was exhausting.

Then we broke for lunch. I thought David was a reasonable fellow so I called him aside and asked, 'David, what is happening? Why are you all being so difficult?'

I forgot the lesson I ought to have learnt in Michael's office months earlier. Even before I finished, David raised his voice: 'How dare you speak to me like that?' and still creating a commotion went outside and created the impression that I had somehow insulted him. I almost wished I had. No, he was in it with the rest of the lads. Their mission was to destroy my presidency and David's outburst was a turning point. They had clearly collaborated on what they would do to rattle me and it worked.

I went back to the meeting that afternoon with a heavy heart. I was tired and stressed and when David and the men complained about the way I had 'behaved' I fought back. They had achieved their goal. Even my good friend Ron Cullen was dismayed and said afterwards that I had put my foot in it. No doubt I had. Part of my failure was being a loner in the way I responded to issues. In retrospect, I wish I had asked someone to come with me when I spoke with David. Hardly a minute afterwards I could not remember what they said and how I fought back. It was said in the heat of the moment and in response to a galling situation—then it disappeared for-ever into the far recesses of my memory.

No-one witnessed the interchange that sparked the uproar. Ron and the other committee members were dumbfounded and unable to support me. I wish I could have articulated my feelings in the way that Julia Gillard did in her 'misogyny speech', but no such luck. I lacked the political experience.

Tony Walters, party ombudsman at the time, received an official complaint from the men, who asked for me to be stood down as president. After Tony considered the complaint, and responded that I had no case to answer, one of the men battered angrily on Tony's home door and berated him.

Some women in the party reported harassment, and a couple thinking about running as candidates said one of the 'old guard' had phoned them and put them right off the idea. When told of this, other more reasonable men were inclined to think it could not be happening and that we were exaggerating. However, one evening when some of us had gathered for a meeting, Marjorie Blair-West received such a call. She quickly gestured to her husband, George, to pick up the other phone and at long last the truth was known. George was a gentleman who tried not to think the worst of people, but after that night he acknowledged that something unacceptable was going on.

Behaviour like this was overt, although conducted in relative secrecy. Other behaviours were subtle, such as deliberately moving too close to women—invading their space, butting in on conversations, mocking and laughing, ignoring women in a group, making sexist jokes and excluding women from key discussions.

Nor was the pressure solely on women. Less-forceful men were also under pressure. One told me: 'The *alpha* males did "bully"—but not just women. I felt it too! Their response no doubt would be “If you can’t stand the heat then get out of the kitchen”.

We met one night to work out a way to reconcile the two groups in the party. John Woodley was nominated to mediate. He was the right person to do it, but I feared then, and believe now, that if people really don’t want to be on good terms and would rather use unfair tactics, little can be done about it. I am convinced that the most positive way to counteract this kind of behaviour is to ensure it is seen for what it is—that it is known about. Then others can make up their minds. Generally, when people have the facts they can make good decisions.

The mediation didn’t happen. Michael and Stan officially moved to shorten the presidential term. ‘It will be better not to have the election in the middle of the year,’ was their catchcry. A new election was called and I nominated. My opponent was David Dalgarno, who had seldom attended a branch meeting since the Democrats began. He was more interested in the campaign side of things, but here he carried the flag for his team. With Macklin’s support, he won by one or two votes.

I tried to be a graceful loser, but his ineptitude as a president raised eyebrows, including mine. He forgot to ensure the hall was booked for the first meeting after his win. We wandered about like lost sheep and the rest of the year in the management committee was much the same. He appeared to have no time for the nuts and bolts of the party. Dalgarno must have been astute as he ran a successful business and had good relationships with his employees. Perhaps he didn’t realise that his new position would require a hands-on approach. Business managers often think others will handle the nuts and bolts. I can imagine him saying, ‘Hall booking? That’s why we have a secretary and a committee’. However, the party at this point had no secretaries and a committee member was likely to work full-time then see to Democrat business in their spare time (after attending to branch matters). In the following year, more often than not, David would attend the first half of a meeting and leave the rest to the deputy president, Marjorie Blair-West.

As security during the ballot process had been poor, I challenged the result, first with the party’s State ombudsman and later with its national ombudsman, but to no avail. The party had made its decision. At the end of the year, however, it was obvious to everyone that David had no real interest in the role.

The party drifted. At the next election in 1985 Cheryl Kernot became president. I was by this time a distressed onlooker, damaged by the whole affair and out of the party.

Three decades after the trauma Cheryl has told me she confronted the lads at her first meeting as president. She stood a tape recorder in the centre of the table. 'I intend taping this meeting,' she said. The tape recorded an indignant outburst from West and Stanley. They threatened to resign and bring her down as president. She more or less said, 'Do it then!' They did. Other management committee members followed. Stanley and West then issued a press release about the 'drama' in the Australian Democrats' Queensland division. Most of the media corps soon fronted up at Cheryl's home to report on the furore.

Cheryl handled the pressure so well that she gained the upper hand. West and Stanley had been highly visible in the party in Queensland and thought members would be up in arms to get them back. They had underestimated Cheryl. She persisted and dealt with them face-to-face during their appeal to the party's national ombudsman. The ombudsman would not let them back into the party and from then, with West and Stanley gone, she began to rebuild the management committee and the party throughout the State.

After an initial unruly and mutinous time, Cheryl turned divisional operations around and put the management of the Queensland party on a firm (and participatory) footing.

Occasionally I mused on why she managed better than Ron and I did. It's really no mystery. More facts had leaked into the open and members knew what had happened. She came to it with her eyes open and worked out how to foil the trouble-makers. Also, she was tough.

The Queensland division was back on the straight and narrow. Ron had done his best. I felt I had done what I could and Cheryl managed to complete the task. It was done at significant cost as I spent a year in counselling trying to work through my tangled emotions.

I had drive, will and knowledge, but was not emotionally tough, nor did I have Cheryl's exceptional communication talents. By the time Cheryl took on the lads she had been successful in many spheres. She was raised in a secure family with a strong mother and a loving father, who taught her to be at ease with men. She had enjoyed freedom in her teaching career to take risks and had confidence to go into areas where 'no-one had ventured before'.

I am grateful for that year of turmoil. I learnt a lot and had much to be proud of. I was beaten, but stood by my values as well as I could.

Macklin finished his Senate term in 1990. Cheryl Kernot faced an uphill battle during the candidate selection process as she seemed not to have Macklin's support. As she says, the 'blokes [were opposed] even right up to my nominating for the Senate when Michael nominated Thomas Roth instead—[There was] always something else happening—[It was] never clear-cut'. However, she pressed on and gained the number one position on the Democrat ticket. Behind the scenes Janine Haines used her influence in support of Kernot.

Mike West went on to be vice-president of the Fraser Island Defenders' Organisation and then to Birds Queensland as their president. I heard Stan Stanley joined the Labor Party, but David Dalgarno seems to have faded from view.

We were creatures of our times. The 'male mafia' played the games they knew although I think they should have focused more on what the Democrats were trying to achieve—a different kind of politics, with respect for truth and civility. I have recently been challenged by one of the 'old guard' about the use of such 'pejorative' terms as *clique* and *male mafia*. However, these are not simply my words, but were in common use at the time. The Mike/Stan/David/Les faction was routinely called the male mafia by other State council/management committee members.

In 1998 David O'Reilly, a Canberra journalist, wrote a biography, *The woman most likely—Cheryl Kernot.*[2] It was well-written and interesting, but I was amazed to see an account of the turmoil during my presidency. It appeared to place all the blame on me. It's a fact in politics that people with access to the media express their views, but others less well-placed have no way to put a story straight. I felt badly done by.

I lost touch with Cheryl for many years, but spoke to her briefly after the biography was published. As we had battled through my presidential year together, she knew well what had occurred, although most likely had not noticed the comments in the manuscript before it was published.

The first comment obviously come from Cheryl herself and was accurately reported.

'She (Kernot) took a phone call from the Queensland President of the Democrats, Bev Floyd, asking her to go on to the party's State management committee. She protested that it would be hard—she had a tiny baby to manage. 'Yes I know,' Floyd said, 'but we'll be flexible. We'll come to you to have meetings at your house at times that suit you, when you aren't feeding. I know this is a big ask, but we really don't have enough good people working on things we need to get done, and I'd just love to have your contribution again.' Kernot said she would think about it, but Floyd persisted, asking her to allow her to organise one meeting and she could see how it went.

Cheryl Kernot's political career was off and running again. Soon she was assistant secretary of the Queensland division as well as editor of its newsletter.'[3]

I thought it possible that the second comment came from Michael Macklin, although Michael says, 'No, it didn't'. The author, David O'Reilly, has died and the origin of this quote will most likely never be known.

> '... around her (Kernot) a major row was brewing among party officials, centring on the role of the talented but rather uncompromising Bev Floyd. Put simply, Floyd's get-up-and-go attitude was resented by some other party people. Moves were hatched to roll her at State executive level. When that failed, a couple of officials resigned and the issue took off in the media. One male official complained publicly about the "feminists digging potholes".
>
> 'Kernot got a call from Michael Macklin who was concerned the Floyd affair was getting out of control. He asked her if she was prepared to speak to the national media in an effort to defuse the row. The Floyd row faded from public view, but Cheryl Kernot's coolness was missed by no-one in the party hierarchy.'

THE FLOYD ROW ...?

What Floyd row? The comment was simply a mishmash of inaccurate details. No doubt this kind of indirect lie is quite common in politics, but this was **my** experience and I felt it deeply—and valued my reputation. The statement itself would have been simple to refute—if I'd had an opportunity.

For one thing, the resignations occurred when Cheryl was president, and by then I was no longer a party member. The 'moves hatched to roll her at State executive level' were just shoddy provocation. Finally, the 'feminists digging potholes' comment most likely referred to Cheryl herself as she just wasn't going to put up with shenanigans from the lads.

'Uncompromising' is an interesting word. If it means standing by a set of values, then I *was* uncompromising. If it means being unreasonable, then it depends on a point of view. A lot is at stake when new ventures are undertaken. At the time I thought it important to defend Democrat values as they were the reason for our existence.

MY RESIGNATION

After serving as president I was in a rather frayed state of mind and quite a bit out of pocket, as most of the previous presidents had been. I intended to resign from the party, but wanted to finish writing the environmental policy before I did so. This was under way with the co-operation of a Greens party member, and earned me more demerit points among one or two members of the management committee. However, he was singularly well-informed and the policy was adopted and retained for many years. Having completed that task, I resigned.

In following years I voted for Democrat candidates and watched with interest how they managed issues in the Senate. At the time I resigned I was disillusioned, extremely tired and somewhat traumatised, but thought it necessary to remove my presence from the Queensland division to avoid dissension. Not that anything would stop the squabbling. Democrats tended to be highly-strung people. We used to joke, 'Wherever there are two Democrats, there are at least three opinions!'

It was 1984—shades of George Orwell. A climate of totalitarianism seemed to envelop Queensland and my personal experiences didn't give me any lightness of heart. However, the joy of being an Australian Democrat was to be in a ferment of new ideas. It was possible to try new methods and participate in a new way; there was a can-do attitude, open to the possibility of change and reformation of political institutions.

Although the time of the Australian Democrats may have passed, the legacy of our efforts can be seen in many changes that occurred during the lifetime of the party. The Australian Democrats had a momentous influence on politics for just on 30 years.*

I had moved into a new house in the western suburbs of Brisbane in 1981 and thought it odd that there were telephone connections and cables everywhere until my neighbour told me the house had been used as an escort agency. I had a visitor once, a young man who knocked on the door and looked expectantly at me. 'Can I help you?' I asked. He said the first thing that came into his head 'Do you have a light?' I didn't even smile, although I thought it rather funny. Funny, but also sweet.

By 1984 I was still recovering from my experience in the Democrats, but during that time residents of my neighbourhood had a fight on their hands over the bushland our houses surrounded. That was the struggle for the *Bardon Bushland.* The Labor council wanted to subdivide the area and turn it into residential allotments. Of course, those of us enjoying the amenity

* See Appendix B. Democrat achievements

didn't think that a good idea, however, there were more serious issues as the bushland contained a rich variety of wildlife and plant life. It was a corridor for birds and animals from the Brisbane City Forest and also a drainage area on the western side of the hills overlooking the city. Residents at the bottom of our street knew all about this as they were regularly flooded by water running down the centre of the bushland and exiting in their back yards.

My neighbour started a community protest group and I joined. We canvassed the political bodies. Sallyanne Atkinson was lord mayoral candidate for the Liberal Party, which was running on local environmental issues. I went to see Joe St. Ledger, the Labor councillor for the area. 'Joe,' I said, 'the council is making a huge political mistake trying to develop this land. The Liberals have identified these types of issues across Brisbane and it will be very damaging for the Labor team in the next election.' He chose not to believe me, but as it happened, I was right. Labor lost the 1985 council election and Sallyanne became lord mayor.

Before this happened we raised the profile of our cause in the media. We held public gatherings to make sure residents in surrounding areas knew about it. We hired experts to profile the bushland and tell us what would be destroyed if it were cleared. Then we hired a lawyer and went to court. Apart from an appearance over a traffic fine in Papua New Guinea, this was the first time I had been a witness in a court. It is certainly awe-inspiring. I was also aware that the people in my committee were relying on me to get our message across. We didn't win our case against the council. The main reason was the lack of laws relating to the protection of the environment. This was still Joh country where the main purpose of trees and animals was to put themselves into the path of a bulldozer. Queensland then knew very little about protecting the environmental legally.

However, our cause wasn't entirely lost. Following the Liberal win in the council Sallyanne honoured her promise and the bushland was declared non-urban open space. It was a roundabout route, but a win nonetheless. This little protest reignited my political instincts; my mood picked up and my focus turned to Queensland politics.

****

6
THE QUEENSLAND GERRYMANDER

A fundamental tenet of the established system of Parliamentary democracy is that public opinion is given effect by regular, free, fair elections following open debate. A government in our political system which achieves office by means other than free and fair elections lacks legitimate political authority over that system. This must affect the ability of Parliament to play its proper role in the way referred to in this report. The point has already been made that the institutional culture of public administration risks degeneration if, for any reason, a government's activities ceased to be moderated by concern at the possibility of losing power.

The fairness of the electoral process in Queensland is widely questioned. The concerns which are most often stated focus broadly upon the electoral boundaries, which are seen as distorted in favour of the present government, so as to allow it to retain power with minority support.

Fitzgerald Inquiry Report 1989. 3.3 Electoral Laws.

The 1983 Queensland State election was a debacle. The National Party, with just 39% of the votes, won 41 of the 82 seats, and after two Liberal MPs defected to the National Party this rose to 43, so they then governed in their own right. From then, the gerrymander issue heated up.*

Labor MPs from Queensland called on the Federal Labor Government to intervene against the gerrymander. In November 1985, the Federal Attorney-General, Lionel Bowen, proposed an Australian bill of rights, but few thought it would be a workable solution.

Democrat Senator Michael Macklin weighed into the argument, saying, 'The special representation for the outback myth had some credibility during the horse and buggy era, but the advent of sophisticated communication and efficient forms of transport have debunked this myth'.[1] On behalf of the Australian Democrats, he introduced a 'one-vote, one-value' bill into the Senate to remove the power of governments to rig the electoral system in their own favour.

A group calling itself The Queensland School organised public lectures at the University of Queensland. The meetings were well attended and attracted many like me, tired of the 'same old, same old'. The malapportionment of electorates still made a change of government unlikely and held back the State. Public policy needed to change because of the long incumbency of the Premier, Joh Bjelke-Petersen.

The meetings at the university offered a variety of speakers, one of whom highlighted the Queensland 'four-zone' electoral system—the 'gerrymander'.

The four-zone system:

- 51 electorates in South-East Queensland had a quota of 19 357 voters;
- 13 provincial cities had a quota of 18,149 voters;
- 8 Western/Far Northern electorates had a quota of 9,386 voters
- 17 country electorates had a quota of 13,131 voters.

Of the country electorates, six were within three hours' drive from Brisbane. With improvement in public transport and communication systems, there was no reason to claim they were disadvantaged. The Premier's own country electorate, Barambah, had 12,750 electors, although it was just over two hours' drive from Brisbane.

A Labor Government introduced the zonal system in 1949 and it was still in force when a Country Party Government was elected in 1957. Before 1949, country and regional areas had large numbers of Labor voters. The

* In the election, with 44% of the vote, the ALP won just 39% of the seats and the Liberal Party with 15% of the vote won 10%.

Labor Party origins, of course, had been in the shearers' strikes of 1890, but by the 1950s the Labor vote in country and regional areas had declined. The advantage of the four-zone system passed to the Country Party.

The Country Party and its successor, the National Party, took full advantage of the system, refining it to further improve their electoral fortunes. With the ALP vote mainly corralled in the south-east and provincial cities, a positive election result was rarely in doubt for the National Party. The Liberal Party in Queensland, unlike in the rest of Australia, was secondary to the National Party. As most Liberal voters lived in the South-East or in provincial cities, the Liberals found themselves in the same boat as the ALP. Both were handicapped by the gerrymander and fought each other for votes.

The National Party's electoral redistribution proposals during 1985 created seven new seats. Associate professor of Government at Queensland University, Dr Ken Wiltshire, predicted the Nationals could win at least five of the seven. The changes would worsen the electoral situation for the Labor and Liberal parties.[2]

Russell James (Russ) Hinze, nicknamed 'the minister for everything' because he held so many portfolios, proudly claimed to be able to 'rig the boundaries'. He was quoted:

> "… and I've always been a little bit boisterous. And I said: "Now, Premier, if you want the boundaries rigged leave it to me. I'm going to make a job of it" and I said: "And if you don't do it, of course, well then of course the people won't give you the opportunity to do it again".
>
> 'I wouldn't make that statement today. But I certainly made it and I'm not backing off it. But if you realise and analyse what I said, that's what governments do'.[3]

Hinze was rotund and jokey. But even if he *was* joking, the electoral boundaries continually improved to assist the National Party, and the department that brought this about came under his ministerial responsibility.

After the meetings at the university, an organisation was formed to combat the gerrymander and press for 'one vote, one value'. The new organisation was Citizens for Democracy.

I felt strongly about the need for electoral reform. My time in the Democrats had given me inside knowledge about issues that troubled Queenslanders. I believed we needed a change of government, but felt it would not happen unless the electoral system changed. I was among those who put up their hand to get the new organisation off the ground.

The name Citizens for Democracy had a history. A group that formed in 1976 after the Whitlam Dismissal and focused on the drafting of a new constitution used the same name. Frank Hardy and Patrick White were high-profile supporters. The question of constitutional change was important after the trauma of the Dismissal. I was amused to discover that, before Don Chipp resigned from the Liberal Party, his party colleagues roundly criticised him for attending a Citizens for Democracy meeting instead of another, with the Queen.

The new Citizens for Democracy had three original co-ordinators—Peter Meggitt, Di Zetlin and me. Its meetings were open to anyone and a variety of folk passed through. Soon after we formed, Di, an ALP member, decided to stand down as co-ordinator. Brian Hoepper replaced her.*

On December 10, 1985, Citizens for Democracy organised its first public meeting in the Ithaca Room of Brisbane City Hall. Mischief-makers were at work and Drew Hutton, a convenor, wrote to *The Courier-Mail* to set the record straight.

No party link for protest group[4]

> I refer to the story under the headline 'ALP organises protest against gerrymander' (C-M, Dec 9)
>
> Tonight's public meeting against the Queensland gerrymander has not been organised by the ALP. It has, instead, been organised by a non-party political group called Citizens for Democracy and any attempt to link us with one particular party badly undermines what we are trying to achieve. –**Drew Hutton, convenor, Citizens for Democracy.**

Speakers included Matthew Foley (Queensland Council for Civil Liberties president), Democrat Senator Michael Macklin and Labor Senator Margaret Reynolds. The advertised list of speakers at the City Hall included Bill Hewitt (a former Liberal member of the Legislative Assembly) but he dropped out and was replaced with David Hamill (Labor member for Ipswich). The hall was full and the speakers' messages were received enthusiastically.

National Party Senator Ron Boswell was booed when he claimed the Labor Party was using the redistribution issue as an excuse for its failure in Queensland and 'Howls of laughter greeted his request for a fair go for the 35 per-cent of people who lived in three-quarters of the State outside the south-east zone'.[5] The meeting passed resolutions calling for the State Government

* See Appendix C for list of Citizens for Democracy foundation committee members.

to drop the proposed electoral redistribution and to introduce legislation based on 'one person, one-vote, one-value' and for the Federal Government to ensure State electoral boundaries were redrawn. Citizens for Democracy quickly set up action groups in electorates throughout Queensland. As I lived in the electorate of Mt Coot-tha, a small group there was soon devoted to the cause.

The organisation aimed to be non-party political. I was no longer a member of a political party, but most knew of my previous affiliation with the Democrats. Our opponents tried several times to make trouble by insinuating that I practised some kind of subterfuge and worked undercover for a cause promoted by Senator Macklin. This was ill-informed nonsense, of course, but many such attacks occur on the edge of politics.

Death throes of Democrats[5]

> The formation of the Mount Coot-tha branch of the *Citizens for Democracy* must be seen as the final death throes of the Australian Democrats. This new organisation, claiming to be non-party political, is in fact an extension of the almost defunct, and fast-failing Democrats.
>
> The inference in the name alone is sufficient to establish the association but when one acknowledges the chairmanship of the organisation and its cause then the subterfuge becomes all too clear.
>
> The organisation is chaired by Ms Bev Floyd, a member of the Australian Democrats and its candidate in recent elections.
>
> The cause advocated is 'alerting the electorate to the dangers of …democracy, Queensland style'. This cause is the one promoted by Australian Democrat Senator Macklin.
>
> Support for the Australian Democrats is now at an all-time low so much so that the Morgan Gallup poll published on March 11 does not afford the party individual status.
>
> The poll result shows figures for the Labor, Liberal and national parties and lists an additional grouping under the heading of 'others' which holds 5 per-cent of the State vote.
>
> One may presume that the Australian Democrats are included in that 'others' grouping, but in politics presumptions are a

dangerous thing and it is possible that the Australian Democrats have actually lost all support in Queensland.

G.M. Colless, Boundary Road, Rainworth.

Citizens hit back[6]

We refer to the letter 'Death throes of Democrats' (*The Courier-Mail,* March 25, 1986)

There is misleading mischief in the claim that Citizens for Democracy is an Australian Democrats' 'front'. Bev Floyd, the one Democrat mentioned, does not 'chair' Citizens for Democracy. She is only one of three co-ordinators. More importantly, CFD is a genuine non-party political group joined by hundreds of Queenslanders crossing all boundaries of party, vocation and location.

What does unite them is their belief in democracy, and their determination to eradicate the scandal of Queensland politics, the gerrymander. Your correspondent's claim that our use of the term 'Democracy' betrays CFD's party allegiance is really a reminder of how the word 'democracy' has been debased in Queensland.

Your correspondent's letter is tragic because it tries to subvert a genuine citizens' movement for real democracy in Queensland.

Marcos labelled the Aquino movement 'communist'. We are labelled a 'Democratic Front'. People power triumphed in the Philippines. In Queensland, the people will also prevail. The gerrymander will be defeated. Democracy will triumph. This is the simple yet powerful message of Citizens for Democracy.

—Peter Meggitt, Bev Floyd, Di Zetlin, co-ordinators, Citizen for Democracy, Archibald Street, West End.

On the Senate's final sitting day before the Christmas break, the ALP and the Democrats united to refer Senator Macklin's 'one-vote, one-value' bill to a Parliamentary joint select committee.

The National Party's proposed redistribution neatly divided ALP strongholds to make Labor victories in western seats almost impossible. The town of Cunnamulla, potentially a Labor stronghold, was cleverly excised from the Warrego electorate and got the name 'Cunnamulla nipple', which was in poor taste, but aptly described the weird electoral boundary.

In February 1986, Prime Minister Bob Hawke gave a guarantee he would introduce legislation to abolish State gerrymanders, but the Federal Labor Party was in two minds on whether the bill of rights or separate legislation was needed. Former Labor leader Bill Hayden from Queensland led the fight for Federal intervention on electoral reform. Eventually neither option eventuated.

Federal opposition leader John Howard was against Federal legislation on State electoral reform and the Federal member for Ryan (my own electorate), Liberal John Moore, announced that he deplored the Queensland gerrymander and subsequent attempts at rigging voting methods, but thought they were matters for the Queensland people and not the rest of the nation. I suppose he had a point, but concerned Queenslanders were looking anywhere and everywhere for assistance.

It seemed Federal intervention was unlikely, so Queenslanders would need to do the job themselves.

Citizens for Democracy felt tensions as extreme left-wing members wanted our mission broadened to include particular issues and tried to exclude the Liberal side of politics. I thought differently on both points as I believed a non-partisan focus on just the gerrymander would gain valuable support across the spectrum. Also, if we could bring in Liberals, many of whom were fed up with National Party dominance and bad behaviour, our group would have more clout. We had little success in bringing Liberal politicians on board, but a significant number of Liberal voters joined Citizens for Democracy.

I had little idea about political leanings of others in Citizens for Democracy. I knew there were some communists, but as they were among our most hard-working and likeable supporters, I found little to criticise. The ALP and unions were behind the scenes. I never found out what their contributions were, but knew they had made some. I focused on our main task. Others could look after finances, politics and publicity.

My chief skill was organisation. So, I organised—meetings, rallies, events, pamphlets, petitions and then activities surrounding the election. If we needed specialist assistance, for example, with production of literature, research and submission drafts, or high-profile speakers at public rallies, many qualified people would offer their services. CFD members were formidable and much skill and talent was available.

In February, members of the Federal Joint Select Committee on Electoral Reform, inquiring into the Democrat bill, were in Brisbane hearing evidence about electoral apportionment. Journalist Matt Robbins reported in *The Australian* that political analyst Dr Peter Coaldrake from Griffith University told the committee he believed a conservative government would be returned in Queensland under a one-vote, one-value electoral system because support for Labor had lagged behind that of the non-Labor parties in all elections except two since the 1950s.[8]

Citizens for Democracy responded to this article with a letter to ***The Australian***: [9]

'We are a citizens' group which is receiving remarkable support given that we have only been formed since December 1985. Membership has grown to more than 800, local groups have formed in 20 of the state electorates and more are in process of formation. A recent public meeting in the Brisbane City Hall attracted 900 people and thousands of signatures are being collected on petitions.

Plans are under way for a significant intervention in the State election due later this year. The real strength of this group, however, is the fact that it is at last drawing its support from across the whole spectrum of Queensland society—workers, employers, teachers, academics, students, liberals, socialists, Democrats and Greens. These people have temporarily forgotten their divisions and are pursuing a common aim—a fair and just electoral system for Queensland.

While Dr. Peter Coaldrake may be convinced theoretically that the conservative forces would be returned under a one-vote—one value system, the rest of us would like the chance to test this theory in practice.

The way it stands now, we will never know. Despite the brave front of the Queensland ALP there is really almost no chance whatever that they can win under the present redistribution. This situation is no longer acceptable to a wide range of decent and talented Queenslanders.

Journalists Quentin Dempster, Peter Morley, Denis Reinhardt, Matt Robbins and Marion Smith in Queensland and Wallace Brown in Canberra were among those who closely followed the electoral reform battle.

In March 1986, National Party backbenchers threatened a revolt against Bjelke-Petersen over his decision to allow private subdivision of a national park on Lindeman Island, but he was resolute. Citizens for Democracy launched a letter-writing campaign. Supporters across Queensland deluged the papers with information about the gerrymander.

Good decision on gerrymanders[10]

> I wish to applaud the Federal Government decision to investigate gerrymanders, especially ours in Queensland. Should legislation follow, it will mean my vote in the Toowong electorate will count more than the present 42.1% of a vote cast in Balonne. Then I hope we will see less of situations like this Lindeman Island affair where the Premier held in complete contempt despite an overwhelming public outcry. Without a gerrymander he would know he is accountable in the public at elections when taking a stand. I will be watching with great interest proceedings of the Human Rights and Equal Opportunity Commission on his issue.—**Chris Griffith, Swann Road, St. Lucia. 4067**

The Cabinet stopped Bjelke-Petersen's Lindeman Island plan. The rebuff for Joh from his party and colleagues promoted a headline in ON THE NATION, 'All the signs point to Premier losing control'.[11]

A group representing major churches in Queensland called for a fair and just voting system. Members included the Anglican, Greek Orthodox, Salvation Army and Uniting churches, while the Catholic Church and Bjelke-Petersen's own Lutheran Church both had observer status.

On April 21 1986, Citizens for Democracy organised a rally in the main auditorium of the Brisbane City Hall, an elegant building that seemed to suit the rally's promotion as 'A festival of music, drama, poetry and talks to highlight the campaign for electoral justice in Queensland'. The artists were: Error O'Neill, Breadline, Steve and Adele Nisbet, Ross Clark, Order by Numbers and Megan Redfern.

Mike Higgins, a South-East Queensland newsreader, chaired the rally. The speakers were Dr. Ian Lowe, an environmentalist and Griffith University professor; Dr. Paul Reynolds, a political scientist from the University of Queensland; and myself.

Years later in an interview Dr Reynolds reflected: 'I could not teach my students about Westminster democracy and see it fouled on a day-by-day basis in George Street … it was impossible for me to stay silent … when what I was saying and lecturing to my students was so antithetical to what was being practised in State politics.'[12]

I had an attack of nerves before I spoke, and I was so nervous I could hardly think what I was saying. Never mind, I'm sure the people listening knew where my heart was, even if my mind seemed to have gone missing. At other times, carried away by emotion and the occasion, I could speak fluently.

Happenings around politics can be hysterically funny sometimes, particularly if you are in the know. One fund-raising event sponsored by Citizens for Democracy was a showing of the film *The Gods Must Be Crazy*. Some of our members believed the movie was racist and took advantage of the bush-men of the Kalahari. I was asked to cancel the fundraiser, but our plans were too advanced.

Besides, the criticism was a little abstruse for me as I thought the film actually made a positive point about the bush-men. So we went ahead, and as we ate sandwiches and drank wine, a cohort of fellow members, with signs and fierce intent, picketed the cinema.

In May, *The Courier-Mail* reported Sir Joh's personal popularity was down 9% to 45% and the National Party's approval at 34% might not be sufficient to retain government at the next election. Labor Party approval had risen slightly.

Denis Reinhart in *The Bulletin* predicted Joh's days were numbered. 'His fitness for leadership increasingly questioned within his own party, external enemies gradually encircling him and amid increasing personal isolation, Bjelke-Petersen is gambling on an electoral redistribution, which he hopes will guarantee the Nationals continuing rule in their own right after the October State elections.'[13]

In July, Citizens for Democracy launched its pre-election publicity in Aspley, one of seven marginal electorates that were targeted for an intensive campaign. All candidates were interviewed on their attitude to a one-vote—one value redistribution. The guest speaker was Drew Hutton. The talk was followed by question time and a video, *The Sunshine System*, which a central committee member, Jeff Clarke, and his students produced.

After the Lindeman Island debacle, the Government's lack of concern for the environment was becoming a significant issue in Queensland and on

August 25, 1986, Fraser Island Defenders Organisation stalwart John Sinclair declared he was leaving Queensland as a 'political refugee'. That same month, John Howard visited Brisbane to support Liberal Party State leader William Knox for the coming election. Liberals pulled no punches in describing the State of Queensland. The headline in the advertisement for their public rally said: 'From a State of Queensland to a State of disrepair'.

By this time, the National Party had internal difficulties preselecting candidates for the October election. The general dissatisfaction even threatened the party's president, Sir Robert Sparkes. Such a backlash would previously have been unthinkable.

One of our supporters, Col Cunnington, was in the publishing business. I went with him to place an advertisement in *The Courier-Mail*. It contained a long list of names of eminent people who supported electoral reform. Our task was to proofread the document before handing it in. Col was very thorough. He was also the chief mover behind one of our most successful pieces of literature—a pamphlet with graphs and illustrations. Simple wording with a black and gold design made the pamphlet a stand-out production. We handed out thousands during the campaign.

The result of the October 1986 election was unsettling, with the Nationals increasing their number of seats in Parliament by eight and winning an outright majority, but we carried on.

In December 1986, I ran as an independent candidate for Brisbane City Council with the main aim to raise the gerrymander issue's profile. The suburbs around the University of Queensland contained many 'thinking people' with influence across the State and we hoped to raise their consciousness about what was needed.

A by-election in the Taringa ward followed the election of popular alderman Denver Beanland to state Parliament. Labor, the Nationals and the Democrats did not put up candidates. A Liberal, June O'Connell, ran against Dr Rupert Goodman, a 'protect the Australian flag' candidate, Mike West and me. West ran as an independent as a year earlier he had left the Democrats after the showdown with Cheryl Kernot. His profile was still high due to the publicity work he had done for the Democrats. West lived and ran his business in the ward. He also had good contacts with environmental groups, so I thought he would do well. The 'gerrymander' handicapped both Labor and the Liberals by diluting the value of votes in coastal and metropolitan areas. In essence, people living there could do little to restrain the State Government.

I realised my chances were slim, but believed my candidature would highlight the gerrymander's effect. While this was essentially a State issue, it did have significant effects on people in the Brisbane City Council area. One issue still in people's mind was the Bjelke-Petersen Government's seizure of the electricity supply from local government control. Eighty per cent of Brisbane residents had opposed the takeover. Another issue was the steep rises in home valuations, a State Government responsibility.

The campaign team was an amazing collection of people: supporters from the Citizens for Democracy movement; Democrats with sympathy for the cause; ALP members with no Labor candidate to support; and friends. In due course we all became friends. The campaign ran efficiently. I worked hard. There were plenty of opportunities for the 'electoral justice' message to percolate. The figures were interesting. After the first count, June O'Connell had just one vote more than 50%; two fewer votes and preferences would have been counted. The Liberal vote was down by over 20%. West came second and I trailed the field, but was not too disappointed as we had achieved our goal of highlighting the gerrymander.

In January 1987, Bjelke-Petersen decided to go into Federal politics and seek a House of Representatives seat. This was not only hubris, but also political folly for the conservative side of politics. The impact on a large number of voters shattered John Howard's campaign to win government. Perhaps this was partly Bjelke-Petersen's intention as the National Party at Federal level, unlike in Queensland, was secondary to the Liberal Party, and Joh had no love lost for his once coalition partner in Queensland. He might have achieved his goal of thwarting Howard, but in Queensland the National Party was starting to question his increasingly erratic and high-handed behaviour.

While Petersen was busy on his Federal crusade, Police Minister Bill Gunn was acting Premier. Fearless reporting by *The Courier-Mail* and the ABC raised questions about police corruption. Gunn realised the need for an investigation into the claims of vice and corruption and established the Fitzgerald Commission of Inquiry.

Rumours had circulated about unbecoming conduct by a police officer, Terry Lewis, for many years, but he had the Premier's support and moved up the ladder to eventual appointment as Commissioner from 1978. Initially an investigation into police corruption and vice, the Fitzgerald Inquiry later had extended terms to cover political corruption and electoral malapportionment. Revelations in the inquiry eventually led the National Party to call for Bjelke-Petersen's resignation.

QC Tony Fitzgerald conducted the inquiry using ingenious investigation methods. Jack Herbert, who had been a 'bagman' in police corruption, received indemnity from prosecution and the police whom he identified fell like dominos, one at a time, to unravel the endemic corruption.

Until 1989 Citizens for Democracy continued to rally supporters with public meetings and functions. It opened an office in St Lucia and we mounted a long campaign for a referendum at the 1988 Federal election. This referendum question was an attempt to rectify the widespread malapportionment and gerrymandering endemic during Joh Bjelke-Petersen's term as the Queensland Premier. Referenda in Australia have a low success rate as the bar is high—a majority nationally and a majority of States is required for the referendum to pass. This one did not pass the test, but public awareness of the issue grew.

> 'A large public interest non-partisan organisation, the Citizens for Democracy, lobbied extensively the Liberal and Labor parties to abolish the gerrymander and to make it a major issue in the lead-up to the landmark 1989 Queensland election.'[14]

With the establishment of the Fitzgerald Inquiry, Citizens for Democracy entered a new phase. Some members who worked in the Department of Government in the University of Queensland started preparing (in their spare time, such as it was) a submission to the Fitzgerald Inquiry propounding that the gerrymander was the key to the whole disreputable state of affairs in Queensland. The writing group included Bron Stevens, at that time a lecturer in the government department, and Tracey Arklay, who would later become a lecturer in government at Griffith University where I met her recently. They and others spent hours writing and amending and polishing the submission.

The completed document was clear, well-researched and compelling. The final Fitzgerald report contained, almost word for word and line for line, material from the Citizens for Democracy submission.

How much credit Citizens for Democracy deserves for changing attitudes in Queensland cannot be quantified. We kept the anti-gerrymander profile high and perhaps helped raise the gerrymander opponents' spirits. Attitudes *were* changing, even before the Fitzgerald Inquiry, but many bodies, including journalists, politicians, academics, church representatives, unions and community organisations, were involved.

From the formation of Citizens for Democracy in December 1985 to the Fitzgerald report in 1989, we toiled steadily—raising money, holding public meetings, creating publicity materials and canvassing. I stepped out in late 1988, but others continued until the task was completed.

Tracey Arklay recounted her experience of the *Hands around Parliament* event that preceded the 1989 election. It was a wonderful example of people power.

'On the Tuesday before the 1989 election, about 20 members of the co-ordinating committee of Citizens for Democracy slept out outside the [Queensland] Parliament. We stayed all night with burning candles.

In the morning the media came down and we called for as many Brisbane people as possible to join us as a symbolic gesture that we were reclaiming Parliament for the people. It was excellent. You can't completely surround Parliament, however, we had it completely surrounded on three sides. People held hands and sang "We shall overcome". It was an amazing way to end a long night.'

Fitzgerald recommended an Electoral Commission inquiry into boundaries and correction of the malapportionment. We were on cloud nine. Our efforts, along with others in the community, had impacted positively on the future direction of affairs in Queensland. Perhaps, we thought, now it can be truthfully described as the 'Sunshine State' instead of the 'Moonlight State'.

The era can be described only as incredible—almost unbelievable. Each day new revelations spread across newspaper headlines and TV screens. Fitzgerald managed to widen the inquiry to include the political and social causes behind police corruption. He identified corruption among politicians and the gerrymander's impact, and eventually came face-to-face with the Premier, who gave evidence and was subsequently charged with perjury for statements he made under oath. The statements concerned money 'in brown paper bags' that had been given to him.

True to form, Joh Bjelke-Petersen's perjury trial turned into a farce. He was acquitted, but the jury foreman was later found to be a young National Party member with links to the ex-Premier. Bjelke-Petersen maintained his innocence of corruption and retained, until his death in 2005, thousands of supporters across Queensland.

I met him once during a protest of some kind outside Parliament House. He was walking past and stopped to chat with some of us, possibly not realising that we were the dreaded 'rabble'. He was a short man with a very pleasant manner and spoke politely. If he had been my next-door neighbour more likely than not I would have taken to him. It isn't surprising that many Queenslanders still thought well of him.

After these political dramas, I decided I had the right to 'retire to my estates' and enjoy the fruits of my labours—that, in fact, the real reason for activism is so we can all enjoy a peaceful and productive life—and I planned to do just that.

But first I would go travelling. In December 1991 I headed to Africa with some friends. My friend and her brother had been born in Rhodesia, moved to South Africa during the civil war and then migrated to Australia. They had been in Australia for several years and were going back for a reunion with their family who still lived there.

We arrived in Johannesburg when the Convention for a Democratic South Africa (CODESA) was in full force. Its aim was to establish an interim government and begin the transition from apartheid to democracy. Nelson Mandela had been released in February of the previous year and discussions were proceeding with De Klerk's Government on issues relating to a handover of the government. There were a number of stops and starts before the talks concluded, but in 1992 an interim constitution had been written and a date was set for an election in 1994.

I was exhilarated by the thought of being in Africa at such a significant moment.

****

7
DEMOCRATS IN THE SENATE 1978-1990

I remember it as though it were yesterday—Don Chipp taking young Adams to lunch to tell me of his plans (hopes? dreams?) to start the Democrats. A wildly improbable, even insane, undertaking. But it happened—and it turned out to be eminently sensible. Though otherwise engaged (in a love-hate relationship with the AL bloody P), I was enthralled by the new party's impacts and achievements. Many of its too many leaders became friends—and on a good day, and the party had many good days, the Democrats were great for our democracy. Without them, Australian politics would have been even more mendacious and mediocre, more sleazy and cynical. That's why I'd like the Dems to rise again, refreshed from their sabbatical. You'll never keep the bastards honest — that's an impossible task — but you can dramatise their deceits and duplicities.'

Phillip Adams, journalist. From *30 years Australian Democrats*

In 1978 when Chipp and Mason first held the fort in the Senate, the emphasis was on environmental issues. During protests over damming the Franklin River in Tasmania, the Democrats were in the first carriage of the green train—with only conservation organisations ahead of them. Chipp was anti-nuclear and opposed to the sale of Australian uranium. He also strongly opposed the hosting of the United States' nuclear submarines and the establishment of American military bases.

He and Mason advocated the need for more workplace harmony between employer and employee. They were among the first Parliamentarians to support Aboriginal land rights. The first elected Australian Democrats were of a progressive bent and strongly raised many ideas that their members felt passionate about.

They were vocal about 'bottom of the harbour' schemes which effectively stripped companies of their assets so they were unable to pay tax. In 1982, the Fraser Government, with John Howard as Treasurer, tabled a bill to allow the retrospective recovery of tax. Without this action, those who had used the schemes would avoid penalty, but the Democrats would not support such legislation. Don Chipp: 'I do not trust politicians to legislate retrospectively. One of the few protections that the ordinary citizen has is that he knows the law.'[1]

Janine Haines was appointed by Don Dunstan in 1977 to a casual vacancy in the Senate; she served until 1978. Janine, an intelligent woman, had been involved with the Liberal Movement party which Steele Hall and Robin Millhouse founded in South Australia.* Haines ran again in 1980 and was returned to serve with Chipp, Mason, Siddons and Macklin. All were very impressive senators.

When Chipp resigned in 1986, Haines, after a contest with John Siddons, became the Democrat leader. She spoke out vigorously and fearlessly and in particular challenged the rise of the neo-classical economic approach which was sweeping the world and would create social hardship and upheaval in Australia. David O'Reilly describes economic rationalism as 'a view that the working of demand and supply—market forces—should be the sole instrument of economic decision-making in society. Government, and its agencies, should exercise a minimal role, without public sector 'intervention'.'[2] Janine resigned her Senate seat in 1990 and unsuccessfully contested the lower house seat of Kingston in South Australia. She left the political scene just as Cheryl Kernot arrived. Janine later wrote a book, *Suffrage to Sufferance—100 years of women in politics,* which begins:

* See Appendix J: What came before the Australian Democrats?

> The day I walked into the Senate chamber in the old parliament house for the first time in February 1978 I was struck by the maleness of the place. Of the 64 senators only seven were women. When the 124 all-male members of the House of Representatives joined us for the official opening of Parliament, the place was awash with testosterone. The Governor-General was male, so was the Prime Minister, the Deputy Prime Minister, the Leader of the Opposition, the President of the Senate and the Speaker of the House; all 124 members of the House of Representatives, all but seven of the senators, most of the clerks and all the attendants. Only one minister was female. [3]

If Janine Haines had walked around the parliament in 2013, she would have seen 65 women members, including the Prime Minister, the Speaker and 14 ministers or Parliamentary Secretaries. The Governor-General and many clerks and attendants were women. Considerable progress has occurred but the work for women's equality continues. I am sad Janine cannot see what she worked for; she died in 2004, aged 59, from a degenerative neurological condition.

After her political career, Janine became the University of Adelaide deputy chancellor. In 2001 she was awarded the Order of Australia.

Janine Haines and Chipp didn't agree on a number of things. Chipp had a tendency to chauvinism. As someone told me, 'Chipp loved women but he didn't respect them.' On the political front, however, he was a genius of public communication. The slogan, 'Keep the bastards honest', is rumoured to have begun in Mike West's cork tiling shop but Chipp made it his own, gaining tremendous public support, thanks to the major parties' behaviour.

In 1981, Chipp had a mild heart attack while the five Democrats were embroiled in the Senate over contentious changes to budget bills. Chipp would always be in two minds about the decision because of his pledge not to block supply. In later years a distinction was made between 'supply' and a budget bill which blocked minor money proposals and particularly spending the Democrats had campaigned against. Their opposition to the bills would not hinder the government's legitimate right to govern, but might mean the Treasurer had to find another way to fund a proposal, or leave it out of the budget.

After ten years as Australian Democrats leader Chipp retired. Janet Powell took Chipp's Senate seat and was elected in her own right the next year.

Chipp was 78 years old when in 2003 he developed Parkinson's disease. He died in 2006. In later years he occasionally intervened in issues, much to the consternation of Democrats' serving senators. As he aged, his conservative roots seemed to strengthen. He wrote a newspaper column and sometimes used it to criticise the Democrats and Cheryl Kernot. Chipp questioned whether the Democrats had a mandate to block the Telstra sale. He thought they were opposing government policy too strongly. Kernot retorted the public had told her in no uncertain terms they did *not* want Telstra privatised.

Chipp phoned Kernot to ask if she wanted him to mediate between her and Treasurer Peter Costello who was worried she would oppose the Federal Budget. Kernot told Chipp, 'No thank you'. The Democrats would not oppose the budget but reserved the right to criticise and amend sections if necessary.

The pair eventually had a public falling out, when Kernot accused Chipp of interfering on behalf of the Liberals while he was considered for appointment as Victorian governor. Tough talk! Chipp probably never forgave her as any chance of becoming the governor had disappeared.

Colin Mason has been another of the Democrats' intelligent senators. He was a journalist and author. An Australian Broadcasting Commission foreign correspondent for 14 years, he had written about the effect of communism in the Asian region. Before joining the Democrats he was an Australia Party convener. Colin was unpretentious but his analyses were penetrating and persuasive.

I met him briefly in 1978 at the Queensland state conference. His wife was unwell and he needed to balance his time to care for her. This kindly characteristic impressed me greatly.

In the Senate, Mason concentrated on defence and foreign affairs but in 1983 he introduced a bill to protect Australia's world heritage sites and he played a significant role in establishing the royal commission that eventually freed Lindy Chamberlain—for which he was both lauded and despised, as the Chamberlain case was extremely divisive.

Colin left politics in 1987 and has written books, including one on Asia and another, *The 2030 Spike: Countdown to Global Catastrophe,* analysing problems facing the world and suggesting solutions.

John Siddons, a successful businessman, was a leading member of the Australia Party—one of the parties that called on Chipp to lead a new centre party. He deserves our gratitude for that as without his drive and persistence, the Democrats would not have come into being. However, he was no match for the wily Chipp. From time to time they had flaming rows.

Siddons, when nominating for the Democrat leadership after Chipp resigned, probably thought his knowledge of economic policy and prominence from the party's beginning would give him the edge over Janine Haines. However, with Chipp's endorsement, Haines won the ballot. Her leadership style was very different from what Siddons' might have been. He resigned from the Australian Democrats soon after the ballot, claiming the party had moved too far to the left. In 1987, he registered the Unite Australia Party, merging two other minor parties, the Advance Australia Party and the remnants of the Australia Party. The Unite Australia Party unsuccessfully contested the 1988 federal election.

Michael Macklin, for eight years before entering federal politics, had lectured at the University of Queensland on the philosophy of education. He was an inspirational speaker, particularly about educational matters, on which he thought deeply. He leaned more towards the anarchist end of the scale in discussions of freedom and public administration. Macklin was elected to the Senate in 1980 and served until the 1990 election. In the Senate he was Democrat spokesperson for education and Aboriginal affairs. He wrote *The Australian Democrats—a major 'minor' party - face the future.*

During his time in the Senate (1981-90) the Democrats held the 'balance of power' and he comments: 'This enabled us to implement, via discussions with government, very many of our policy objectives'.[4]

Macklin's Electorate Officer, Cheryl Kernot, was elected as a Queensland Senator after his term ended.

Macklin was involved later in fundraising for several organisations including the Democrats and the University of Queensland. He was involved in a project to benchmark private school finances and in 2002 became the professor and Dean of Arts at the University of New England. He has played a role in official tribunals and committees and published articles and books.

Jack Evans a West Australian was elected in 1983 but lost the seat in 1985 when Greens Senator Jo Valentine was narrowly elected. Evans wanted to be 'a people's voice in the parliament to balance the conflicting extremes of powerful unions and wealthy big business'. During the 1981 election he 'initiated High Court actions against Malcolm Fraser and Bob Hawke—both for misleading advertising in the lead-up to my election campaign—and the rulings are still used by lawyers and academics to illustrate the stupidity of the law'. [5]

David Vigor, from South Australia and elected in 1984, was in the Senate until the 1987 election. Meg Lees said: 'I suspect that, if one goes back through the Hansard, one would see that he held close to the record for the largest volume of questions ever placed on notice in any 12 month period. He was a central player in the move to self-government in the Australian Capital Territory and a tireless advocate for the science community within public life.' David died in 1998.[6]

Norm Sanders, originally from the US, was elected in 1985 to a Tasmanian Senate seat and served until the 1990 election. He found the Senate frustrating as at that time the 'balance of power' was shared with another Tasmanian, the independent Brian Harradine and the National Democratic Party (NDP). Sanders notes: 'We did manage to untangle the mess of civil aviation. We put up a bunch of amendments. I held the balance of power on this issue, and the Democrats managed to set up the Civil Aviation Authority, which was a great step forward'.[7]

Norm's chief claim to fame preceded his Senate role when he was elected as a Democrat member of the Tasmanian House of Assembly. In his words he 'actually managed to bring down the government—that was pretty cool'. This took place during the Franklin Dam dispute when both major parties favoured the dam.

Norm held the 'balance of power' in the Tasmanian State Parliament but it wasn't much use with both major parties on the other side of the issue. In the referendum over the dam, Tasmanian Democrats told the people to write 'NO DAMS' on their ballot ticket. 'When more than a third of the people wrote no dams, and at the opening of parliament—with bands playing and everything—I moved a motion that brought down the Labor government which had been in power for 46 years.' Norm was a large personality and a fervid environmentalist.[8]

Janet Powell, a Victorian, was appointed to Chipp's Senate position after he retired in 1986. She became party leader after the 1990 election. I stayed with Janet and her husband on one of my Melbourne visits for a National Executive meeting. They lived on the city outskirts in a rural area. Janet, like other Democrats, cherished the environment and clearly understood the Democrats' role in the Senate. 'Something of which I am personally proud', she writes, 'is the fact that we exercised our balance of power in a very sensible way (which) did give comfort to people in the community. Often, a much more global perspective was taken, rather than a selfish party perspective, which I think is something to be proud of as well'. She also writes, 'I was the first woman to have a private member's bill passed through the Commonwealth parliament and that was the Smoking and Tobacco Products Advertisement Prohibition Bill in 1989. It banned the print advertising of tobacco products'.[9]

Powell resigned from the party in 1992. In 1996 she campaigned for Greens leader Bob Brown and in 2004 joined the Australian Greens. In 2006 she was an unsuccessful Greens candidate in the Victorian state election.

Janet Powell has been a member of the Patrons' Council of the Epilepsy Foundation of Victoria and is a life member of YWCA in Victoria. She was an inaugural appointee to the Victorian Honour Roll of Women in 2000 'for services to the community'.

In the 2012 Queen's Birthday honours list, she was appointed a Member of the Order of Australia, in recognition of her service to the parliament and people of Australia, including through leadership of, and support for, YWCA Victoria.

THE 1987 FEDERAL ELECTION

Evans came and went after one term as did Vigor, but in 1987 John Coulter, Paul McLean and Jean Jenkins joined Haines, Mason, Macklin, Sanders and Powell to give the Democrats seven senators—a high point.

John Coulter came from South Australia. He and Norm Sanders were dedicated environmentalists and in the Senate highlighted environmental issues. According to Kernot, 'Some of the things he talked about I think have been proven to be very sensible' but John treated [issues] as if everybody should understand.[10]

Coulter led the Democrats to the 1993 election. He resigned through ill-health in 1995; Natasha Stott Despoja was appointed to the casual vacancy.

Paul McLean was a NSW senator from 1987 to 1991 and handled the business portfolio. He said in 2007: 'My all-consuming issue was bank malpractice and corruption, and it climaxed in the tabling of the Westpac letters, which was one of the most spectacular events in the parliament for many years'.* McLean resigned his Senate seat in 1991 and was replaced by Karin Sowada.[11]

Jean Jenkins represented Western Australia in the Senate from 1987 to 1990. She said, 'As a parliamentarian, my pet cause was always human rights and social justice. My concern with what was happening to the environment was part and parcel of that. I believed, and continue to believe, that we as citizens of Australia are entitled to a clean, unpolluted environment.'[12]

****

* The Westpac bank lent money to farmers in Swiss francs just before the franc fell in value. Letters and internal correspondence within Westpac (and between its associate Partnership Pacific and the clients) revealed a poor attitude of bank officials. Westpac eventually paid the farmers a generous amount to compensate for their losses, but not before the affair badly damaged the bank's reputation.

8

DEMOCRATS IN THE SENATE 1990-1995

Senators and State Parliamentarians (1990): Front row: Vicki Bourne, Elisabeth Kirkby, Jean Jenkins, Meg Lees, Janet Powell and Janine Haines; middle row: Paul McLean, Sid Spindler, Cheryl Kernot, Michael Macklin and Richard Jones; back row: Ian Gilfillan, John Coulter, Michael Elliott and Robert Bell.

THE 1990 FEDERAL ELECTION

The 1990 election, with Janine Haines as leader, gave the Democrats their highest vote, up 4.15% on their previous result. Although they lost the leader in her failed bid for a House of Representatives seat, five new senators—Robert Bell (Tas), Vicki Bourne (NSW), Meg Lees (SA), Sid Spindler (Vic) and Cheryl Kernot (Qld)—were elected, raising the number to eight. Five Democrat senators had six-year terms, which meant the party would hold the balance of power for some time.

By 1990, Senators Haines, Chipp, Mason, Macklin, Siddons, Vigor, Evans, Jenkins and Sanders were gone. West Australian senator Jean Jenkins lost her seat in the election, as did Norm Sanders, Tasmania. Only Powell, Coulter and McLean remained of the first two sets of Democrat Parliamentarians. Powell was elected leader.

Although the Senate now had eight Australian Democrats, the changing of the guard was not smooth. Newly elected Democrat senators felt Powell relied excessively on Sid Spindler's support and advice. Sid had been a long-term member of the Australia Party and Chipp's assistant. He was knowledgeable and experienced, but the other senators felt he had too much influence.

Powell was maligned—to the point of receiving death threats—when she opposed the first Gulf War, but she had the privilege of calling the parliament to task over not debating the decision to enter the war. She told the Leader of the Opposition in the Senate (Robert Hill) that the Democrats would vote to recall the Senate; this put Prime Minister Bob Hawke in a difficult position so he recalled the whole parliament.

Powell remained party leader until 1991 when a movement to replace her began. She had been negotiating a controversial merger with the Greens. Another issue placed Powell in an ambiguous position. The matter came to light when a letter from the Finance Department went to someone else instead of her. 'We need to draw your attention to this anomaly. It's an extraordinary amount of over-time, being claimed'.[1] The suggestion was that her two staffers had a quiet arrangement with her that they would claim it and pass it on to the Victorian Division, but nothing came of the claim.

Tony Walters, who was Queensland president at the time, has said the move to replace Powell began in Tasmania but a Queensland executive meeting decided to circulate a petition asking for leadership positions to be thrown open. The outcome was that John Coulter replaced Janet Powell as leader.

Meg Lees told me, 'I think, looking back, [the party] should have just let her go with the leadership. It was more damaging to challenge her'.[2]

In 1992 Powell resigned from the Democrats but sat as an independent until her defeat at the 1993 election.

Tasmanian **Robert Bell** was in the Senate from 1990 to 1997. Natasha Stott Despoja says of him: 'Robert Bell was my friend, colleague, mentor and former boss. He was a tireless campaigner on education, rural and indigenous issues. From King Island products to free education and industrial democracy, he was a great advocate as well as passionately representing Tasmania'.[3] Robert died in 2001.

Vicki Bourne, a NSW senator from 1990 to 2002, had been involved in the setting up of the Australian Democrats. She explained why she joined the Democrats: 'There was a feeling—at least at university which is where I was at the time—that the main political parties were run by small groups of anonymous old blokes and that having any influence was virtually impossible. The idea of setting up a party from scratch was very exciting'.[4]

Meg Lees, South Australia, was in the Senate from 1990 to 2002. She shared with Bourne, Allison and Murray the distinction of being among the second-longest-serving Democrat senators—12 years. After her resignation from the party she spent three more years in the Senate. Only Natasha Stott Despoja with 13 years represented the Democrats longer in the Senate.

Lees followed Cheryl Kernot as leader, holding the position from 1997 to 2001. Although Lees lacked Kernot's public charisma she was a very principled and effective leader.

Sid Spindler, senator from 1990 to 1996, had been an Australian Democrats foundation member and previously had been an Australia Party member. As a child, Sid was affected by the events of a war-ravaged Europe. He felt deeply that another catastrophic event such as the Holocaust could be prevented only if 'every human being is respected and treated equally, regardless of race, religion gender and sexuality'.[5] Spindler entered the Senate in 1990. He retired through ill-health at the 1996 election.

Spindler and his family set up the Towards a Just Society Fund, which distributes $200,000 annually to help Aboriginal students. He was 78 when he died of cancer in 2008.

Karen Sowada was in the Senate from 1991 to 1993. She replaced NSW senator Paul McLean, who resigned his seat in 1991. At the time, Sowada, 28, was the youngest woman to have a seat in the parliament. Karen trained as an archaeologist and continued this work after leaving the Senate. She says: 'I joined the Democrats because of the party's focus on long term environmental and economic solutions rather than short term political gain'.[6] In the Senate, she worked on education issues and opposed the Labor government's Higher Education Contribution Scheme (HECS). In 2007 she wrote, 'Democrats have an important role to play in the wider body politic as a voice for the marginalised and as a generator of ideas'.

Cheryl Kernot entered the Senate after the 1990 election. In previous years, she had built up considerable experience—as party organiser, Queensland division president and Michael Macklin's electorate officer. She had been a candidate in the Queensland state election and a Queensland policy co-ordinator.

Kernot focused on portfolios including finance, superannuation, transport and regional development and Aboriginal affairs, which she particularly sought and later played a pivotal role in the Labor government's Mabo legislation.

THE 1993 ELECTION

The Democrats' support fell 7.32%. Their campaign was mainly about environmental issues. In retrospect, that was an error. Their leader at the time, John Coulter, did not realise that casting the Democrats solely as an environmental party might diminish its appeal—particularly in an election where economics would play a large part.

Paul Keating had moved to the right on economic policy—and Coulter's approach failed to get traction. Sections of the media mocked the Democrats as 'fairies at the bottom of the garden'. In Western Australia, the Green's Jo Valentine beat Jack Evans; this was the first inklings that the Greens party was on the way up. The Rev John Woodley was elected as a second Queensland senator, taking Democrat numbers to seven. He told me, 'I was elected in Queensland because of Cheryl. There's no doubt about it … Cheryl was just the darling of everybody'.[7]

Kernot was elected as the Australian Democrats parliamentary leader in a 'participatory' ballot after the 1993 election.

John Woodley, a Queensland senator from 1993 to 2001, had become interested in politics because of injustice to indigenous people.

Before his election to the Senate, Woodley met with Drew Hutton, a Greens spokesman in Queensland, to arrange a coalition between them and the Democrats. Drew was a decent fellow and a good spokesman for his party, but a coalition was not to be. Neither Cheryl Kernot nor Bob Brown wanted it. Cheryl was no fan of the Greens, who were fighting the Democrats for the final Senate seat in each state. She thought their methods gave a bad reputation to minor parties.

Woodley's final task as a senator was to chair an inquiry into the dairy industry deregulation. All the information received by the committee pointed to a disaster if the industry was deregulated but economic rationalist ideas drove both the Government and the Opposition; nothing the Democrats said could change their minds.

****

March 1983: Jack Evans, Colin Mason, Michael Macklin, Don Chipp and Janine Haines (left to right).

March 1983: Jack Evans, Colin Mason, Michael Macklin, Don Chipp and Janine Haines (left to right).

Janine Haines, Australian Democrats senator for South Australia, 1977-8, 1981-90.

John Siddons
Australian Democrats senator for Victoria, 1981–3, 1985–6.

Jack Evans
Australian Democrats senator for Western Australia, 1983–5.

The party's 21st birthday (1998): Meg Lees (leader), Don Chipp, Colin Mason, Natasha Stott Despoja (deputy leader) (left to right).

The party's 21st birthday (1998): Meg Lees (leader), Don Chipp, Colin Mason, Natasha Stott Despoja (deputy leader) (left to right).

Cheryl Kernot
Australian Democrats senator for Queensland, 1990–97.

Meg Lees
Australian Democrats senator for South Australia, 1990–2008.

John Woodley
Australian Democrats senator for Queensland, 1993–2001

Natasha Stott Despoja
Australian Democrats senator for South Australia, 1995–2007.

Federal parliamentary team (1991): Cheryl Kernot, John Coulter, Janet Powell, Meg Lees, Paul McLean, Robert Bell (upper), Sid Spindler (lower) and Vicki Bourne (left to right).

Federal parliamentary team (2001): Meg Lees, John Cherry, Vicki Bourne, Andrew Bartlett, Natasha Stott Despoja, Lyn Allison, Aden Ridgeway, Andrew Murray and Brian Greig (left to right).

9
DEMOCRATS IN THE SENATE 1995-1997

We need a third force like
the Australian Democrats.
Australians need honesty, tolerance
and compassion injected into the parliament.

Natasha Stott Despoja

Natasha Stott Despoja, a South Australian Democrat senator from 1995 to 2008, said in 2007: 'I was inspired to join the Australian Democrats because of the party's commitment to human rights, social justice, sustainability and accountability in government'.[1]

Stott Despoja was appointed to the casual vacancy created by the resignation of John Coulter through ill-health. She completed the rest of Coulter's term, was returned at the 1996 election and re-elected in 2001 for a six-year term. When she entered the Senate in 1995 at the age of 26, she was the youngest woman to have been elected to the Australian federal parliament.

She led the Democrats in the Senate from April 2001 to August 2002. In 2004 Stott Despoja took 11 weeks' leave from the Senate after the birth of her first child before returning to full duties as Democrat spokesperson on status of women, higher education, and work and family.

She did not contest the 2007 election but by the time her term expired she had become the Australian Democrats' longest-serving senator.

Stott Despoja in 2011 was made a Member of the Order of Australia for service to the Australian parliament, particularly as a South Australian senator, through leadership roles with the Australian Democrats; to education; and as a role model for women.

THE 1996 ELECTION

Democrats, under the leadership of Cheryl Kernot, raised their vote by 5.51% and won five Senate seats keeping their total at seven. Sid Spindler did not stand because of ill health; Robert Bell stood but was defeated. Andrew Murray won a West Australian Senate seat and Victorian Lyn Allison joined the Democrat senators.

The national campaign manager, Steven Swift, urged Cheryl to buy into the GST debate. Swift believed the Democrats needed to be 'players' or the media would ignore them. Although Cheryl was unhappy with the approach, she brought the Democrats into the tax debate. 'While not willing to prescribe a GST, [Kernot] was 'prepared to see it discussed in a wider discussion about what we do about tax reform in this country'.[2]

After the 1996 election, Kernot was responsible for the treasury portfolio when privatisation of Telstra became a key issue. After a three-year apprenticeship in the Senate, her ideas on the economy were well-formed and she had the energy, talent and inspiration for the challenge.

Kernot's campaign not only targeted city voters but also looked to regional areas, and the policies she emphasised fitted in well: support for areas affected by economic rationalism and competition policy; opposition to privatising Telstra; and concern about Keating's tax proposals. Her handling of the first Keating government budget made a significant mark and, having established her economic credentials, she didn't look back.

She was fully involved with negotiating the native title legislation and towards the end of 1996, during the Howard government, worked with Peter Reith to devise industrial relations legislation that would be acceptable to the Democrats.

Victorian **Lyn Allison** was a Democrat senator from 1996 to 2008. Lyn recalls: 'Meg Lees did a huge amount of travel into country areas, including many visits in Victoria with me before the 1996 election'.

Lyn was the fifth woman to lead the party and one of the last Democrat senators. She led the party from 2004 to 2008. She was progressive in the area of women's rights, winning the fight against a veto over RU486, the non-surgical abortion option. The struggle showed the importance of women in the parliament because many men opposed RU486, which had the support of almost 90% of the women Parliamentarians. Allison says: 'It took months of patient negotiation to even get a vote on anything to do with women's reproductive health despite the serious threats by the health minister and others to limit access to abortion. We could have gone it alone but opted in the end for co-sponsorship because, although the accolades would have to be shared, this made a win on the ground much more likely'.[3]

Andrew Murray was a Democrat senator from West Australia between 1996 and 2008. He gained considerable respect for his breadth of knowledge and intellect during his twelve years in the Senate.

After his education in Rhodesia and South Africa, Murray went to Oxford University on a Rhodes scholarship. As an office bearer in the National Union of South African Students he was deported for his opposition to the national apartheid policies. He migrated to Australia in 1989.

Senator Murray dealt with an enormous number of bills, including those relating to tax, industrial relations and electoral matters. However, he considers: 'My most important work on the social justice side of things has been for adults who were institutionalized as children'.[10] He had experienced this himself when sent from the UK to Rhodesia as a young child migrant in the 1950s. Early in 2013, Murray was appointed as a commissioner in the Gillard government's royal commission into child sexual abuse.[4]

From 1996 to 1999, during John Howard's first term as PM, the Democrats either held the balance of power in the Senate or shared it with other parties and independents. The Democrats opposed the sale of the national telecommunications body, Telstra, on the grounds that most Australians did not want it sold and those in rural areas believed their service would suffer. All sides attacked Kernot for arguing this in the Parliament and accused her of obstruction and acting without a mandate.

Eventually, an ALP senator, Mal Colston, defected from his party and agreed to support the sale in a deal that resulted in his appointment to deputy president of the Senate. Colston, sitting on the cross-benches as an independent, changed the balance of power in the Senate. His vote with the government on the Telstra issue was distressing for the Democrats and in particular Cheryl Kernot, who had fought long and furiously against the sale.*

The change in the Senate's composition made the fight to restrain the Howard government's excesses difficult, if not impossible, and contributed to Kernot's decision to leave the Senate to seek a House of Representatives seat for the Labor Party.

Ex-prime-minister Malcolm Fraser was extremely critical of the Liberals. He denounced their policy on refugees, terrorism and civil liberties. He opposed the Iraq war. Years later, in December 2009, he resigned from the Liberal Party, but in 1997 he told Woodley, 'John, this is not the party I joined, and as for John Howard, I put him where he's got to today and I couldn't talk to him now. He's so far away from what I believe'.[5]

In the 1996 election, the voters of Ipswich and surrounding areas elected a populist politician to the House of Representatives. Pauline Hanson had been a Liberal candidate, but the party dis-endorsed her before the election for making racist comments. Hanson was a one-term member (1996-99) but with the founding of the One Nation Party her name resounded throughout Australia and overseas for many years.

One Nation won over 20% of the vote and 11 seats in the 1998 Queensland election. In the federal election in October that year, a One Nation member, Heather Hill, was elected as a Queensland senator but was obliged one year later to retire in favour of another One Nation member, Len Harris, when her citizenship status was challenged. Harris had the seat from 1999 to 2005, the end of the original six-year term.

* According to Lyn Allison: '*and interestingly it was Labor that goaded Colston into voting for the Telstra sale because they thought it would be to their political advantage at the following election and were keen to have access to the revenue. Also the coalition had a deal with Harradine trading off spending in telecommunications in Tasmania and restrictions on the abortion drug RU486 for his vote to sell Telstra*'.

Hanson appeared to embody the frustration and pain coursing through Australian society. Both major parties supported economic rationalism. Jobs had disappeared; competition policy threatened businesses, education and health; and policy-makers no longer seemed to listen to the electorate. The government simply pressed on with change after change, much of which was destructive.

Hanson gave voice to their fears and pain. That she made Aborigines, refugees and foreigners the scapegoats was unforgivable, but the electorate's strong support for her indicated a mood which needed to be assuaged. Howard initially said little to rebut her arguments until it was obvious that her attitude to Asians impacted on Australia's reputation and economic fortunes.

****

10
DEMOCRATS IN THE SENATE 1997-2008

I have called this press conference today to inform you of my decision to resign as leader of the Australian Democrats, and as a member of both the party and the Senate.

I fully appreciate this decision will come as a shock to members of a party I have served for 17 years, but it is a decision which, in the past 18 months, has grown unavoidable for two reasons; One, my personal and growing sense of outrage at the damage being done to Australia by the Howard government, and two, my limited capacity to minimise that damage.

I have reached the conclusion, that, for me, the imperative at the next federal election lies not in battling to extract a share of the third party vote to keep the balance of power in the Senate. It is to play a more direct role in the removal of the Coalition government. It is to stop the enormous damage the coalition parties are doing to the fabric of this society.

Cheryl Kernot's resignation speech. October 15, 1997.

From *Speaking for myself again* by Cheryl Kernot

CHERYL KERNOT LEAVES THE DEMOCRATS

Kernot resigned from the Democrats on October 15, 1997, and joined the ALP. The stunning blow to Democrat members was totally unexpected.

She waited for the press conference with Beasley and other senior Labor politicians in the Parliamentary Labor offices—a woman among men with many different agendas. They had counselled her not to tell anyone what was about to happen and she accepted their advice.

However, some in the media apparently had already caught a whiff of what was about to happen. Political parties implant 'spies' in other parties, and journalists use the same tactic. A staff member who had been recently appointed to the Democrat team phoned a particular journalist before the press conference which Kernot called to announce her move. The staff member had worked for the journalist as a researcher and went back to a position with him after the Kernot move.

Andrew Bartlett, from Queensland, took the casual vacancy left by Cheryl Kernot in October 1997. Bartlett describes his reason for joining the Democrats: 'The key thing that appealed to me about the Democrats above other parties was their open-mindedness and ability to think outside the square—to not just mindlessly follow a pre-determined ideological line'. He saw the participatory ethos as a key example of this. Bartlett replaced Stott Despoja as leader in 2002.[1]

After a poor electoral result in 2004, Bartlett resigned the leadership and Lyn Allison led the party to the 2007 election.

Bartlett was defeated at the 2007 election and left the Senate when his term expired in 2008. He joined the Greens and in 2009 was a Greens candidate for the House of Representatives seat of Brisbane. He is now a convener for the Greens in Queensland.

THE 1998 ELECTION

With Meg Lees now leading the Democrat team, the party won four Senate seats, although the Democrat vote went down by 2.37% Ridgeway and Greig joined the team to take Democrat numbers in the Senate to the highest they had ever been. From 1999, there would be nine senators—Allison, Bartlett, Bourne, Greig, Lees, Murray, Ridgeway, Stott Despoja, and Woodley.

One candidate almost made it into the Senate; Rick Farley* in the ACT. John Schumann** in South Australia came within two percent of taking Liberal foreign Minister Alexander Downer's seat of Mayo in the Adelaide Hills.

Following the departure of Cheryl Kernot*** to the ALP, the results of the election were a credit to Lees and her team and an acknowledgement by the public that they appreciated the role Democrats had been playing in the parliament.

THE GOODS AND SERVICES TAX (GST)

The GST played an important part in the 1998 election. Andrew Murray was a keen advocate of a modified GST; John Cherry (economics adviser to Cheryl Kernot and Meg Lees from 1993) supported the view. After long consultation with state divisions, a membership ballot supported the inclusion of a tax on 'services'—an indirect reference to the GST.

The Democrats would pass the tax reforms of whichever party won the election but would support the GST only if food and other necessities of life were exempted.

The Howard government introduced the GST bill soon after the election. According to Andrew Bartlett, the Democrats were surprised to have to deal with the GST issue. 'We weren't expecting to be in that position, but from the moment Brian Harradine said he wouldn't do it [support the GST], it was like three weeks, and before Harradine said no, the government hadn't come near us'.

The Democrats proposed a series of compromises to fulfil their promise to the electorate before supporting legislation. Murray and Cherry accompanied Meg Lees to the talks.

Lees and her team achieved many but not all the concessions she wanted. The bill passed in June 1999 (prior to Ridgeway and Greig taking up their position in the Senate) after Lees agreed to support the legislation. Two Democrat senators, Stott Despoja and Bartlett, crossed the floor to vote

* Rick Farley, among other achievements, was executive Director of the National Farmers' Federation and later a member of the Council for Aboriginal Reconciliation.

** John Schumann was lead singer in the Australian band Redgum and song-writer/activist/intellectual who contributed significantly to public culture in Australia.

*** Cheryl Kernot also did well to win a seat in the House of Representatives. However, as the Labor Party lost the election, she progressed no further and in the 2001 election lost the seat and left Parliament.

against it. Bartlett told me that because the Democrats were in an invincible position they could have achieved everything they wanted and this was one of the problems he and Stott Despoja had about voting for the negotiated package. That and the fact they saw the GST was extremely unpopular with the electorate.

The government did not handle the GST's implementation well and some interest groups were unhappy. Small business people had masses of unfamiliar paperwork to collect the tax; hotels copped flak because of increases in alcohol prices. Petrol prices rose from unrelated causes but the rise was blamed on the GST.

Treasurer Peter Costello took every opportunity to blame the problems on the Democrats' insistence on exempting food and the necessities of life from the tax. 'All the complexity, blame it on food' he said. This was blatantly untrue as the complexity of the quarterly compliance statements, Business Accounting Statements (BAS's), was a large part of the problem.

However, the problems had ramifications for the Democrats' future, feeding later concerns about Lees' leadership and subsequently leading to the short-term leadership of Natasha Stott Despoja, Brian Greig and Andrew Bartlett.

The post-GST confusion also extended to the Liberal-National Coalition, which suffered a fall in electoral standing. My local member in the Ryan electorate, Liberal John Moore, resigned from parliament when passed over for the position of defence minister. In a by-election in January 2001, the ALP's Leonie Short had a shock win in the blue-ribbon conservative seat.

By 2002 Howard realised decisive action was needed to reverse the loss of support before the 2004 election so he pulled out his cheque book and 'made amends' to every interest group with a range of concessions, so got the GST off his back. He lifted petrol indexation, doubled the home buyers' grant and introduced many small business concessions.

It worked. The GST was no longer an issue for Howard and the coalition, but the same was not the case for the Democrats.

Although the Democrats had been clear on their policy and managed to have many essential items exempted, the media represented the decision to support even a modified GST as a betrayal. It was difficult to counter this impression, although Democrat polling showed they were doing well among voters in typical Democrat areas and it is possible that had Meg Lees retained the leadership the GST question could have been put into perspective during the 2001 election campaign.

Looking back soberly, we can see the GST has worked effectively. The Democrat compromises softened some of the tougher aspects and the public soon adapted to the new tax.

LEADERSHIP STRUGGLES

Meg Lees battled through 1999 and 2000 until April 2001 when she was replaced as leader by Natasha Stott Despoja. Lees eventually lost the leadership by a margin of 70/30, which John Cherry said 'reflected a view at the time that the GST was hurting, the polls were down and Natasha's time had come … From day one in that ballot [Meg] knew she was going to lose and it was a big vote. A lot of people who supported the GST deal still voted, reluctantly, for Natasha'.

The campaign for the leadership was damaging and Stott Despoja found it difficult to bring the party-room along with her. One of the downsides of the membership electing a leader is that if the person elected is unacceptable to most of the parliamentary team there will be conflict—and there was.

THE 2001 ELECTION

Natasha Stott Despoja led the party for reasonable results, only 1.20% less than previously. The party won four seats and after the election there were eight senators: Stott Despoja, Allison, Bartlett, Cherry, Lees, Murray, Ridgeway and Woodley.

Long-standing NSW Democrat Vicki Bourne lost her seat after ten years in the Senate. Queenslander John Cherry joined the team after the departure of John Woodley. Cherry was the last Australian Democrat elected to the Senate.

John Cherry from Queensland entered the Senate in 2001 after John Woodley's term ended and served one term. Before his election, he was a key economic adviser during Cheryl Kernot's leadership, then with Meg Lees. He worked on superannuation and pressed to ensure the tax office better recognised charities. He said, 'It's absolutely crucial that no one controls the Senate. The strength of the Senate for the last 30 years—it has been one of the most effective houses of parliament in the world—has been because the Democrats have held the balance of power'.[2]

Aden Ridgeway was a Democrat NSW senator from 1999 to 2005. He is of Aboriginal descent. He said, 'There were three key things that stood out for me about the Democrats at the time I joined. One was the party's policy on Aboriginal affairs, the second was its policies in relation to the environment and the third was its policies on education. I identified with the policies the party had established, but most of all I identified with the way the party worked. It was more open than other parties and it was democratic in the way discussions were held. The Democrats presented an alternative voice that most Australians agree with'.[3]

Since leaving the Senate, Ridgeway has worked on projects in the indigenous community.

Brian Greig was an Australian Democrat senator from Western Australia from 1999 to 2005. He joined the Democrats because of their policy and platform on gay and lesbian rights, and Sid Spindler's introduction of a comprehensive private member's bill on anti-discrimination laws and partnership recognition. Greig said, 'Whether I liked it or not, I was always seen as the gay senator. My agitation both within the party and the parliament saw John Howard give in and include same sex equality in the Super Choice legislation for the purposes of death benefits … For many gay and lesbian people I was their voice and hope. I was able to bear witness to discrimination and tell their stories'.[4] Greig became acting leader after Natasha Stott Despoja's resignation.

REPLACING STOTT DESPOJA

Brian Greig was appointed Acting Parliamentary Leader to replace Stott Despoja. The National Executive overlooked Aden Ridgeway, who had been the deputy leader and should have taken the leadership. Democrat senators were amazed as most were prepared to support Ridgeway.

MEG LEES' RESIGNATION

In July 2002 Meg Lees had resigned to sit as an independent. She says proudly, 'When I left the Democrats I went off and worked on health care. I got psychology into Medicare, and it's still there. No one's taken it out'.[5]

The next year she founded the Australian Progressive Alliance. The APA contested the 2004 election in four States with candidates including former Queensland senator John Woodley and Elisabeth Kirkby, a former Democrat member of the NSW Legislative Council. None of the other candidates won. Lees continued in the Senate as the sole APA member until her term ended on June 30. 2005.

John Coulter initially supported Natasha Stott Despoja and was publicly critical of Meg Lees' leadership, especially her handling of the GST legislation. However, he later changed his mind about Stott Despoja, deciding she had reduced internal party democracy and taken the party further from its grassroots. He then resigned from the party.

John Woodley admired Meg Lees' straightforward and intelligent approach to her tasks, particularly when leader from 1997 to 2001. He was distressed over the campaign in which she eventually lost the leadership.

Soon after retiring from the Senate in 2001, Woodley left the Democrats and joined the APA. He served as national president of the APA, which wound up after unsuccessfully contesting the 2004 federal election. In retirement, Woodley continues to be active in church circles in Queensland.

THE 2004 ELECTION

The party went to the election under Andrew Bartlett's leadership. The vote dropped significantly and they lost three Senate seats. Cherry, Greig and Ridgeway were not returned.

Four Democrat senators remained: Allison, Bartlett, Murray and Stott Despoja. Before the election an altercation between Bartlett and a Liberal Senator, Jeannie Ferris, during a Christmas party had caused poor publicity. The significance of the event appears to have been exaggerated but the negative publicity lowered the standing of Bartlett and the Democrats.

The coalition won a significant majority in the Senate. While the number of Green senators rose by two to equal the Democrats' four, there were not enough to block any bills the government wanted to pass. In these circumstances Howard introduced his infamous workplace legislation, Work Choices, which passed both houses of parliament to become law.

THE 2007 ELECTION

This was a fierce battle between Labor and the Liberal-National coalition over industrial relations policies. Labor won the 2007 election and replaced Howard's severe industrial relations legislation with something more acceptable to the majority of voters.

Smaller parties are often squeezed out in this kind of struggle and, although the Greens managed to increase their Senate numbers from four to five, the Democrats had no new senators. With the terms of the Democrats' sitting senators elapsed, the party was no longer a force in the Australian parliament.

Between 1999 and 2003, internal conflict had sapped energy required for the party's promotion. The party of balance was balanced precariously on the edge of oblivion.The demise was complicated. The senators were asked to do almost inhuman tasks. They had to work closely with each other and while they were, no doubt, conscious of the fragility of the organisation, their own stresses and strains and human needs must have been at times almost overwhelming. Perhaps in hindsight, we must simply appreciate the marvellous way in which this amazing organisation rose, persisted and achieved what it did for so long. Given all the pressures, it is a virtual miracle that it survived so long and did so much good work.

ROUND UP

Twenty-six Australian Democrats were elected to the Australian parliament between 1977 and 2008, and many others in local government and State Parliaments.* South Australia, Victoria, New South Wales and Queensland each elected five senators. Four were elected from Western Australia and two from Tasmania.

Don Chipp led the parliamentary party from 1977 to 1986; Haines followed from 1986 to 1990. Michael Macklin was interim leader for several months before Janet Powell, 1990 to 1991. John Coulter was the leader from 1991 to 1993; and Cheryl Kernot from 1993 to 1997. Meg Lees took over in 1997 and led the parliamentary party until 2001. She was followed by Natasha Stott Despoja from 2001 to 2002. Brian Greig was Acting leader for several months in 2002. The final leaders were Andrew Bartlett, 2002-04, and Lyn Allison, 2004-08.

****

* See Appendix B Electoral Results

11
THE BEGINNING OF THE END

Brutus:
There is a tide in the affairs of men.
Which, taken at the flood, leads on to fortune;
Omitted, all the voyage of their life
Is bound in shallows and in miseries.
On such a full sea are we now afloat,
And we must take the current when it serves,
Or lose our ventures.

Julius Caesar Act 4, scene3

Some thought the departure of Cheryl Kernot in 1997 and the surrounding media frenzy was the beginning of the end for the Australian Democrats. Liz Oss-Emer, President of the National Executive between 2001 and 2002, told me that was not so:

> 'I think.. the time when Cheryl actually left.. was an event that brought everyone together.. Tightly together.. I remember the first National Executive meeting happened to be in Brisbane after she left, and the feeling of cohesion was very strong there. Everyone was very focussed on making sure that we stabilised and Meg came in as Leader then and she was a very good leader—she worked very hard to keep everything together….'[1]

The following year Meg Lees lead the Australian Democrats to the 1998 Federal Election and nine Democrats were returned to the Senate—an excellent result. Meg was confirmed as leader by a members' ballot and Natasha Stott Despoja was her deputy.

Prior to the election John Howard announced his intention to legislate for a Goods and Services Tax and the Australian Democrats prepared by sending teams to each State Division to discuss the issues. A membership policy ballot took place to determine Democrat policy on the GST. Although the question on the ballot paper was difficult to interpret, a majority voted for a GST if it was modified to exclude food and other essential items. John Cherry was an advocate of the GST as was Andrew Murray.

After the election, the Prime Minister John Howard pressed Brian Harradine, the independent Tasmanian Senator, to vote for the GST in the Senate. When Harradine declined to support the government the focus turned to the Australian Democrats.

Meg Lees, John Cherry and Andrew Murray met with John Howard and his treasurer, Peter Costello, to negotiate terms on which the Democrats might support the Bill in the Senate. This process dragged out and gave the media (and the government) the opportunity for a great deal of negative publicity about the Democrats and their role in bringing in a new tax.

Also in the mix, was the lack of agreement among Democrat members about the policy of supporting the GST. The constant negative publicity served only to heighten the anxiety of members about supporting it. Liz Oss-Emer says:

> 'It wasn't just their vote in the Senate that was really the issue that caused a lot of division. It was actually the policy ballot that preceded that. It was the most confusing thing designed not to actually elicit a clear result. I think there were pockets of members from that time that just didn't accept that it was the right way to go.

> 'I remember when.. the GST was being debated at a Queensland State Council meeting (which is about 40 or 50 people), Andrew Bartlett just took a straw poll of the room to get a (and this is branches from all over the State) feeling of it and it was split one-third 'accept the GST as it was proposed', one-third 'oppose under any circumstances' and one-third 'modify'. So, I think that was pretty indicative of how members were feeling. [2]

The GST negotiating process damaged the Democrats and it also damaged Meg Lees' image. Whether she could have recovered ground for the party is difficult to determine as other factors entered the equation. In the Parliament Natasha Stott Despoja and Andrew Bartlett voted against the Bill and differently from their Senate colleagues. It was not unusual for some Senators to vote differently as Democrat Senators always had the right to vote according to their judgement of what the electorate wanted or as their conscience dictated. However, on this occasion, it may have been wiser for the Democrats to vote together. The votes of Bartlett and Stott Despoja could not change the outcome. They would only further split the membership on the question of the GST. And that is what happened.

For and against factions developed among the membership. Loyalty to the serving leader was lost in the ensuing melee. As often happens in such circumstances, emotions ran high; good sense and civility was lost. It came down to a question of changing the leader. Stott Despoja's supporters were urging her to run for the position. She wasn't sure if she wanted to do that before the next election.

Natasha was a charismatic figure. She attracted attention everywhere she went. She was the popular media's darling—attractive, exciting and an excellent communicator. Her support was increasing—particularly as younger voters were won over. Eventually the barrage for her to run seemed irresistible. The National Executive President at the time was Michael Macklin (previously a Democrat Senator) and he urged her to run. The idea was that a change of leadership would lift Democrat ratings and unify the Party room.

Don Chipp did not support Meg. There was a history between them and Chipp was not one to forget a rebuff. His subsequent support for Stott Despoja almost guaranteed her success in a ballot.

However, Democrat leaders were selected by members and it was necessary for a number of members to petition for a leadership spill before there could be a vote. Eventually, The ACT division brought that about and nominations were called.

It was Meg or Natasha.

The electioneering process was damaging for the party. As the contest sped to its inevitable outcome, Meg was denigrated by some anti-GST supporters. It must have been galling, not only to lose the leadership but also to have her record and integrity challenged. Those who were sensitive to the treatment Meg received were resentful. Five of the nine Senators prepared a letter to send directly to members saying they supported Meg, but were told by the National Executive they were not to send it. Meg had been a good leader—competent, principled and effective. The results of the 1998 election were the best the Democrats had ever had. She had carried out the wishes of the majority of the members by negotiating changes to the GST. Now the party was being divided by arguments over whether the GST should have been passed.

Natasha was well-placed to benefit from the anxiety over falling polls and lost membership. She, along with Andrew Bartlett, had voted against the Howard bill. Her own personal stocks were high; she was constantly exposed on the media and she had support among senior figures in the party. The ballot reflected these advantages and she won by a significant amount.

After the results of the April 6 leadership ballot, Natasha was the new leader, but she would inherit the damage the leadership change had incurred. It seems she thought Meg would step down and pass on the baton. But Meg was not of a mind to do that. As was to be expected the relationship between them was strained.

Natasha needed to re-unite the party under her leadership but five of the eight Senators were not happy with the way things had been handled. To add fuel to the fire, in the first months of her leadership, the allocation of staff members caused friction. Some new staff members were insufficiently aware of the way matters had been handled previously and stepped on toes. While she was good at policy and communication, Natasha couldn't find a way to deal with tensions in the party-room. There was a time allocated to 'party matters' on the agenda of the Senator's meetings, but critical issues still existed and grievances went unresolved. The party-room did not come to grips with the essential difficulties everyone in the team faced as a result of the unpleasant way the change of leadership had occurred. Her 'presidential' style grated with others in the team and she was difficult to contact. Her schedule was hectic, her phone was often in silent mode and had no voice mail and when messages were received Natasha did not always return calls.

Despite the pressures and strains, people endeavoured to pull together in the time leading up to the 2001 Federal election, but there were uncontrollable factors. Jack Evans previously a Democrat Senator from

West Australia, was drafted in at the last minute as campaign director and proceeded to arrange preferences in a way the Democrats had not done before. It is unclear where his authority to do this came from, but it caught Stott Despoja flat-footed. Also, towards the end of the campaign, her one-time mentor and supporter John Coulter resigned publicly and caused some damage with his comments of her being too 'left-wing'.

In the November 10 election the Democrat vote dropped, and they lost one senator, Vicki Bourne. There were now eight Senators—Stott Despoja, Aden Ridgeway (who was Natasha's deputy), Lyn Allison, Andrew Bartlett, John Cherry, Brian Greig, Meg Lees, and Andrew Murray. The Greens vote rose and they elected two senators. Comparisons were drawn between the two parties. The following day, Stott Despoja was asked why she thought the electorate had punished them and she responded—the GST. After a tiring campaign and a somewhat disappointing result, this was a comment by Natasha unlikely to mend fences within the Party room. Meg responded furiously. Andrew Bartlett rebutted her criticisms. Any reconciliation was now unlikely.

Perhaps also, it was a generational issue. Natasha was firmly in the new generation. She used new media; was post-modern in many of her approaches; did not have the same pre-occupations as slightly older members. Generational issues can be very divisive. The question many of her opponents at the time raised was the way she dealt with the media and her personal style which was unfamiliar to them. Some, like John Howard, thought she was more 'appearance than substance'. I doubt this was so, however perceptions can be powerful.

While Natasha had a lot of exposure on the popular media, it seemed difficult to get positive coverage from journalists in the Canberra press gallery. Alison Rogers—media adviser to Stott Despoja during her time as leader—noted in her book *The Natasha Factor*, that the Canberra press gallery wasn't as supportive of Natasha as her media team would have liked.

> 'Politicians arrive in Canberra usually as an unknown quantity and earn their stripes and their reputation through the messages of the press gallery. Natasha had bypassed the press gallery in her political career and used more popular media to communicate with people who weren't just the Canberra observers.' [3]

Moreover, from time to time Democrat senators let slip remarks that were unhelpful and might best have been suppressed in the interest of unity. Aden Ridgeway was reported as saying he thought it had been a mistake for Natasha to become leader and the Democrats would have been better off sticking with Meg Lees. He was being consistent as prior to the leadership change he had told Natasha he didn't think a leadership spill was advisable as the party needed stability. He claimed he had thought his remarks were 'off the record', however the media gaffe didn't go down well with members of the National Executive who, by this time, were struggling to settle the issues down.

The South Australian State election followed closely on the heels of the Federal election. It was due in February 2002 and a decision had to be made about Natasha's role in the campaign. Both Meg and Natasha came from South Australia, so there would have been some tensions over the issues of the GST and the leadership spill. Natasha was still experiencing a considerable amount of negative publicity from certain parts of the media and even from people who still supported Meg, but for whatever reason, voters in South Australia turned against the Australian Democrats and the result was very poor. There was a swing of over 9% away from the Democrats.

The year was a roller-coaster for Natasha. In March she was diagnosed with Glandular Fever. Then in April she and Ian Smith, a long-time friend, were engaged. As the months passed, the struggle in the party-room did not resolve itself.

By July 2002 tempers were completely frayed.

In the lead-up to the budget a disagreement occurred over the Democrat position on the sale of Telstra. In response to an announcement from the Greens leader, Bob Brown. Meg Lees mused on the option and was reported as advocating the sale of Telstra. Stott Despoja felt undermined and sent a complaint to the National Executive.

The pot had boiled over.

The National Executive asked their Compliance Committee to investigate Meg's comments and Natasha's complaint. Meg complained of unfair treatment and the majority of the Senators stood behind her on the issue. Natasha had lost control of the party-room. Lees declined an invitation to put her case in person to the Executive. Instead she wrote a letter which was critical not only of Stott Despoja's leadership, but of Stott Despoja's staff as well as the role of the Executive. Meg felt her role as a Senator was being limited and that the National Executive had been used to undermine her. She was told 'Support Natasha' but she also had grievances that were not being dealt with. It couldn't continue. Something had to be done. The role of Democrat Senators was difficult enough without all the unresolved tensions.

The Executive, at their wits end, suggested mediation between the two protagonists and their supporters but Stott Despoja was not agreeable.

The media avidly followed and reported on all the twists and turns of the Democrat troubles. Natasha's high profile and the grumbling of the Senators made sure of that. At the time Natasha became leader, Sam Hudson, foundation member and long-serving Secretary of the National Executive became her Chief of Staff, but following the Federal election Sam had left both roles. She was not around to do what she had done, so often and so well, before—bring harmony and good sense to situations. Perhaps she could see this was not a situation amenable to ordinary solutions. Only the Wisdom of Solomon would have sufficed—and Solomon wasn't anywhere to be found.

Andrew Murray, re-elected as the Democrat Senator from West Australia, was a forthright and intelligent man but angry with the complaint against Lees and at odds with the way the party-room was functioning. He and Natasha locked horns. Neither knew the meaning of the word 'retreat' so the difficulties escalated. The pro- and anti-GST forces was now clearly the 'for and against Natasha' factions.

A personal matter eclipsed the issues for Natasha. Her fiance's father had cancer and his condition was deteriorating. Natasha and Ian needed to travel to England to see him. They left in late July and had been there for short time when the situation worsened in Australia. Before her journey to the United Kingdom, Natasha and Aden had asked the National Executive to drop the inquiry into Meg Lees but the Executive refused. Now it seemed Lees was on the point of resigning and Murray was also considering his options.

While Stott Despoja was still overseas, Murray and Bartlett had a very public and very damaging exchange.

Natasha needed to return to Australia. Ian, of course, would have preferred to stay, but loyally went back with her. In Australia matters were out of hand. From Alice Springs Meg, unwell and feeling seriously aggrieved, announced her resignation from the Australian Democrats. None of the other Democrat Senators were at hand to talk to her. At the same time, Andrew Murray was on the verge of resigning and four colleagues took him aside to try to talk him out of it. He agreed to stay if a series of motions were accepted to address some of the problems. These motions became known as the Ten Resolutions and were tabled in the next meeting of the Senators but, according to John Cherry:

> 'The problem was to get [Natasha] to discuss them. She deferred it for three party meetings. She kept saying that she was developing a response then rejected every single point.'[4]

Meanwhile Murray, who was outraged when he heard about the loss of Meg Lees from the party, launched a wide-ranging and stinging attack. He told the media the leader no longer had his support.

Saying he was a 'Senator in exile', he took himself out of the party-room and retired to the Democrat 'back bench'. This was an irony as there were always so few Democrats that the Senators all had multiple policy portfolios and couldn't afford the luxury of a 'back-bench'. However, Murray was determined to bring about change to the way the Senators were functioning. He and Stott Despoja engaged in a very public interaction where she asked him either to return to working with the other Senators or to resign. The National Executive was also in the mix and asked to mediate between them.

The Executive had tried to rein in the 'rebels' but events had overtaken them. Following his press statement, Natasha wanted Andrew Murray out of the party and intimated she would resign if this did not happen. The National Executive would not agree to expel Andrew Murray. According to Liz Oss-Emer:

> 'National Executive … at that stage.. felt that … to try and reconcile everyone our attitude was we follow the processes.. if this is what our documented processes are .. we have to follow them. So that's where it got to be.. '[5]

STOTT DESPOJA RESIGNS THE LEADERSHIP

Eventually the Ten Resolutions were discussed and then supported by 5 of the 8 senators. Most of the resolutions were reasonable but some presented a challenge to Stott Despoja's authority and she decided to resign. After advising her staff members and the other Senators she stood up in the Senate on August 21 and announced her resignation as leader.

Stott Despoja's leadership lasted only 16 months, but the surrounding events were extremely harmful. Leadership requires maturity and insight. Clearly, the other senators were unhappy with Natasha's leadership and their needs were not resolved. Actions of the National Executive seemed to worsen the situation. This struggle between the Executive and senators is bizarre. It sounds remarkably like the difficulties Calwell and Whitlam had with the Labor Party equivalent of a National Executive in 1963—the one that led to the 'faceless men' tag.

Menzies and the Liberal Party solved it neatly by ensuring the administrative wing and the Parliamentary wing were totally separate, depriving members of immediate input into day-to-day political decisions. In parties with a participatory ethos, the National Executive's role is meant to represent the rights and interests of the members and give them a say in what goes on in Parliament. On the other hand, Parliamentarians have duties to the Parliament and it is illegal to interfere with their freedom of speech and action.

After Natasha's resignation, the deputy leader, Aden Ridgeway, according to normal protocol would have become acting leader. He had the other Democrat Senators' support and they conveyed their opinion to the National Executive, which chose to ignore it and appoint Brian Greig as leader. Why?

I asked Liz Oss-Emer this question and she replied:

LOE: 'Because, well.. I can remember someone on the National Executive.. actually saying at the meeting where we had to appoint an interim leader that we didn't want to reward bad behaviour..

BF: So, had he gone public?

LOE: Yes. He had. He had. There was a big.. front page newspaper Sydney Morning Herald or something.. off the record comments from Aden Ridgeway..[6]

The decision to overlook Ridgeway for the acting leadership had serious repercussions. Although urged by numerous people, Aden decided not to put his name forward in the ballot for the leadership position. Cherry believes the Democrats would have survived the following election if Aden had become leader. He had a friendly and open way of communicating that appealed to voters. Being relatively new to the Senate, he might not have been confident about leadership, but there were ways that could have been dealt with.

With Aden not standing for leader, members elected Andrew Bartlett. When he replaced Stott Despoja as leader in 2002, relative harmony returned. Democrats held the Senate balance of power and won concessions on Medicare and superannuation for gay and lesbian couples. Then disaster struck. Bartlett's leadership was marred in December 2003 when he was accused of drunken behaviour and verbal abuse. This was a 'beat-up' of an incident involving a prank by his staffers. The media magnified the affair, which damaged the reputation of the Democrats in the 2004 election a year later. Perhaps Bartlett should have been asked to step down, but Lyn Allison, the deputy leader, could not bring herself to do this. After the previous shocks, this was the last straw for the public and the Democrat image was smudged. The party contested three Senate seats and lost them all with the lowest vote the Democrats had ever received; it dropped by 5.16%. Cherry, Greig and Ridgeway were not returned. Four Democrat Senators remained—Allison, Bartlett, Murray and Stott Despoja.

The Liberal/National coalition won a majority in the Senate—39 of the 76 seats. The Greens' representation rose by two to equal the Democrats with four each. Now the Coalition would have a free and unfettered path for legislation they wanted to pass through the Senate and soon introduced severe workplace legislation—Work Choices—which went through both houses to became law. This legislation caused bitter conflict across the nation.

The anguish for Democrats was that the legislation could only pass the Senate because they no longer held the balance of power.

****

12
WORK CAN BE HELL

Economic rationalism isn't rational and isn't economic either

They just see part of the picture and count part of the cost. The total picture eludes them; they have narrow accountant minds which bind them when it comes to all the things that make life worth living. They're not interested in the bigger scene; they're mean and unholy. Everything sacred is profaned and violated in the name of the game called money. That doesn't seem funny to me. I don't want to play their game. I'll insist there are things in this world worth having that cannot be bought with money; things without price; niceness and kind deeds done with a generous and co-operative heart. These are the truly rational deeds and down the track when we've been there and back, they're probably economic too. If you want to know my philosophy I'll tell you. It's all about people; you and me—us. We aren't just items on a debit and credit ledger or cogs in a wheel. No—we feel, and hurt and smart; there's an art to be learned in dealing with us. We aren't just 'things' for nasty children to pull off our wings and neither are we made of steel. No—we feel, and all the ridiculous stuff being done makes us reel. We are flesh and blood and thought and ideal; we're real. We're not just items on a debit or credit ledger or cogs in a wheel; we matter. It's people who matter not this dreary natter and chatter constantly about money.

Floyd, B. *Political Poems* 2012.

John Howard's unfettered control of the Senate lead to policy excesses that affected everyone in Australia. The Work Choices legislation was just one example of this and I would like to describe what happened in my own workplace.

I want to describe the detrimental effect of an economic theory—neoclassical economics, or economic rationalism—in a workplace, the South Brisbane Technical and Further Education (TAFE) College where I worked from 1983 to 2003. It is a case study of the before and after—the impact of government decisions and economic theories on people.

David O'Reilly describes economic rationalism as 'a view that the working of demand and supply—market forces—should be the sole instrument of economic decision-making in society. Government, and its agencies, should exercise a minimal role, without public sector intervention.'[1]

My university studies were finished and I had an education degree, but I had not been entirely settled since my return from Papua New Guinea. I enjoyed the university experience—lunch in the student union canteen, coffee with acquaintances, cold days rugged up in the sun with a textbook at hand, examinations in halls that held hundreds of students and walks to the nearby shopping centre, but although I knew quite a few people I felt disconnected and lonely.

In 1976 I worked part-time at the Queensland Health Department's Indooroopilly Rehabilitation Centre as a tutor to patients recovering from trauma, and in 1977 joined the Australian Democrats. It was an exhilarating time and my mood lifted. In 1979 I was a candidate in the Brisbane City Council election and in 1983 I started teaching in TAFE. During the early part of the time there I was deeply enmeshed with Democrat politics, which used up a lot of spare time and energy.

The first person I met at South Brisbane TAFE in 1983 was the principal, Col Marsh. He was involved with a charity for homeless youth and had founded a course at the college to give them an opportunity for education. My first assignment was with this group, the Skills for Living and Working (SLAW) course. They were a tough bunch. Classes were held in a building due for renovation and as the kids walked up the stairs into the classroom some would beat holes in the walls. We once found a few of them under the building—drinking rum and throwing rocks at passers-by. Something had upset them. I could understand their anger as I had some myself, but such events were disconcerting.

TAFE in those days was revered as the workers' way up. Fees were moderate. The teaching was practical and classes were small enough for each student to receive personal attention. The small college, with just one campus, taught mainly trade courses from prevocational to diploma. Col knew every staff member by sight and name, and probably knew all our foibles too. He managed the finances. His word was law, which might not have been good if he made a mistake.

Staff took part in group projects related to their courses. A plane was rebuilt, cars remodelled.

At Christmas we had a feast before a concert with skits, choirs and solos. Weeks before the event singing echoed in the corridors and secret rehearsals took place in empty rooms. The sound of jingling money tins also wafted along the corridors as we sang carols while collecting for charities. The college training boat went to sea to catch prawns for our meal.

After the Christmas celebrations we went home satisfied, feeling part of a team, a family. We thought what we did at the college was worthwhile. We were training workers for the future and it felt good to be part of that.

Of course, to equip the projects, some bolts, wood or steel may have been appropriated from college resources. But what did the public purse receive in return? Staff were contented; students saw their teachers working together on projects and could join in too; the plane, when flight ready, took us across the State to meetings. The Piper Cherokee was bought second-hand for $2700 and by 1987 it was worth $40,000. I am told that it recently sold for $75,000.

There was give and take. We worked overtime and sometimes took time off. Very few abused the privilege and if one did, a supervisor or the principal himself soon knew and dealt with it.

However, in later years the groups' activities came under investigation by the Crime and Misconduct Commission (CMC), which would be called in over matters like this and as a union delegate I spent hours accompanying staff to meetings where they were interrogated like criminals, but without the protection accorded to people accused of crimes. Some sessions with investigators ran for hours and I had to insist on regular breaks. The investigators passed on hearsay and the 'evidence' they noted was obviously not confidential.

In my first years at South Brisbane TAFE, Col and senior staff would share morning tea and lunch with us. We would chat, joke and discuss ideas. There was mutual respect. Col had an open mind as well as an open door and encouraged senior staff to act similarly.

GLOBALISATION STRIKES

By the mid-1980s trends that would later shake our working world with tectonic force started to affect us. Britain was turning more to Europe so Australia had to disengage its terms of trade. The Quality movement was beginning. At South Brisbane TAFE we went to lectures on globalisation and the need for productivity and efficiency. Some presenters were a tad overbearing, but there was no escape as attendance was compulsory.

The Hawke/Keating Government deregulated the banks. Unions were amalgamating. Awards were redrafted to deal with the increasingly competitive nature of trade and employment around the world. Some of my classes dealt with these matters. I was interested in the changes and thought them reasonable. The Labor Government, while deregulating and stressing the need to be competitive, had entered into a pact with unions to ensure a social wage. The plan was to cushion the workforce as the Australian economy made a transition to the modern global economy.

The struggles with Joh Bjelke-Petersen in Queensland were over. Michael Ahern was a decent Premier and committed to reform within the police and political areas. His party did not support him completely, but the changes he set afoot would remain. Then, at the 1989 election, after a period of instability of leadership in the National Party, Wayne Goss led Labor to government and took up the cause of reform.

Finally, change was coming to Queensland. The next two decades would be filled with not only 'change', but also turmoil and upsets—most unnecessary or even downright stupid.

We first noticed an increase in paperwork and meetings. Under the lawyerly Goss Government we were inundated with a raft of new forms and papers and needed forms to get forms.

As the computer was coming into its own we also found demands could be made instantly—and results expected sooner. A computer management system was instituted but, as with some other earlier systems, left a lot to be desired. We realised the computer age treated robots better than people. A person with an idiosyncrasy or a novel idea had a hard time fitting into a computer management system.

During its first term, the Goss Government was preoccupied with enacting legislation that Fitzgerald recommended. They established the Electoral Reform Commission and various commissions with an ongoing brief against corruption in the public service. In its second term the Labor Government turned its attention to the public service. Because the Federal

Government pressed on with competition policy, Labor in Queensland had little choice and also took a hard line on the issue.

This meant TAFE colleges competed with industry groups for the funding of courses. The money came through industry groups which sometimes had financial interests in allocating it to their industrial and commercial cronies. Some TAFE colleges came close to bankruptcy. Valuable courses ended because they could not 'compete'. The aeronautics section went to private industry.

Some evening classes were expensive so they were cancelled to save money. Students with day jobs could no longer attend; numbers and income gradually deteriorated. For a small saving, we lost valuable courses. For some reason this always reminds me of Mao in China commanding people to capture sparrows for hygiene reasons, only to disturb the balance of nature and cause ecological disaster.

Some colleges amalgamated, with economy of scale as the rationale. South Brisbane joined with two other colleges. The $5 million supposedly 'saved' was taken from the overall budget. This meant more scrimping and saving just when we needed to re-establish the amalgamated college. We struggled on all fronts. For several years the merged college had no internal phonebook. The TAFE head office was also culled so a phone book was no use for them either, as the next day their jobs might go. Management at top levels changed rapidly, sometimes overnight.

Directors were moved sideways against their will. The organisation was in turmoil. Restructure followed restructure until we totally lost count of the number of times it had happened.

Nothing, however, stopped the economic rationalist juggernaut. Staff lost jobs or were at risk of losing them. Work was 'outsourced'. We lost our cleaners. We were in danger of losing maintenance staff. We were out of our depths. Shady figures at round tables planned their next action while we still fought the previous ones. Then like a bolt of lightning they would strike. We would say to each other, 'Well, it can't get much worse', but it did. After which, we would say again, 'Well, it *really* can't get much worse than this', but it did again.

The stress, stupidity and turmoil just kept getting worse. I spent hours of my own time each week listening to seriously distressed staff members who were almost at the end of their tether trying to work in the chaos.

Someone above us thought older workers were likely to resist change so hundreds were made redundant, leaving huge gaps in the knowledge base. Few newcomers knew what had happened previously or what worked, so almost everything had to be reinvented. Youth may have energy, but misdirected energy can be very disruptive—as we found.

The economic rationalists won that battle against the rest of us, but the war will continue until a sensible balance is reached between economics and the people's needs. The bottom line cannot be the only consideration.

Our college was no longer small and friendly. Small teams could be a haven of co-operation and support, but the institute overall was now a large-scale organisation cloaked in uniformity and anonymity. Through my union duties I had regular contact with most levels of management, but the management structure was a mystery to staff. It stretched far higher than most could reach. The aim of uniformity supposedly is to save money and increase productivity, but the loss of diversity and friendliness deadens people's spirits. Diversity can be difficult to manage, but it is immensely important.

The institute operated from a relatively new building that a company including 'friends' of the then Queensland Premier had constructed. The building began to deteriorate badly. It had concrete cancer; the roof leaked on to expensive pianos in the top floor; tiles in the canteen had buckled and needed replacing and the walls of the underground garage had cracks. Joh Bjelke-Petersen had retired to his home near Kingaroy, but his legacy remained. I marshalled my students and armed with a video camera we toured the building, climbed on the roof and snuck about in the underground garage getting evidence, all of which appealed mightily to my students. We sent the edited video through channels to those responsible for maintenance.

The Goss Government decided not to prosecute the builders, but rather to spend the money on repairs, which were so extensive they took a year or more. It is a pity prosecutions didn't occur, but the times were not conducive. Many Queenslanders still thought Joh and his methods were OK.

Teachers love to teach so our work continued despite every hindrance. Surveys showed students appreciated their efforts even when just about every other item on the form received a negative tick. But the system began to treat teachers as 'units' in a profit and loss ledger. Because teachers were expensive, much effort went into maximising their contact with students. Teachers were gradually isolated from institute planning and management. They attended fewer meetings and were consulted less. In an organisation where the purpose is to teach and to train, this was a serious error. Information needed to run the institute effectively and to improve quality was not sought or readily accepted. Teachers were unimpressed.

The number of administrative and managerial staff increased. The TAFE system became top heavy; teaching experience had been customary for senior managers, but was no longer a requirement. Their expertise was now more business oriented.

The nature of the institute changed—it became a stepping stone for people using it on their way to future promotion. New managers wanted to show their mettle and would introduce new systems or reinvent systems previously tried and found wanting.

There was no continuity or even time for serious consolidation of new systems or for developing relationships. Managers came and went, leaving us with the rubble of their 'new' ideas. It was disconnection at its worst.

Susan Hawthorne describes an alternative in her book *Wild politics*:

> *'What I hope for is a world filled with richness, texture, depth and meaning. I want diversity with all its surprises and variety. I want … multiversity which values the context and real-life experiences of people. I want a world in which relationship is important, and reciprocity is central to social interaction.'* [2]

Formerly close to management, teachers now were at the bottom of the pile and effectively locked out. Their voice was unheard. Teachers were an opinionated lot and would have been difficult to control if they had power within the new system—better to sideline them.

Life under the new regime was almost impossible for me. Uniformity was a religion; diversity was frowned on: Don't have an idea, just go along with the way things are; don't try to right injustices, leave it to someone else. I just wasn't like that. I wanted a co-operative approach, one valuing people and their contribution.

THE SITUATION WORSENED

I belonged to the Queensland Public Sector Union (QPSU), the major public service union. As working conditions deteriorated and conflict grew, I was drawn further into the union movement. The number of casual or contract staff increased dramatically. Someone had realised people whose jobs are insecure are unlikely to rock the boat, but they had not also figured out that the frightened will stay silent for quite a while, but then the dam bursts. We held several successful union stop-work meetings in the early 1990s. These were a joint effort between the Public Sector Union, the Australian Liquor Hospitality and Miscellaneous Workers' Union of Australia [ALHMWU] and the Queensland Teachers' Union [QTU]. Workplace delegates organised them and the turnout was terrific. I think they shook management; I don't think much immediate change occurred within the institute as a result, but perhaps they had some impact on political change.

Staff worked under heavy pressure. Absence and illness from stress were increasing alarmingly. Management decided something should be 'done' and set up a confidential counselling service. Anyone could have six free sessions. I suppose the scheme was better than nothing, and perhaps showed good intentions, but it dealt with symptoms rather than causes.

By now, with assistance from a supportive manager, I had opened a learning centre. I had dreamt of such a project—basically a large room with computers around the walls and plenty of space for groups doing self-paced study. Our pride and joy was the Adult Tertiary Preparation Program allowing adults to gain Year 12 certificates. Some industry courses could also be taught online or individually (in the gaps).

The centre became a place for people with disabilities to have computer tuition. Study assistance was provided for both Australian and overseas students. The place had a wonderfully co-operative atmosphere, but it was a false hope to think we could exist securely despite the chaos around.

The learning centre team was often at work by 7am and left late in the evening, but categorising the variety of activities was difficult. Self-paced learning was quite new and the computer-managed system could not capture the hours. We were frustrated, but should have realised the tide flows slowly in a public system. Novelty and ingenuity have an uphill battle until they become the mainstream.

Because they could not see the numbers and perhaps because I was a highly visible union delegate, some managers believed I was cribbing hours for my union work. Nothing could have been further from the truth, but when someone wants to believe something they will soon think it is true. So the centre was closed, and vultures gathered to get the rooms and to pick up some of the courses.

I was devastated. One should not care so much about a project, but this one had captured my heart and soul. At short notice I organised six months' leave for a world trip.

GOING OVERSEAS

It *was* good for my soul. But more than that, I returned with renewed determination to be a better advocate for workers' rights. A kind of steel possessed me and people seemed to notice. I wanted to fight injustice on my own terms and do it as fiercely as I could, but wherever possible without bitterness or malice. I was outspoken and stubborn. I intervened. I said things as I saw them. Some might have said I was nigh on impossible. Unless they had earned it, I gave managers no more respect than I would any ordinary person. Some managers began to fear the possibility of my entrance into issues. I smiled secretly at this because I didn't consider myself an ogre, but injustice was a red rag to me and I had many opportunities to challenge it.

Soon after my return I slotted into my new team and began teaching at Advanced diploma level. This was a pleasant change from the battles with my beloved scallywags in the prevocational and SLAW classes.

I found my new students, particularly older ones in evening classes, quite inspirational. We learnt together. We explored and discussed what was happening and students worked to improve processes and practices in their workplaces. It was adventure again, just a different version.

Unfortunately, my team came under the control of negative, abusive and incompetent behaviour by one of the worst managers I have ever encountered. One of the victims took the manager to court, and a verdict of negligence was made, but later quashed after an appeal.

I believe the manager could have been a sociopath and should have been removed from the position. However, as the budget was balanced, the institute looked no further. Time and again I complained. Others complained. We were ignored. Our team made an escape by organising a transfer to another faculty with a decent manager.

Those on contracts were targets for overwork and bullying so we advised them to leave issues to permanent staff with at least some security of tenure. This, however, was hard in circumstances as bad as those. A significant number of mistreated contract staff lost their jobs for simply telling the truth as they saw it. Some left to find jobs where they would not be harassed.

Dissatisfaction and stress levels were still rising. The picture from the annual staff survey was so bad one year the results were not publicly released. They became even worse. Staff on stress leave cost the institute a lot of money and excellent people left because of the chaos. The cost of staff turnover must have been significant. Regular staff stopped filling in the survey forms as they saw no significant efforts to improve the work environment.

Conditions improved under the Beatty Labor Government. The pressure went off competitive funding and issues regarding permanency were tackled. A new institute director managed to bring the funding crisis under control. However, across the organisation and especially within the teaching ranks, a sense of deprivation existed. Some joy had gone from the teaching role because of the changes we had experienced.

The counselling staff had been cut from six to three and they were instructed not to counsel on personal matters. How do you chop a person in half? 'I can only discuss your course with you, not your anxiety or your problem with finding money to buy food.' Well, the only way to deal with this instruction is to ignore it and do what you think is best for the people who come to you for assistance.

The Crime and Misconduct Commission made some of our lives a misery. I appreciate honesty and it is sometimes necessary to have a body to ensure public servants behave correctly. However, I came to believe such an organisation with significant powers—search, surveillance and seizure, and to conduct coercive hearings—should not be ongoing as it can itself become a problem. I also believed their inquiries should be restricted to matters at a certain level and minor issues dealt with at a local level.

A union colleague and I were assisting a teacher in the hospitality area who had allegations relating to the serving of alcohol made against him by another staff member. He was harangued by the investigators and I thought their behaviour seriously out of order. But who monitors the monitors? We won that round, but only after a great deal of persistence.

Not only did managers treat staff poorly, but their example was copied by others below them. Compared with my early experiences at South Brisbane, the institute was a bleak and unfriendly place. I felt certain types of people were not being considered for managerial positions. If you cared about your staff more than your budget you were not suitable. I was by now teaching business principles to Diploma students and found myself teaching my students one thing and experiencing another within the organisation.

By the time I left in 2003, the institute was too large for the kind of human interaction we enjoyed in the 1980s. No real thought was given to ensuring the wellbeing of people in the organisation. A sullen rapprochement settled across our activities with little chance of those at the workface being in touch with senior managers at a human level. Size is an issue that needs careful consideration. Signing a paper to amalgamate campuses or smaller units into one large organisation will not ensure the new body's success. Effort is needed to ensure bonds grow; relationships are established; and there is life instead of disconnection and sterility.

I blamed economic rationalism for the decline in co-operative behaviour. Federal governments since the 1980s had adopted the theory wholeheartedly and Prime Minister Howard refined and intensified it. Competition policy, 'efficiency' and 'cost-cutting' became the order of the day. The theory treated employees as units whose output must be maximised then maximised again, not as people with human needs and families.

Across Australia others tackled economic rationalist ideology in their own spheres. The Australian Democrat Senators highlighted its shortcomings; commentators such as Eva Cox, in the 1995 Boyer lectures, outlined the importance of the civil society and how it was being lost in the impulse to make economics the key to everything.

I am a fervent critic of economic rationalism. In its name Australia was devastated; country towns lost businesses; manufacturing industries collapsed; constant restructuring made people fearful of losing their jobs. I think that was the idea, as Hugh Morgan, a powerful mining executive, once famously intimated: Workers should be in fear of losing their jobs as it would make them work harder.

During my 1991 overseas trip, I looked carefully at its effects in other countries. Everywhere I went I spoke with ordinary people who suffered fallout from this simplistic theory. It is simplistic for many reasons, but the main one is it places too great a responsibility on the shoulders of the 'free market' to be the sole pillar to support a productive economy and healthy society.

It is also my view that the economic rationalist ideology was responsible for the great financial crisis that began with banks in the United States of America and their greed for profit. It is an ideology without a soul, and consequently no real understanding of the world most people live in. Proponents of economic rationalism loosened regulatory frameworks so corporations could operate freely. Many of these corporations followed the 'greed' route that led to their downfall and the subsequent financial fallout that rapidly spread across the world.

Economic rationalism undermined democratic conventions as bureaucrats and politicians became less willing to listen to the voice of people who were striving to modify policies. The views of these officials were set during their university studies in a period dominated by theories from the Chicago school of economics and Milton Friedman.

'After Friedman's death in 2006, Keynesian Nobel laureate Paul Krugman praised Friedman as a "a great economist and a great man," but criticised him by writing that "he slipped all too easily into claiming both that markets always work and that only markets work. It's extremely hard to find cases in which Friedman acknowledged the possibility that markets could go wrong, or that government intervention could serve a useful purpose"'.[3]

My reading revealed a clear process in favour of this view of economics was under way across the world. It was not left alone just to seep into societies; it was parachuted in with the heavy artillery it needed to succeed.

I first noticed this in a book I discovered in New Zealand,* where the author, Jane Kelsey, wrote about the role of the roundtable in the strategic war to promote economic rationalism. And it was war, carefully planned and ruthless. Anyone who wanted promotion needed to adhere to the new ideology. It was marshalled through the Parliament with military precision, using a variety of tactics and in particular the 'blitzkrieg'—strike hard and suddenly, then strike again while the enemy does not expect the next blow.

Nothing we foot soldiers could do would turn back the tide. It reached its most abominable point while John Howard was Prime Minister. Emboldened by its control of the Senate, the Liberal-National coalition delivered a determined assault on unions and working conditions. A vigorous public outcry and a strong Labor/union campaign returned Labor to government where they could return the balance to ordinary working people from the extremes under Howard.

Although many spoke out strongly on these matters, we still had to endure Work Choices during the Howard years.

I sometimes ponder how different life would have been if the Democrats had maintained the Balance of Power in the Senate in John Howard's final term. There would have been no Work Choices and none of the anguish faced by countless employees during that time.

The worst aspects of economic rationalism retreated during the six years of Labor Government. I am certain, however, that if given an opportunity they will rear their heads again in Queensland.

> **STOP PRESS**: Brisbane. Campbell Newman the Premier of Queensland is planning a complete overhaul of … A recent report by … from the Resources Council of Queensland has recommended practices that sound similar to those …….. from…….. A freeze on new positions is being used to … **secret … individual contracts … TAFE**

We must still compete globally and we need to be productive. However, this will remain difficult unless managers accept that happy and secure employees are more likely to be productive. Our fight continues as our leaders remain under the sway of what they learnt during previous years.

Managers everywhere are between a rock and a hard place. Expectations are placed upon them and technologies allow closer scrutiny of results. They and the people they manage are constantly expected to cut costs and improve

* Jane Kelsey's *The New Zealand experiment.*

outcomes. But the emphasis is more often than not on cutting costs rather than on imaginative approaches to improving outcomes.

If the knowledge and imagination of frontline workers was liberated by involving them in planning and decision-making, we could see an explosion of improved productivity and better workplace relationships. But it is difficult for disempowered workers to change their work culture for the better. Unless the sterile blanket of right-wing economics is lifted, we will continue to have dissatisfied workers, unacceptably high stress levels and excessive staff turnover.

The extent of workplace bullying still bothers me. I am pleased a report into workplace bullying has been made public. While I worked in TAFE and was an elected union representative I saw dozens of examples of bullying—demeaning, unjustified and unforgiveable attacks. I recorded them and reported them. I complained. I appealed to managers, but the climate of opinion was against us. I have seen lives seriously affected, some tragically. There were several suicides. Those who recovered and worked on were diminished by what happened to them.

It would be enormously satisfying to see such behaviour reduced in Australian workplaces. Trends have started to correct wrongs of the past (for example, the 'stolen generation' and forced adoptions), but the process will take several more eras to set right. In the case of workplace bullying, the economic experiment provided a happy breeding ground for workers to be manipulated and mistreated. Much needs to be done to restore safe and harmonious workplaces. The report into workplace bullying may be a step in the right direction and needs the support of all right-thinking people.*

****

* Appendix H. A quote from the Foreword of the Report on Workplace Bullying, 2012.

13
CONVERSATIONS WITH DEMOCRATS

What follows is taken from interviews with a number of Democrat Senators— Cheryl Kernot, John Woodley, John Cherry, Meg Lees, Andrew Bartlett, Aden Ridgeway and Michael Macklin. I also spoke with Liz Oss-Emer who was president of the National Executive of the party during 2001-2.

I didn't manage to interview Natasha Stott Despoja and Andrew Murray as their other commitments meant that was not possible. I have had to rely on written records and Newspaper articles to fill in the gaps.

From what I learned, I pieced together the 30 year history of the party appearing in the previous chapters and the role played by individuals in its formation and progress. In the writing I tried to be fair and objective but that can be quite difficult when someone has been involved in the story themselves. If I have erred in some particulars I ask forgiveness of the people involved.

I hope this account will prove helpful for anyone with an interest in politics. In their 30 years in the Senate The Australian Democrats were a powerful force for progress and good sense. Their demise was disappointing but perhaps in some form or other the phoenix will rise and a better form of politics will emerge from the ghost of a party that meant a lot to those of us who were involved.

CHERYL KERNOT

I flew to Sydney to meet Cheryl Kernot and we renewed our friendship after being out of touch for years. The interview was conducted over lunch. Cheryl ate while I asked questions and I took a doggy bag afterwards. The noise in the café was ferocious and when I tried to transcribe the tape at home I faced a daunting task.

I like Cheryl. She is herself. After everything the political process and the media have thrown at her, she is still the person I knew in Brisbane many years ago. At one point while sitting side by side at the computer we looked at each other and said, almost simultaneously, 'It only seems like yesterday that we were doing this together'.

By the time she entered the Senate Cheryl had built up considerable experience as party organiser, Queensland division president and Michael Macklin's electorate officer. She had stood for the Queensland Parliament and been a Queensland policy co-ordinator for the Democrats.

Cheryl notes, 'I gave my maiden speech on, say, Wednesday evening and I had to speak about the deregulation of the airlines the next morning. I remember Bob Collins looking. He told me afterwards that he was really surprised that someone who had just come in could get up and talk about it and, you know, the irony of it. The only reason I could was because I won that political exchange trip to America and I observed the way the privatised airlines worked. So, it was lucky'.

After her swift dive into the deep end, Kernot focused on portfolios including finance, superannuation, transport and regional development and Aboriginal Affairs, which she particularly sought. She jokes that those in the major parties would run a mile before taking on Aboriginal Affairs. Because of her involvement with the portfolio, she was appointed to the Council for Reconciliation—which she saw as a great privilege. Her knowledge of the people and problems led to her pivotal role in the Keating Labor Government's Mabo legislation.

Kernot was elected as the Australian Democrats Parliamentary leader in a 'participatory' ballot after the 1993 election.

'That was a shock,' she said. 'I didn't think we had the numbers. Being from Queensland, I didn't think that even if Queensland supported me strongly that it would be enough. Pleasant shock.

'... I think one of the hardest things about being a Democrat leader was the party-room—keeping together what would be in any other circumstances a kind of loosely aligned independents.' I asked: 'Because they had the right to a conscience vote?' 'That's right! It was intense. It was great that we met every day unlike the other parties. We all had to speak and we had to know what was happening in Parliament.'

Kernot wanted the best always and was sometimes difficult to work with, as her fellow senators would admit, but according to John Woodley, 'After the 1993 election they knew they were on a hiding to nothing if they didn't pull together, and they knew Cheryl was doing well. The polling had shown she was doing exceptionally well. Past the 1993 budget, she had enormous authority in the party-room. She was helped by having an exceptionally good staff. There were people who had been there for a long, long time'.

Cheryl described some ways she managed the party-room. 'One thing I changed was to bring the national secretary into the party-room so the gap wouldn't be so big between the Parliamentarians and the party, and the other thing I did, to try and deal with some of the "ramblings", was to have a rotating chair of the Parliamentary meetings so when "ramblers" were the chair, they had a different discipline.

'You get good processes and you stick by them and you always fall back on the process. That will usually guide you through pretty well. I've introduced them to some other organisations because they were good processes in the main.'

She was a great communicator, but essentially wanted to be herself even in the political hothouse and she was fortunate to lead a party that gave her the opportunity to showcase her talents. Cheryl was widely admired and seen as a breath of fresh air in a stale and virulent political atmosphere. She appeared to embody all the promises that the formation of the Australian Democrats in 1977 had initiated—politics of reason and civility.

Cheryl Kernot has not yet received the recognition she deserves for the years she spent with the Democrats, first as a member and electorate worker and later as the leader. She is a great Australian and her life and work strengthened Australia.

In the 1996 election, Democrats under her leadership raised their vote by 5.51% and won five Senate seats, keeping their total at seven. Sid Spindler withdrew because of ill health; Robert Bell stood but lost. West Australian Andrew Murray and Victorian Lyn Allison were the new senators.

After the election, Kernot had the Treasury portfolio when privatisation of Telstra became a key issue. A three-year apprenticeship in the Senate had well-formed her ideas on the economy and she had the energy, talent and inspiration for the challenge.

She was fully involved with negotiating the Native Titles Legislation, and near the end of 1996, during the Howard Government, worked with Peter Reith to devise industrial relations legislation that would be acceptable to the Democrats.

I asked Cheryl what her emotional attitude was during 1997: 'Mal Colston voted with Howard to sell Telstra. You must have been very upset about that?' She replied, 'I was. I was. I was personally very, very upset. My emotional state was quite shocked that he was dealing with the Liberal Party'.

Cheryl continued: 'With the Labor Party, you felt like you had a starting point, but with the Liberal Party it was like foreign territory. For example, when the Howard Government removed dental hospital services for the poor.

I didn't think I could do it as leader. There was not much at all as a starting point. I didn't want to have to be dealing with them.' Kernot believed the Democrats were in good shape and as she told me, 'I wanted to make sure [that when I left] they were in a strong position'.

Cheryl Kernot's walkout from the Democrats' offices on the morning of October 15, 1997, to join the ALP was a stunning blow. When I first heard about it I felt very sad for her Democrat colleagues and dismayed at the process by which she had left them without any warning of her plans.

I believed then that her defection to the Labor Party was the beginning of the end for the Australian Democrats. However, the Democrats did exceptionally well under the leadership of Meg Lees in the 1998 election.

Cheryl's Democrat colleagues knew of her contacts with Labor's John Faulkner as both were members of a Parliamentary walking group, but none knew of her intention to join the ALP.

The Labor Party wasn't easy street for Cheryl. BF: 'You had a rough time in the Labor Party, didn't you?' CK: 'Yes… I learnt a lot about raw, brutal politics. The Democrats were ahead of [their] times on so many things. One of the things when I joined the Labor Party I was promised I could be involved in regional issues. I wanted to learn, but when I'd say things they'd say, "You're not in the fucking Democrats now." I'd expect things to be voted and agreed. You know what the irony is? Now they elect their national president…the members [do].'

In most respects, the Australian Democrats were an exact fit for Cheryl Kernot. She thrived in an atmosphere of participatory democracy, social justice and progressive ideas. She was an 'innocent' in as much as the kind of struggles facing politicians in the major parties had not knocked the stuffing out of her. However, when facing the difficulties of the Howard era, she desperately felt the inadequacy of the Democrat presence in the Senate;

it was unable to stop the Liberal/National Coalition juggernaut and the risk they posed to her values. She wanted to be in a position to do more, or to put the ALP in a position to win.

As we know, that did not happen. The next decade saw the coalition shamefully overstep the mark with its Work Choices legislation and inappropriate and damaging applications of economic rationalist ideology. But, like Janine Haines, Cheryl took the risk of doing something outside the frame. She put it well with her final comment to me, 'I wouldn't want to be living a life of mediocrity because of timidity. I really wouldn't want to do that'.

The ALP lost the 2001 election and Cheryl was not returned in the seat of Dickson, which she had won for Labor in 1998. In 2002, free at last of political responsibility, she wrote a book, *Speaking for myself again,* in which she was critical of her treatment by the ALP and also of the way the media had dealt with her.

Over lunch, Kernot had some strong words about the media. 'I think social media is going to change politics. [It] can bypass the mainstream media in a way that's powerful. I think that's so important because at the moment an unelected, unaccountable media has so much power. Alistair Campbell [Tony Blair's press secretary] said to me as we sat on the comfy sofa at Number 10: "One has to decide who is running the country, the elected politicians or the media." He said, "We're going to have to pick a fight with the media"'.

Cheryl: 'What's wrong with the media? When I first went into politics, most journalists would not publish all of the assertions unless they had an opportunity to check out whether they had some basic reality or not, but now news is 'he said that about her', 'she said that about him' and it goes on and on and on. We must never lose sight of how unaccountable the media is. I was and I wasn't a good politician for the times. I was because people trusted me; I wasn't because I wouldn't spin. [Everyone] on my staff was given instructions, "When you go and explain this to the press don't spin"'.

REV. JOHN WOODLEY

Many years had passed since I had spoken to John Woodley, but here we were again, sharing a coffee and it felt like the clock had stopped. He is a Uniting Church minister who still plays a role in Queensland, but from 1993 to 2001 he was a Queensland Senator who had become interested in politics because of injustice to Indigenous people.

John Woodley

My first memory of John was from a Redcliffe meeting he facilitated in the Democrats' early days. He introduced each representative, then described me as 'incredibly idealistic, but perhaps a little naïve'.

I later challenged the word 'naïve', arguing I was instead 'innocent'. It seemed that the 'naïve' foolishly do not calculate the outcomes of their beliefs, whereas the 'innocent' have not yet experienced sufficient knocks to destroy their belief in what may be possible.

Over our coffee John and I shared some great yarns and I learnt more than I needed to know about the inner workings of the Australian Democrat party-room during the 1990s.

He says of his political career, 'I would do it all again. I felt I was doing the thing I should do. If you like, I felt I had a call, that it was the next stage of my vocation. I never stopped being a Uniting Church minister. Cheryl challenged me one time. "When are you going to stop being a minister and start being a politician"?'

I also heard about the book he had researched and written on the role of fundamentalist religions in Australia and their influence in right-wing conservative politics. It hadn't been published yet. I told John he needed to get cracking!

Then I asked him what had happened in the leadership battle between Natasha Stott Despoja and Meg Lees.

Democrat party rules had three ways to instigate a leadership ballot: a petition by the membership; a vote by the National Executive; or a vote by the party-room.

Meg Lees received significant support in the leadership ballot after Cheryl Kernot's resignation from the party, but then faced two more ballots during her term because of membership petitions. In the first ballot she was re-elected unopposed, but in the second ballot, Stott Despoja won 70% of the votes. Lees told me that party policy was 'basically to re-ballot policy … re-ballot … same thing with the leadership'.

This was a critical point in the Democrat journey, as I learnt from others who knew the whole story.

> JW: One of the issues that was really strong for me was that the National Executive of which I was a part for some years, and which I enjoyed, when it came to Meg Lees, and the Natasha issue, overstepped its authority very significantly, and really they put themselves in jeopardy of being found in contempt of the Senate. But the National Executive forbade us from putting out any statements about Natasha or Meg during the leadership ballot and in the end we agreed. They tried to totally gag all the senators except Natasha. I went to the clerk of the Senate and gave him some information and he said, "No. That's not on. They can't do that".
>
> BF: It's sad, isn't it?
>
> JW: Ah … It's actually illegal, but we let them get away with it.
>
> BF: How come?
>
> JW: Too soft. Too naïve.
>
> BF: You needed me there!
>
> JW: Did. You see. I'll give you an example. There had been a lot of criticism of Meg which had been going through in emails … which was really organised by Natasha's supporters. In the Senate we had decided out of the nine of us, six … said, "This is ridiculous. We must put out something to say that we support Meg." We prepared a letter for the membership from the six senators saying, "We support Meg—not saying vote for her but simply "we support Meg". Some of the stuff that was said about her was just untrue.
>
> BF: Have you got a copy of that?
>
> JW: No. Anyway we had … whatever membership there was then … 5000 or something. We had the letters all prepared to be sent out from the Whip's office … Vicki Bourne. She was excellent too. The National Executive forbade us to send them out and we had them all destroyed. We didn't send them out. Stupid. We should have. We should have because it was the truth. It was right and probably our duty to say that

> the majority of the senators don't want Natasha, we want Meg. We weren't even saying it as strongly as that.

Soon after retiring from the Senate in 2001, Woodley left the Democrats and joined the Australian Progressive Alliance, a breakaway party set up by Meg Lees after she left the Democrats. He was national president of the APA, which wound up after unsuccessfully contesting the 2004 Federal election.

He said, 'One of the lasting benefits of the Australian Democrats is that people are now comfortable with the idea of alternatives to the two major parties and are happy to vote for third parties. A lot of that is because they discovered the Democrats were able to negotiate for better outcomes. That's one of the things the Greens have never done. They've never been able to do that.'

JOHN CHERRY

I drove to Brisbane to see John Cherry and arrived after threading around every other street in his suburb. I believe even my vehicle was out of breath. He and his wife Nicky and their family were charming. I felt at home immediately. We sat at the kitchen table while John answered my questions and corrected my misunderstandings. Nicky, whom he teasingly called 'Dr Jones', joined our conversation from time to time when it became too interesting to resist!

John, a Queensland Democrat Senator from 2001 to 2005, said the 1998 election had been 'great': 'It was a hard election—a very, very hard election. Cheryl had just left. I think what we put together for that election was, in some ways, our finest hour. [We were] up against Hanson so [were] getting no media at all. Jeff Dodd, who was our media officer at the time, did a media report on our media coverage and for the first three weeks the media was just following Hanson. We got no media at all and all of our media was in the last week and a half after the Press Club appearance where Meg released our tax policy.'

I commented, 'That's when people realised you would be in a position to block the GST?' 'That's right' said John. 'That's right. It was high odds whether the Liberals would ever agree to take food out. Stephen Swift [the campaign manager] in his heart of hearts never thought the Liberals would agree, but it was necessary to stay in the game.'

We discussed the GST. John was an economics adviser to Cheryl Kernot and Meg Lees from 1993 to 2001 before his election to the Senate. He said:*

'John Howard had been thinking about a goods and services tax for about 20 years. He launched the debate again in 1995. In the 1996 election campaign he said, "Read my lips [never, ever]". About a year later he said, "We should have a debate; I won't introduce it without an electoral mandate", so he said he would take it to the next election.

'What I think reignited it was an alliance between ACCI and ACOSS during 1994-5 when Julian Disney was the president of ACOSS. They started a dialogue about tax reform, then released a joint statement calling for reform of the indirect tax system. ACOSS was prepared to put their skin in the game by saying, "We would be prepared to support a GST as long as it excluded food and the necessities of life". They did say they also wanted a suite of changes to income tax to make it more progressive.**

'The Democrats' approach was to keep an open mind on the issue and to rule nothing in and nothing out, just to say the tax system had to be progressive and had to raise enough tax to actually pay for all the things we wanted to do—health and education.

'The Democrats ... were reviewing their tax policy. A key question at the time was whether the indirect tax ... should be expanded to include the services sector. The old wholesale sales tax was very narrow in terms of the goods it picked up. Different rates on some. It was a bit of a mess actually and importantly, it also fell on exports, which put our exporters at a disadvantage around the world because the VAT actually doesn't apply to exports. But it didn't apply to services that makes up about 60-70% of the economy and employment. The Democrats signalled they were particularly open to a discussion about services.

'There was a long debate within the party that resulted in a ballot which went out, bewilderingly confusing as Democrat policy ballots were. The result that came back in September 1998 said that the mix between direct and indirect taxes needed to be more towards direct taxes, closing loopholes and all that and that the indirect tax system should be expanded to include services.

* The Goods and Services Tax (GST) in Australia is a value added tax of 10% on most goods and services transactions. GST is levied on most transactions in the production process, but is refunded to all parties in the chain of production other than the final consumer.

** ACCI (Australian Chamber of Commerce and Industry) and ACOSS (Australian Council of Social Services).

'When the Coalition won government in 1996, John Howard was adamant he would never introduce a GST. During the 1998 election campaign he reneged. Many countries had implemented a GST or similar system.

In Australia, goods were already taxed, but the increasingly important area of services was not. 'The indirect tax system needed repair; Queensland was about to bring in a bed tax, so Howard decided that the GST was imperative and it became Coalition policy at the 1998 election.'

George Megalogenis in *The Australian Moment* says, 'The GST had two things going for it as a reform. It replaced less-efficient taxes, and the revenue it generated would increase more or less in line with economic growth, thus relieving future governments of the burden of inventing new levies to balance the budget each year'.[1]

Before the 1998 election, each Democrat State division held forums where Cherry and the taxation spokesperson, Senator Andrew Murray, explained the background to the Coalition's plan. In a subsequent policy ballot, party members accepted the inclusion of a tax on services, but wanted food and other necessities of life exempted.

In 1999, after a Coalition election victory, the Howard Government introduced a GST bill. Labor, the Greens and Senator Harradine were opposed, which meant it needed Democrat support to pass in the Senate. This gave them the balance of power.

Lees was in a strong position and proposed a series of compromises to fulfil her promise to the electorate before the legislation was passed. Andrew Murray and John Cherry accompanied her in the negotiations.

Cherry described the atmosphere in the room during the negotiations: 'Howard and Costello were an interesting combination. Costello was still a classic barrister. He was the smartest man in the room and everyone had to know it, and there wasn't a lot of give or take, so every concession Howard made was over Costello's dead body. I recall one part … where Meg was talking about the importance of taking food out for social justice perspective. Costello was objecting—body-language like this [agitated demonstration] and trying to correct Meg. Howard was taking notes with his pencil on a pad, then put his hand in front of Costello and said, "No. No. Let Meg speak".

'Were [Costello] negotiating there would never have been a GST, but the GST was too fundamental to [Howard's] election. He was prepared to take a half measure. A loss on the GST would have been too devastating to his standing as Prime Minister.'

Six of the eight Democrats agreed to pass the legislation, but Stott Despoja and Bartlett crossed the floor to vote against it. The Democrats had a 'conscience vote' and could, at any time, vote as they thought right. Nevertheless, on such a significant issue, the media made much of the appearance of a rift in the party.

The GST had its birthing pangs and the resulting fallout damaged Democrat support. In April 2001, Stott Despoja won the leadership of the party and replaced Meg Lees.

John Cherry said party-room difficulties had followed the Natasha/Meg leadership battle.

'Natasha has an enormous inability to work in a team. She has incredible communication skills policy-wise. She's pretty smart. She had great networking ability. A communicator par-excellence, but her political management skills were hopeless ... Her capacity to work in a team ... very, very difficult. I came in August, just before the October 2001 election, and was helping Natasha and Andrew Bartlett with running the election campaign [and] desperately trying to broker an accommodation of Meg as an ex-leader of the party. If you look at the task of the leader: when the former leader stays on the ex-leader has got to be accommodated. You've got to find them a meaningful role. Typically it's Foreign Minister! But Natasha just wouldn't. She assumed Meg was going to retire and was trying to facilitate that. She didn't openly attack Meg when she [Natasha] became leader, but she didn't make her overly welcome either.

'[Meg] was Health spokesperson, but her Health research person was removed, for example. Things like that. Meg was writing her own speeches. She wasn't being given the research support she felt entitled to. An ex-leader should be given a little bit of latitude to speak out on issues. That wasn't allowed and Natasha ... by that time she had strong support and would use the National Executive to cause issues.'

John also explained the series of resolutions that six of the senators had devised to resolve some of the internal issues.*

'The centre of it was to return the party-room back to how it had been. A lot of it was about access to staffing resources. It wasn't just Natasha, although throughout the year and a half that she was leader, I don't think she ever rang me. The only way I could talk to her was by text message. Have you ever tried negotiating your way through a political crisis by text message? Nowadays that's the only way you can talk to politicians. She was the first one. These were the early days. I never liked text messages. Throughout that whole period the party-room hardly ever discussed the issues of the party floating around it. It only discussed the legislation and the agenda for the day.

* See Appendix G: Ten point plan.

'Going back to the 10-point plan, one of the things I was trying to get rid of (not written in the plan but underlying) was a complete lack of faith in virtually all Natasha's staff. They weren't party people. They were largely acolytes. They put her ahead of the party. One of them had a reputation for [going into the other senators' staff rooms and treating the staff badly]. The leader wasn't perceived to be acting as part of the team and doing things a bit unilaterally ... it all added up.'

I asked John why he believed the Democrats 'died'. He thought for a while then replied, 'They died because politicians put their own feelings ahead of the good of the party'.

MEG LEES

I flew to Adelaide and spoke with Meg Lees. Meg remembered me from a visit she had paid to Brisbane in the early days of the Australian Democrats. She was generous with her time and assistance. We drove to Glenelg Beach, ate cake in an attractive café by the beach and talked.

Like other Democrat leaders she experienced enormous pressures while steering the party through tough times: Cheryl Kernot's resignation, the GST decisions, and leadership challenges. Someone said to me, "Meg was dogged". I translated that as Meg deciding on the right thing to do and *not giving up*. After a serious health issue, Meg now works on behalf of youngsters and anyone who needs legal help but cannot afford it. That is typical of Meg and, indeed, of most Australian Democrats I have known. They have a penchant for social service and trying to change the world for the better. I felt privileged to meet her again.

She studied at the Sydney University as a mature-age student and then worked for a time in a metallurgy laboratory. As a female she was on half the wage of males in the laboratory and was refused promotion because she was a woman. Meg told me ['When] I realised what was happening 'it was one of those moments'. She decided to stand up and be counted.

In South Australia and around the rest of Australia the Australian Democrats were on the rise. Meg joined and was soon a Senate candidate. Meg says 'I joined the Democrats because I believed Australia needed more than two major political parties. As we look around the democratic world, we see very effective governments built on consensus and real policy debate. In Australia we have a winner takes all system, where parliament and policy debate is largely irrelevant'.[2] She won a Senate seat in South Australia and was a Democrat Senator from 1990 to 2002. Following her resignation from the party she remained in the Senate for three more years.

Lees followed Cheryl Kernot as leader and held the position from 1997 to 2001. Like most of us Lees had strengths and weaknesses. Her temper was sometimes uncertain (particularly with reporters) and she lacked Kernot's public charisma but was a principled and effective leader. The party was in good hands.

Kernot broke the news of her departure in a phone call to her then deputy, Meg Lees, just minutes before it was announced publicly. Lees was out on a limb, about to go into a press conference, when she realised the room overflowed with reporters. The conference was delayed until she and other staff made urgent phone calls to Democrat figures around Australia. They needed to inform as many in the party as possible to allow them to respond adequately to the sudden news. Then she faced the reporters, as the party's acting leader.

In the 1998 election, with Lees leading the Democrats and with opposition from One Nation (Pauline Hanson's party), the party's vote fell by 2.37%, but Democrats won four Senate seats. Aden Ridgeway (NSW) and Brian Greig (WA) joined the team to take Democrat numbers in the Senate to the highest they had ever been. From 1999, there were nine senators, also including Allison, Bartlett, Bourne, Lees, Murray, Stott Despoja and Woodley.

After Kernot's departure to the ALP, the election results were a credit to Lees and her team and an acknowledgment by the public that they appreciated the Democrats' role in the parliament. The Democrat message during the campaign had been clear. They would pass the tax reforms of whichever party won the election but would support the GST only if food and other necessities of life were exempt.

'John Cherry ... was the one on the ground. He went to every division to talk about the Good and Services Tax (GST) policy to get the ballot through... at least. I deliberately didn't vote because I wanted to wait for the membership. I didn't do a lot canvassing. All I did was answer questions. [the membership ballot] agreed to pass the GST. 'What was happening, as we saw it, was that services were a growing part of the economy. Every other country had a GST or something similar, except America who was doing it on a state by state basis, ad hoc (and it's still a mess).

'Queensland was about to go with a bed tax on services, Northern Territory [had] some sort of a services tax. We were running a risk. We looked around the world and asked 'Where was it doing the best?' Meg told me that Chipp and Siddons supported a tax on services. She said, 'I respected

John Siddons. I think he was looking further ahead than I was with the risk we took with the Party. He told me, as Chipp did, that they were fully supportive of taxing services. It was only when we came to it that they got a bit shaky. John said "You were absolutely right. It's the best thing for the country, the only thing we could have done". [About Chipp] Meg said 'I respected what he did, but personally I never got on with him. That was to my cost later on.'

The government did not handle the GST implementation well and some interest groups were unhappy. Small businesses had masses of unfamiliar paperwork to collect the tax; hotels copped flak because of increases in alcohol prices. Petrol prices rose from unrelated causes, but the GST was blamed.

Michael Macklin told me how he saw that time. 'Meg stepped into the breach after Cheryl walked and did it very well. She handled the media very well. By that stage she was a fairly proficient with the media. Meg however, didn't suffer fools gladly lightly or any way at all. She was always pretty tough on them. I thought it was perfectly reasonable because what they were doing was personifying Cheryl walking as the Democrats walking and she had to be tough to say, 'Well. Look. Cheryl was the leader and she's gone. The party's still here. We still have the balance of power so she had a very, very difficult juggling act. And I think the approach she took was probably the right one … to be tough, but, journos don't like that. That gets their goat. They want people to think they're lovely and they know all these things. Meg ran into increasing difficulties with the media as a result of that very strong approach. But I think she held the party together. She increased the membership.'

However, the misplaced blame had ramifications for the Democrats' future. The criticism later fed concerns about Lees' leadership and led to the short-term leadership of Natasha Stott Despoja. Although the Democrats had been clear on their policy and had gained concessions for a considerable number of essential items, their decision to support even a modified GST was represented by the media as a betrayal. It was difficult to counter this impression, although Democrat polling showed they were doing well among voters in typical Democrat areas and had Meg Lees retained the leadership, the question of the GST could possibly have been put into perspective before the 2001 election.

Meg was not impressed with the role of the Labor Party.

'Look at what they were doing. They knew. The Labor party was well-aware. They knew the problem. They knew they couldn't keep racking up debt. If they kept going the way they wanted to go which was a politically easy option we would be where maybe not where Greece is but maybe where Spain and Italy are in terms of our debt to equity ratio.

'We did support the GST but not much else. We were regularly opposing particularly industrial relations and a raft of social matters on and on and on. I know that was frustrating, but that was our job. That's why we were there to give a voice to those who weren't having a voice.

BF: How do you remember your time in the party after Natasha became the leader?

ML: Natasha's inexperience and getting rid of staff, some of whom had been there since Janine. In the party if you disagreed with her, it was as if you were against her. There had been a collegiate approach in the party-room closely involving long-standing staff, but the way it was run after my time was one of the issues I had. Qualified staff members were sacked and other people brought in. They would go into a Senator's office and say "Just do as we say". Only once did they come into my office and they didn't come back. Let's just say, no-one ever intimidated my staff again.

'Natasha didn't get everything the way she thought it was going to be. No-one forced her out. I'd given up. We were doing absolutely nothing. I came into politics to make a difference. I wanted to work on legislation. I wanted to go to the media. Natasha had the numbers on the National Executive. Several on the National Executive basically said, "You do what Natasha wants. We want Natasha not yourself. You just behave yourself" and I thought Nuh, I'm not playing the game anymore. I went off separately and worked on health care. I got psychology into Medicare, and it's still there. No-one's taken it out.

'I thought Michael Macklin was part of the problem. He said he was supporting me, and told Natasha he was supporting her. I would have confronted them if I'd realised how much damage was being done behind my back. How would I do it differently? I would watch my back. I was far too trusting. Natasha kept undermining those other Senators—seven of her colleagues—endlessly, every media door-stop, constantly.

'The party genuinely got worried. The polling in the party dropped but in the leafy suburbs polling showed support for the Australian Democrats. [Democrat Senators] had discussions about all leaving, as the party wasn't going to survive. The brand was so tarnished when Natasha and Andrew had finished with it. Andrew Bartlett took over a party that was on the skids. '[I had a] lot of time for Lyn Allison. She got left with the mess.

'I'm pretty sure that when we got to the next election, I would have done better than [Nathasa] did. I don't think we would have lost a seat in New South Wales. I would have been safe for another year at least and by then the

GST would have bedded down and I would have had another year before they challenged again.

I asked Meg why she thought the Democrats had failed and she responded:

'It wasn't the GST that brought the ship on the rocks; it was the ship itself and the structure. Unless the people of Australia are prepared to put at least some of their time and energy where they say they want politics going we can't do what we did with the Democrats. …People are enthusiastic but the work ends up being done by so few…'

NATASHA STOTT DESPOJA

I attempted by several methods to contact Natasha. It is likely that one or more of my messages reached her, but I had no response. What follows is an analysis of information from others and from my reading. It would be good to hear her side of the story, but I respect her right to decline.

****

Senior party members saw Natasha as young and vibrant and attractive and the future of the party. She *was* young and *was* vibrant and *was* attractive to the media, but was she ready? Those qualities do not necessarily add up to the substance necessary for the leader of a party such as the Australian Democrats.

From her Senate debut, Stott Despoja was comfortable with the media and the media befriended her. She was constantly available for interviews and opportunities for publicity. Journalists more or less told her (and the public) they thought she was destined to lead the party. Alan Ramsay, a senior journalist, was not of that opinion and wrote, 'She was all about herself … She paraded herself … it wasn't about politics, anything she could get herself on to, particularly television … She was the leader, and you thought, hang on, what about the Democrats? … What about the party; what about policy?'[3]

Michael Macklin thought Alan Ramsay wrong. He said: 'Natasha *was* good at publicity.' 'Well,' I said 'as long as you get the essential Democrat message across' and Michael replied, 'She was very much Democrat. Her value system and so forth very much up and down the line. She had been mentored by Janine for a long period of time. She came out of student politics of course where she'd done very well and Janine picked her up and got her into the party.

'I think the problem with Nat was she was young. Nat turned a lot of people off because she was young. End of story. It is not surprising. I can tell you about Janine because it was exactly the same problem that she ran into that Nat ran into. It is about what we tend to call in young people "brashness" and we tend to call in older people "confidence". Nat's big problem was her age.

'There was resistance to her because of her age. Remember, she was almost the same age as Janine when she [led the party], but I was deputy. I ran the Parliament; Janine ran the stuff outside and in the four years we operated, Janine did not ever have a problem from the Parliamentary side because I'd been whip for six years so I knew precisely [what needed to be done].

'She [Natasha] needed a backup.'

Macklin again:

'My general approach would be (having been in there) is that it is easy to be critical. What was going on at the time was always extremely difficult. We were a small group with the balance of power and, if one hasn't been in those circumstances, it is almost impossible to describe the pressure that one comes under—and with very, very minimal staff compared to what the Government and Opposition had. So our staff just had to work day and night in very difficult circumstances. My view is that the leaders that we had were always going to fail. Where they succeeded, we were lucky because the pressures were just inordinate.'

The GST debate divided many in the party. Natasha and her supporters campaigned against it. The National Executive was divided and unable to give a clear lead. The party-room felt the division, although by six to two the senators supported Meg Lees in the decision to pass the bill.

After the GST legislation passed there was continuing media pressure on the Democrats. Its introduction took a long time and seemed chaotic. The media forgot it was a Government bill and had actually needed the Government to pass it.

It was a stressful time. Kernot's departure, a hectic election campaign and then the pressures arising from the introduction of the GST put Meg Lees in an invidious position. As Michael Macklin said to me, 'Meg really got all the odium and none of the kudos, I mean, just imagine where our tax situation would have been if we hadn't had the GST.'

Polling showed the Democrats losing support. The tide turned against Meg's leadership and a movement began for Natasha to replace her. A leadership struggle is bound to be difficult. Tensions increased. There were two ballots and the second one saw Natasha become the leader.

Meg Lees told me: 'She had to divide the party to get the leadership and she couldn't put Humpty Dumpty together again. To get the leadership she had to [distort the facts] about the GST and it divided the party'.

Lees said Don Chipp had agreed with her statement that: 'Had Natasha waited, I wasn't going to be around for ever, perhaps just for one election and another couple of years, then she would have had a united party, but she couldn't (or wouldn't) wait.'

Natasha had Don Chipp's support to replace Meg, but Chipp later admitted in an interview on the Andrew Denton show that he thought he had made a mistake and she had not been ready.*

In 2001 Natasha Stott Despoja led the party to the election. Democrats held four of the five seats contested and after the election there were eight Democrat Senators: Stott Despoja, Allison, Bartlett, Cherry, Lees, Murray, Ridgeway and Woodley. Vicki Bourne had lost her seat. The results were 1.2% lower than the previous election, but not unreasonable given the negative publicity about the GST. However, this was the second election in a row that had seen the Democrats' vote decline.

One of Stott Despoja's first actions on becoming leader was to replace long-term staffers. John Cherry: 'There [had been] enormous continuity in the staff through numerous leadership changes. I think when Cheryl took over from Coulter she made minimal changes. Most of the advisers she took on were Coulter's.

When Meg took over from Cheryl there were minimal changes. When Natasha took over there were a large number of changes. It was a whole new crew and most of them, in my observation … hadn't come up through the party. They owed their first loyalty to Natasha, and from the beginning this caused difficulties.'

The party-room atmosphere, which had been friendly and collegiate from the party's beginnings, deteriorated. The loss of long-term staffers meant the loss of expertise and the harmony of people who had worked together for many years.

Several people have told me that Natasha, despite her incredible communication skills policy-wise, had an inability to work in a team. In the regular meetings, concerns and team issues were not discussed. It is sad that Natasha made no accommodation for the former leader, Meg Lees. As John Cherry and others have noted, Natasha probably believed Meg would retire.

* See Appendix F. Interview: Chipp on the Andrew Denton show

This is clearly a downside of the membership electing a leader. If the person elected is not acceptable to most of the Parliamentary team, there will be conflict—and there was.

Some of this account may appear negative but, to put it in perspective, I tried to think what many of us were like at the age of 32. We were probably ambitious, thinking the world was our oyster. We may have thought we knew everything and could do anything. If we were thwarted we thought people were picking on us even though we were doing our best. Despite her brilliance and attractiveness, Stott Despoja made errors of judgement.

ANDREW BARTLETT

I was keen to speak with Andrew Bartlett, who was not only the Queensland Democrat who took Cheryl Kernot's place in the Senate, but also one of two senators who voted against the GST. I was curious to know his reason for doing so and needed his point of view to round out my account. I had not met Andrew previously as he came to the party after I had left.

Nowadays he plays an important role in the Queensland branch of the Australian Greens. In 2009 he was a Greens candidate for a House of Representatives seat and gained just over 21% of the vote. In 2002 he was a candidate for the position of lord mayor of Brisbane. On both occasions, the Green vote rose.

For a while I thought I had missed my chance to meet him. After we spoke earlier in the year I caught a virus that laid me low for almost two months, then heard no more. One day, out of the blue, he called and we arranged to meet. A day or so later I drove to his unit overlooking the Brisbane city skyline. After we had a coffee I turned on the tape recorder.

At first he was hesitant. Perhaps it was difficult to think back to times that were so eventful, stressful even. Perhaps he wondered if I was trustworthy and how much he should share with me. Then as the interview went along we began just to chat.

In 1990 Andrew joined the Queensland division management committee as assistant secretary. He soon became secretary. He was also on Cheryl Kernot's staff when she was elected and went on the Senate ticket as a result of Cheryl leaving, which he said had been 'a hell of a thing and totally unexpected'. In total, he was part of the Democrat family for 18 years or so as staffer and in party roles. He was formerly a Social Security Department social worker.

I asked what he regarded as a highlight of his time in the Senate. He replied: 'Improving the Federal environment laws, the Environmental Protection and Biodiversity Act. Unfortunately we did that and got that passed at the same time as the GST. It was a big advance, but Bob Brown opposed it as it wasn't enough.

We couldn't get anything agreed to about regional forestry stuff. Forest is evidently his thing, so we also had the Greens attacking us, a bit ironic for me, I suppose, so it was hard for people to think we were getting something positive done because quite a lot of our supporters were already at that time a bit leery about us [because of the GST].

'The most difficult times were the [GST issue] and then after the 2001 election—Meg Lees … I often think [about] the GST that there were things I should have done. I'm sure I could have stopped that happening if I had anticipated it right. But, that is, getting it passed.'

I questioned, 'Would you prefer the GST not to have been passed? Andrew: 'Yes, although … you could have the policy argument and I think there are arguments in favour of it, but my view is that if we thought it was a good thing we should have campaigned in favour of it, but we said it would not be passed if certain things weren't exempted and there were a lot [of items we didn't press on for]. We were in a very strong negotiating position. John Howard didn't have anywhere else to go so we had no need not to insist on everything and it was obviously going to be very controversial if we did agree with it, and for me it was the problem that we were doing something that we said we wouldn't.

'It was against the policy we had balloted and we did a pretty comprehensive year or so engagement with the members a couple of years earlier and that's one of the [reasons] I should not have accepted it. In the ballot we [did] not have a question that explicitly named the GST so we had all this arcane stuff, a mix of direct tax … indirect options.

'The GST was explicitly, deliberately, not mentioned in the ballot because it was expected if we had a direct question that it would have come out with a negative. That would have meant that we had no negotiating room. It was more about political positioning. It sent the message that we could walk both sides of the street.

'Andrew Murray genuinely believed it was a good idea, but all the rest, in my view, ended up being talked into it, partly because it was very explicitly said, in the party-room and some of the discussions we had, this would be a brilliant strategic move that would show that we were in the main game and … just stupid, so stupid. It was difficult, not so much because we disagreed, it was difficult for me, particularly for a party that had the tag, "Keep the bastards honest", to go and do something that was obviously against what we'd given the impression.'

I asked if Meg and her team campaigned very strongly in the 1998 election on GST. Andrew: 'Not in the sense they were saying GST is a good thing as long as we fix these things, but [rather] if Labor wins, here's our response to that and here's our responses to the Libs' stuff. Actually … our big message was who is going to control the Senate: us or Pauline Hanson? That was our slogan and that was our core message. The GST was just positioning.

'The core message for Liberals and Labor was the GST, but the core message for us was the Senate—keep it safe versus One Nation, and we got a fair bit of coverage around that.

'We weren't expecting to be in a position to decide 'yes' or 'no', but from the moment Brian Harradine said he wouldn't do it [pass the GST], it was like three weeks, and before Harradine said no the Government hadn't come near us.

'We sort of got manoeuvred into it by Stephen Swift [campaign director], John Cherry and others and convincing Meg that it was a strategic move—which was insane.'

I asked, 'What did the National Executive think about the GST and what Meg was doing?' 'Well, there was a debate about it and a vote that narrowly passed and [a lot of] emotion. Meg and Natasha were on [the executive], but they cancelled each other out. John Cherry was on it and he held two positions, State representative and deputy national president. [There were also] three or four votes [from people who] were staffers of Meg.'

'Was Chipp still around—I wonder what he thought of it?'

'He was around and I suppose it was a bit sad for him to see all that happening, but he sort of stayed [out of it]. He was good. He just sort of left it to us.'

I asked Andrew about Natasha. 'She was getting an enormous amount of media publicity and she obviously knew how to get that. But it was also coming to her—some of which she didn't want. 'Do you think that planted ideas in her head that she would eventually be leader?' 'Oh no, I think even before she got into the Senate she had a profile in South Australia, but more broadly'.

'Had she run for anything before in South Australia?' 'No. From the day she arrived there was an expectation that she would likely end up leader at some stage, which was why there was also massive paranoia about it. Natasha was obviously very charismatic and very good at communicating, but as I say there was that paranoia about her. She certainly was not good at organising and building alliances within the party-room. Natasha had a lot of people [who] were supporters of her, thought she was fabulous, but she wasn't good at the internal stuff.

'I'm sure to this day, although Meg thought differently, she was not pushing to be leader. There were all these young people joining [and some thought] that there was some "stacking" thing going on. Concern about people joining! When people get that paranoid that they don't like building membership numbers then it's so counterproductive, and even when it all happened, when she finally got there she was … very apprehensive.

'After the GST vote happened (there were quite a few members unhappy about it, of course) there was a member petition thing where they got enough numbers. A lot of people wanted a leadership spill, but [Natasha] didn't run then. It was just Meg running on her own. She got 80% in a yes or no vote. After another year or so another membership petition happened and she had to then, but she certainly wasn't manoeuvring for it. She wasn't campaigning for the leadership. But the third time … you can't keep spilling and spilling, you've got to give them a choice.

'[Natasha] liked to be liked. She was always worried about people criticising her or whatever. Rather [than] saying "that is it; we'll go with it even if some people are upset", she would put a toe out then come back a bit … and that sort of thing. She couldn't have kept the party-room together in the way Cheryl did because there were people there who just refused and were so antagonistic to her.'

I suggested, 'Andrew Murray and Natasha didn't hit it off?' 'Ha ha, no, and Aden as well. From the day he got in he had that extra focus on him. People who loathed Natasha swung behind him and tried to build him up quickly to position him as someone else who could be a potential leader. And again, it just meant that if that's what is driving your strategy then you can get a whole lot of stupid things happening. [When he was first in the Senate] he didn't have that background that I have. It was a new experience for him so you can understand.'

I wondered why the National Executive put Brian Greig in as Acting leader and not Aden, and Andrew replied: 'Yeah. That was a weird thing that. Then Aden decided not to run. He [Aden] also was sensitive to being criticised. I was part of the National Executive, but I was amazed, shocked, when it happened. Very odd! The reason they went for Brian was that a lot of them were pissed off with it [the disharmony]. But I think it was because people felt he was part of a [move against Natasha]. About August 2002, you know, they had that 10-point plan. She had no option but to quit really. That was what Natasha had to resign over in the end—basically the majority of the party-room demanding that [the 10-point plan be accepted].

I explained that I had a copy of the 10 points and felt they didn't seem to be excessive, particularly if a party-room was not functioning properly, but Andrew believed the party would never function while Natasha was leader as people would just not basically accept her.

I asked 'Did you enjoy being Democrats leader?' 'Not overly. It was interesting.' Did things settle down a bit? 'Yes. In terms of the party-room stuff they did. Our polls never recovered from the day Natasha was forced out. We never went above 2% ever again. Yes, I think the party-room settled down quite well and we did a lot of good stuff. I think that I had some capacity in enabling that to happen, but in terms of the public media stuff and that sort of thing I think our well was so poisoned by then I'm not sure that anyone could have recovered it. That wasn't my strength. I didn't have a problem doing it, but compared to people like Natasha and others that have that sort of charisma, I didn't have that'.

Should the leader have been Aden? 'Oh well! He didn't nominate … yes … and in terms of having enough grasp of all of the issues, I'm not sure he had that skill. But if had run he would have won.'

It was time to broach a sensitive topic: 'We come to that horrible night … I'm pretty sure what they wrote in the newspapers isn't the real story.'

'No. I would handle that differently. I would have just stayed right away from certain people. I'm a bit apprehensive talking about it particularly because Jeanne Ferris has died since then so I don't want … If I had my time again, in terms of responding … very differently, rather than just say typical social work, "Democratty" sort of thing. Um, but I didn't put forward my side of the story at the time … so it's too late now … now that she's died … Looks pretty poor form to add some stuff now … well, you know, that she can't respond to.'

Finally, I asked if Andrew had a view about why the Democrats folded. He said: 'I think (obviously) we lost public support. On a very macro level I think "Keep the bastards honest" was quite a strength for us, but also a weakness. People thought you are sort of an umpire and our own policy and philosophy in its own right was harder to communicate. We didn't really encapsulate our core values in the way the Greens can and have. The Greens got slowly stronger and stronger so we had that competition. People had somewhere else to go. They had that consistency and stability with us falling to bits and people had somewhere to go. But I think overall we lost our support partly by the GST and partly because of all that brawling.'

ADEN RIDGEWAY

I visited Aden in Sydney and after a warm greeting we went into a boardroom and I turned on the tape recorder. You sense at once that he is a man with gravitas. He considers his words and is careful not to be overly critical.

Ridgeway was a member of the Democrats for eight years before his election to the Senate. He told me: 'The reason I joined was essentially around policies. The main parties had developed policies on the environment, education and Indigenous rights. The Democrats stood out, by far. In terms of the progressive nature of the policies, as well as the way those policies were developed, there was an engagement of the membership to participate in that process. It stood out as something significant and in many ways akin to what I was familiar with, that is, growing up in a community where decisions were made collectively, rather than one chief making decisions.

'According to my mother, I used to talk about becoming a Member of Parliament when I was 10 years of age. I kind of put that down to the time when the late Liberal Senator, Neville Bonner, from Queensland, was elected and that stayed in my mind. Two great things were happening, and the other was South Sydney were winning the rugby league grand finals! I guess that was the seed that was planted in my early years and grew during my upbringing and mentoring in my own community, particularly by my grandmother, who was involved in politics and especially land-rights campaigns.'

Aden is New South Wales born and bred. During his adult life he has held some very responsible positions, and since leaving the Senate has been involved in attempts to improve the representation of Indigenous people in the corporate sector and to open up pathways there. He and his partners have built up a company that works as consultants to government agencies. More than half the team are young Indigenous.

He told me a little about his family's values. 'I'd grown up in a family where everybody in those days always supported the Labor Party. My grandfather worked on the railways. He was a fettler. He used to say three things, "Be good to your mother; be a good Catholic; and vote Labor".

I'm sure if he was alive at the time he would have approved of my joining the Democrats and members of the family voting for the Democrats, so there were similarities in that sense.

'I was the New South Wales policy convenor probably for eight years. My [view] was there was no point in putting up your hand as a candidate for an elected position unless you were involved in the party, and there was some authenticity about having become familiar to the members and also understanding the working of the party and the development of policy itself.'

Aden was preselected by Democrat members in New South Wales with 90% of the vote. The eight other candidates shared the 10%. However, at the time he was also the CEO of the New South Wales Land Council and in the media for a number of other reasons, appearing at ICAC inquiries and working against corruption in the Land Council system, so that added to the attraction.* Aden did not go into details about his involvement with ICAC, but Michael Macklin told me: 'He was the only person who really took on the crooks in the Aboriginal welfare industry and had them jailed. Other Indigenous leaders he had jailed because they were ripping off their own communities. Everybody else used to say, "Oh, oh. You can't do that because they were Indigenous." Aden said "They are *bad*! It's criminal what they're doing. I will not stand for it".'

When I began to ask about the difficult days leading to the Democrats' decline, Aden said the most important principle should always have been what was in the party's best interest. He was unwilling to blame the party decline on any one individual. However, he did comment on the Meg/Natasha leadership struggle.

> AR: I remember having a conversation with Natasha that we shouldn't be having a leadership spill no matter how much there were these disagreements about the GST, and the main reason for that was I think we needed to show stability rather than allowing the party to fall apart. But also [we needed to] be disciplined [and] to show the right sort of leadership required to keep the party together. Parties are going to go through a range of different issues and this happened to be one of them.
>
> It was *the* biggest test of being able to demonstrate that we were a party that could manage the difficulties. Meg wouldn't have stayed for ever.
>
> BF: Meg told me that herself.
>
> AR: She [Natasha] would have been the leader … and of an even more successful party. That's the thing that frustrates me about what happened.
>
> BF: Well. Do you think she *would* have? There has been a lot of critique of Natasha—the fact that she didn't have good internal capacity to guide a team of people and didn't seem to care about the needs of the group.
>
> AR: She was young. She was bright. She was popular.

* ICAC—Independent Commission Against Corruption.

BF: The 'young' thing is what seems to me to be the crux of the problem. If, as you say, she could have been persuaded to … or if people in the other segments of the party could have slowed her down a little bit so she was mentored through it until she was ready. Chipp himself said he didn't think she was ready.

AR: [Perhaps] she thought there was going to be another Costello thing where a promise was made and she was going to miss the boat, but I don't think that was going to happen.

BF: Do you think Natasha was keen on being the leader—as keen as everybody seems to think? Andrew Bartlett said everyone was mistaken. That she didn't really want to be the leader.

AR: If she wasn't then she ended up like me—being in a position she didn't want at that time. She ended up getting pushed into it by all the people around her, her supporters.

BF: And then, of course, you were deputy [when Natasha resigned], and they put Brian Greig in [as acting leader]. What a slap in the face.

AR: Yeah. That's why I stood down as deputy. I made the statement at the time to the media… well, if my National Executive doesn't have confidence in me to put me in as acting leader how can I be deputy leader. I don't think they expected that I was going to step down then not run for the leader's role.

BF: Why on earth would they have done that? Do you have any insight into that at all? That's another inexplicable thing.

AR: The National Executive at the time were pro one camp and anti another. I was perceived as being part of the camp that they didn't support. Therefore putting me in that role would have been doing what they didn't want to do.

BF: It shouldn't have been anything to do with them really. It should have been automatic. You should have been acting leader.

AR: Yeah. It should have been convention as it has always been in the party. That to me is a public demonstration of lack of discipline and appropriate courtesies.

Aden didn't put his name forward on the leadership ballot although he was encouraged to do so by a number of people in the party. Michael Macklin said:

'Aden was a marvellous man, marvellous man. I pushed him to become the leader … He could have run as leader and he would have won and we would have had the first female leader of a political party and the first Indigenous leader of a political party.

'He was a good performer. He would have made a great leader. If we'd put him in there may have been a bit of a splutter, but I think we would have recovered and I think, given his background and what he's done … he was a strong enough personality to go over the top of that internal party individualism and pull the media to him as party leader, which is what party leaders had to do.'

Ridgeway finished his term in 2005 and the opportunity was lost. But as Aden himself told me, 'Politics is a time and place thing'.

'For me, the … learnings were that we needed to understand and respect the role of the leader of the party.

One of the things we didn't have was a kind of reverence for the position and an understanding of what was required to be in that role. Some party members never really paid due to Meg or others before her about the responsibilities that involved. The second thing was we didn't display enough maturity as a party after those decades we'd been there to show the sort of discipline and mettle if you like to hold our ground as a party, even though there was disquiet. I take the view that if we had, we would still be in the Senate. We'd probably be stronger than what came out of it. Unfortunately, the reverse side of that was that we undercut ourselves so much that the fallout meant that we were never going to be there. We weren't going to get the support because voters could see that.'

MICHAEL MACKLIN

I left the interview with Michael until last. If you have read the rest of the book you will understand why. I was anxious about meeting him—knowing I meant to raise the issue of what had happened so many years ago and unsure what his response would be.

We came face-to-face at last prior to a meeting we were both attending. Michael greeted me warmly; I responded similarly and the meeting went ahead. Afterwards I gave him the chapter 'My year as president' along with my email address and asked if he would respond to what I had written. 'Don't read it now,' I warned. 'Read it later and then tell me what you think.'

Michael responded fairly quickly and said he had a radically different view of events that I had described in the chapter. Not really surprising.

However, our engagement had begun and I wrote back asking if we could meet for an interview. He agreed, and I promised to send him a list of questions. Michael said he didn't want some of his responses recorded and with some trepidation, I agreed.

I had arranged the questions from general to specific so thought we might be able to discuss his role in the party and in the Senate before coming to the more delicate subjects. Perhaps he would agree for the first questions to be recorded and then we could discuss the final matters without the tape recorder.

Michael wrote back quickly with answers to all the general questions and with a wealth of material from personal memoirs he had already prepared. The generous amount of material contained much of interest, but there was still no clear response to the questions I had asked about that certain chapter. So I sent another chapter, 'We finally have a party'. Michael responded to some points and I answered his critiques. I also asked him directly about his involvement in the issues I wanted to discuss.

Our email exchange went like this—

> BF: I suppose if you are in a 'clique' you might not notice. It's a bit like being a fish in water. Only those outside the water feel a bit left out. It's true that the members elected the officials, but if you look at what happened in practice, the first to come to the party were elected and re-elected and they helped each other to stay in the top positions.
>
> MM: You may make such a judgement, but I did not experience any clique at that time or later and it wasn't the "fish in water" exercise. I had experienced cliques previously in university politics and subsequent[ly] in business, so am very familiar with the approach. It simply didn't happen in the party in Queensland for the very good reason that we were so thin on the ground that we couldn't work except to include everyone. Again I tend to feel that evidence is necessary in making such assertions in print. It might also be useful to define what you mean by "clique" given its pejorative connotations.
>
> Perhaps some evidence of this would be useful. My view was that alliances were pretty fluid at this time and the democratic nature of the party worked against such alliances.
>
> BF: I think they [members of the group] developed a sense of ownership (and even secrecy) that locked many others out—particularly people who were of a mind to be more fully involved. In the case of a couple of those first-timers (named in chapter 6) there was, at the very least, school-yard bullying at a significant level, and at the most, one could say discrimination. I have given quite a bit of evidence of how these people behaved in chapter five.
>
> As in the case of Janine's feminism, only a small number were involved in this bad behaviour, but what is really serious to me is that they were very close to you and you appeared to take no action to restrain them.
>
> In my case, you seemed to be opposed to me from the time I became President.
>
> MM: Your perception. It isn't mine.

THE DAY OF OUR MEETING ARRIVED

The venue was an elegant city café. I arrived early. Michael soon came and we began our conversation with coffee. Michael had told me of his interest in writing 'mini' books for his children so I took along a few of my own to show him and first we discussed the ins and outs of getting books published. He agreed to me recording the first of the questions and I agreed to turn off the recorder towards the end when I hoped we would have a frank discussion of the chapters I had given him. Michael's account of the first days of the Democrats in Queensland astonished me as I knew very little of what had happened before the City Hall and Dendy meetings.

'Why do you think there was such an explosion of support in the beginning for the Democrats?' I asked and Michael replied, 'I think we were riding on not only on some political issues that were around at that time, but we were [also] riding on some social issues that were around at the time ... the social upheaval overseas. We were delayed in Australia. Everywhere else got it in the late 60's, we got it in the mid-70's. There was a ferment going on that attracted the type of people who were in the party. The social reformers, the middle-class do-gooders ... they were happy to interfere in people's lives to make them better.

'The fact that we managed to do what we managed to do, quite frankly, was extraordinary. It was an historic accident—plus a strange coming together of a strange group of people. I'll give you an example of that—John Siddons, multi-millionaire. One of the things that he had done in his own company was he followed through the policies we [the Democrats] were talking about of industrial democracy. They weren't just theoretical.

'If you have workers then those workers ought to share in the outcomes of the profits of the company. If you do that you make more money. They make money. You make money. He truly believed in that and when he got excited about it he would always go back to Sidchrome and you could see that what he was talking about were actualities. Nobody else had a person like him. In the entire Parliament there was nobody like John. So when he did get up to talk about industrial democracy, everybody else could sit down and shut up because John knew about it. He'd done it. He'd been there. He'd made it work.

'Then there was Norm Sanders. Norm Sanders established *the* major environmental group in America and had been thrown out of university as a result in California. He put his family on a boat and brought them to Tasmania. Actually ran into Tasmania. They beached. Norm ended up becoming first anchor for *7.30 Report*. He became the first Democrat elected to Parliament in the Tasmanian Parliament. So here was this person whose environmental qualifications were second to none and if you wanted to talk about anything on the environment just talk to him. We were very, very lucky to have this strange group of people come together at this time *with the balance of power.*

> BF: It was like a vortex drawing in people who had something to say.
>
> MM: It was mind-bogglingly difficult. We met every day and debated in the party-room. Not once a week like the Labor Party or once a week the Liberals. Every day we debated every bill. The media used to come around and ask us about legislation because we were the only ones who'd read the blasted stuff.
>
> Michael showed me an example of work on a bill. 'Fine detail. We always had somebody there for the committee stages of the bill. We would go through clause by clause. What was going on was a phenomenal amount of work with a group of individuals who should never have been got together in the same room and then we say, "We appoint you leader. Oh, come on!"
>
> Author: How did the first five of you get on? Janine, Siddons, you, Chipp and Mason?
>
> MM: Siddons was a huge man. He would occasionally slam his papers on the table and then walk out the door and slam it. [The regular meetings] were almost an endless brawl and that was when Don was running it. Remember, he was the longest-serving manager of government business in the Australian federation. He wasn't a wilting lily. He knew how to organise in a Parliamentary context. It was under him. He was probably the best, most knowledgeable, organiser of Parliamentary business in Federation. Don used to say to me, 'Michael. You're the whip. Use your whip" So you had all these [individuals] and you had someone trying to lead them. It didn't work. As I've said many times, it's like herding cats. It doesn't work.

Michael seemed to warm to the detail of the era and continued:

'There was a split in the Parliamentary party. Splits in the party weren't that unusual. It happened with the taxes on the necessities of life when we had the balance of power. Chippie was in hospital with a heart attack. Poor old Colin says, "We've got to pass it". We all go back to our electorates, talk to the party, discover they're dead opposed to it, come back and I said, "Look. I've canvassed widely in terms of the party in Queensland. I'm unhappy with the tax. I don't propose to support it". So then Janine says, "I've canvassed and I don't propose to support it either". Ah. All hell broke loose because Colin, quite rightly, said "I've gone out on a bloody limb, you know." Don had just gone off to hospital. "Come on, you bastards, you're hanging me out to dry"—which was true. On the other hand, I said, "Well, look Colin, I know we're hanging you out to dry, but I can't support something on the basis that you will feel embarrassed. I'm sorry, I'm going to oppose it." Jack Evans then moved to opposition. Chippie comes back and decided to change it. It all worked out in the end. We didn't vote for it.

'What I had tried to do at the beginning was to say, "Let's start talking about what's best for the party". Every senator had a right to vote according to their conscience, then according to the electorate and then according to party policy. That was the standard operation we used for the 10 years I was there. If their conscience said this, then that's how they had to vote. That wasn't a problem? People used to vote different ways when I was there. We didn't have a problem. We came into the party-room the following day and there wasn't an issue. However, the media never, ever liked that. It wasn't black and white.'

'The money bills were difficult,' I observed, and Michael agreed. He outlined some of the Democrats' economic themes. 'It's an area where we were very pushy. Every election we went to we argued for increased taxation. Every election. Because our view, mantra really, was if you want to spend it you have got to earn it. We would never put up a proposal to spend money unless we could actually show how you could earn the money. The public are supportive of that—for example, the increased Medicare levy. It was a popular move. Here's taxation being popular! Why is this so? Because what you are doing is directly showing, we're not just taking money and putting it into a big coffer.

We're spending it on X; we're spending it on Y; we're spending it on Z. People are happy with that. They were happy with the Medicare levy because it goes into health.

'And then the GST (a consumption tax): in hindsight, you might say, a tax on consumption might be a bad idea, but we had production proposals which were much more radical and they were part of party policy at the time, much more radical than the GST and much more comprehensive. The difficulty at the end of the day with the GST is that it penalises poor people as they pay exactly the same as the rich. It is very regressive.

'We put up one that was a progressive consumption tax. It was a very good model, would have raised more than the GST.

'It [the GST] is a 'broken' tax. It was never a good consumption tax because it was regressive. There are [better] ways of dealing with that whole thing.'

BF: We're coming to the decline of the party.

> MM: I would go back to the original demise when Cheryl left. That had a rumbling effect. It wasn't noticed in terms of the vote. Meg did very well. She held it together, but the second big hit was the GST. I think we could have survived one or the other. I think trying to survive both was very, very difficult. I think what happened was with the group that followed, quite frankly, was the advancement of personality politics. That's not unusual in the party because that had started in 1977, however, it was kept in check by strong leaders in terms of the public persona. When Don went on, he was the face of the party; when Janine went on, she was the face of the party; when Cheryl went on, etc. So, in a sense, prior to that there had been protection by these leaders who were exceptional and strong enough out there in the public arena to draw attention to themselves and away from what was essentially a dysfunctional group of people.

Michael expanded on the theme: 'All of the people were working like little beavers, but they could have worked like little beavers as independents. They would have been quite happy, because they all had their own agendas. And they were going to push their own agenda come hell or high water and they did.

That was lucky because they would work 24 hours a day and the agendas were pushed. Agendas were massaged into some type of platform. They were in the party because they had a general ideological view, so much of these didn't cause much noise with other people in the party.

'If I came in and said I wanted to do wholesale electoral reform everybody goes clap clap, "Go for it, Michael". Janine says, "This is an extraordinary situation with regard to retirement villages". So clap clap "Away you go, Janine". We were all about reform. People came in and said we had to reform something. So everyone said, "Good on you. Go and reform something. While I get on with my bit over here". So we could have all been independents, but we *weren't.* We just had this general ideological view. The media was prepared to wear the context because those strong leaders stood up in the media.

'Once you removed those strong leaders … I think it [Cheryl's departure] was half of the context. After that, the individualism that was always there, gained the upper hand. Without a strong leader who was able "in the mind of the press, not necessarily in the party-room" to say this is "a unitary party". Once that happened we were in all sorts of trouble and Bartlett wasn't able to do it. Lyn wasn't able to do it. Then there were those little incidents which were blown up because the media wasn't brave enough.

'They didn't have a chance in the end because a strong leader, from the media point of view, hadn't emerged. Didn't emerge. They were dead.'

REFLECTIONS

As I pressed the off button of the recorder I had emotionally braced myself for what might be an angry response. Here was a person who had opposed me many years before. He had shown a reluctance to put his response on the record and cited 'pejorative connotations', but the off-the-record segment of our discussion was cordial.

Plates clicked and the afternoon traffic hummed in the background as Michael gave his version of the events. A waiter cleared the table as we had a very personal discussion. I had just completed an interview that I hoped would give Australians an insight into the nation's political history; suddenly I was closing the door on old wounds, and it felt very satisfying. We passed gradually into a discussion of day-to-day events. A siren went off and a fire-engine roared past. The rain thrashed down. I said to Michael, 'Well, that will put the fire out', and I suppose it did.

As I've grown older I've mellowed and realised there are many more ways than one of looking at circumstances and that probably no particular view can do justice to the whole. Each of the people I've spoken to in writing this account had their own values, their own experience of the world and were at a certain point of their lives when these events occurred. Most probably each did what they were able to at the time and felt that what they were doing was the best they could. I have tried to reflect that in the way their accounts are written and my hope is that it will be acceptable to those who have done me the honour of sharing their viewpoints with me.

****

14
BACK TO SHAPING THE FUTURE

There lives the dearest freshness deep down things;
and though the last lights off the black west went
Oh, morning at the brown brink eastward, springs
because the Holy Ghost over the bent
world broods with warm breast and with ah!
bright wings.

Gerard Manley Hopkins, 'God's Grandeur'

A lot changed between 1977 and 2013. Joh was gone from Queensland. He had tried to dismiss Ministers who opposed him and to replace them, but the Queensland Governor at the time, Sir Walter Campbell, would not swear in the replacements. Meanwhile, the National Party voted for Michael Ahern to lead their Party and Joh was no longer Premier.

The Australian Democrats were gone from the Senate; economic rationalism had almost run its course; a hung Federal Parliament was bitter and divisive and segments of the media were making a meal of anyone prepared to raise their heads above the parapet, its tone cynical and arrogant. What comes next? Does the Parliament need major changes? Do we need another centrist party? Did the Democrats fulfil their potential? Could the Democrats re-emerge?

IN QUEENSLAND

Joh Bjelke-Petersen had been gone since 1987, after which some who had campaigned against his regime for 20 years had a chance to move on.

Police malfeasance and corruption within the political arena was exposed. One can't say it was eliminated, but the stables had a good muck out. A Police Commissioner had been jailed as well as numerous high-ranking police officers. Several politicians—Don Lane, Brian Austin, Leisha Harvey and Geoff Muntz—served jail terms as a result of disclosures during the Fitzgerald Inquiry. Russell Hinze died in 1995.

Electoral reform diminished the role of the National Party and its power declined. A stiff broom swept through the public service, particularly after the Labor Party came into office.

The defeat of the gerrymander was an achievement in which thousands of Queenslanders and other Australians participated. Street marchers; investigative reporters; unions; church-members; academics; Citizens for Democracy members; Fitzgerald staff working for the inquiry as well as all who attended rallies, publicity and protests were vindicated when Premier Mike Ahern committed his government to legislate all the recommendations of the Fitzgerald Commission report.

Ahern did not go unchallenged by other members of the National Party. Russell Cooper stood against him in a ballot for the National Party leadership and won. We were desperate to think that the commitments Ahern had made might be undone by Cooper, who appeared an unmitigated Joh clone. However, an election intervened and the National Party led by Russell Cooper was beaten decisively.

For the first time since 1957 there was a Labor Government in Queensland. Goss and his Labor Party team delivered the reforms recommended by Fitzgerald, which included electoral reform and reform of the public service.

It is interesting to note that the Labor Party won the election even before the gerrymander was eliminated. The exposure of scandals and corruption and the publicity given to the Fitzgerald recommendations was sufficient for the good people of Queensland to understand they needed to change also.

The Labor Party had been out of office for 32 years, but it was popular initially and rid Queensland of many corrupt processes in the public service. As a consequence it went on to win a second term in office. Future Prime Minister Kevin Rudd began his political career as the Goss Government's chief of staff. However in 1996 as the Goss approach became increasingly authoritarian, the Labor Government had a narrow win and governed with a one-seat margin until it was replaced by the conservative coalition lead by Rob Borbidge. The democratic process worked as it should to change governments when the majority of the population wanted a change.

ECONOMIC RATIONALISM-HAS IT IMPROVED OUR COUNTRY?

In my view economic rationalism with its lack of recognition for civil society and community harmed the Australian psyche and led to selfishness and incivility. Society was impacted negatively and will take time to heal.

When the Labor Party came to power in the Federal arena following the 1983 election, Hawke and Keating deregulated the Australian currency and the banking system; we were threatened with the spectre of 'globalisation'; were told there was a need for competition and a reduction of tariff protection; told we would have to change our working habits if Australia was to retain its economic position in the world.

No doubt all this was correct and needed solutions, but when a certain mind-set expressed as 'economic rationalism' put itself forward as the sole solution, we ran into difficulties. This single-minded and overbearing ideology captured the high ground and deprived the rest of us of a voice.

CHANGING POLITICS FOR THE BETTER?

Following the 2010 Federal election, Labor governed with the support of independents. This was a time of a fierce, ongoing (and unedifying) battle between the Liberal/National coalition, the ALP and the Greens in an effort to gain the upper hand. Trivial incidents were magnified; policy differences exaggerated; individuals attacked ferociously. Do politicians realise how hollow they seem when they play these political games? A majority of people see through it all. Some are more aware of the particular causes of it, but all feel its essential falsity, so when people like Cheryl Kernot or Malcolm Turnbull come along who endeavour to remain true to themselves instead of playing games, the public warms to them immediately. But the system has its ways and means of battering such people into submission and few have the capacity to resist.

This might be an appropriate point to discuss issues of morality within politics. If truth is the first casualty of war then kind-heartedness and sociability seem to be the first casualties of politics. Some politicians deal with the political environment by cutting themselves off emotionally and being suspicious of every exchange. At the same time, it is necessary for them (in order to maintain support from voters and colleagues) to exhibit the appearance of emotional closeness. This is a schizophrenic place to inhabit. No wonder many Parliamentarians and potential Parliamentarians behave in a way that is often inconceivable to ordinary Australians. The sad fact is that they (and we) have come to accept this as the natural condition of politicians—to lie, to conceal and to undermine.

Whatever our beliefs, most of us teach our children not to lie. There is a practical reason for this. The social contract is broken if we cannot trust those we rely upon. Why should this be different for our representatives in Parliament? Lies destroy the trust upon which our whole society depends.

Nor is this unsociable behaviour limited to lying to the electorate or to the opposition. It extends to lying about people in the same party—to gain an advantage in a leadership battle or to win a policy debate. It extends to undermining anyone standing in the way of what we desire. Instead of kind-heartedness and fair debate, the arguments descend to the pits of gossiping and spreading untruths.

Given the heat and the passion of politics, is it reasonable to expect any better? My view is that we *must*. If our Parliament is to be the best possible, then we must insist on the highest possible standards; not just what is a legal requirement, but also what is a reasonable standard of behaviour expected by the community.

As we work towards these higher standards, it is imperative that examples of poor standards be exposed. I think when perpetrators realise poor behaviour will, sooner or later, be exposed then they might think more carefully about such behaviours. Perhaps some of them can be persuaded that kind-heartedness and sociability are more appropriate. Our Parliament, our leaders, set the tone for our nation; they need to do better.

The present climate of politics is brutal. Jeff Bleich, the United States Ambassador to Australia, commented recently 'We have made it into a blood sport'.[1]

A side-effect of the poor standards of behaviour surrounding politics is that members of the public who excel in their fields and who could become successful Parliamentarians are unwilling to put themselves into such a damaging environment. Others, in particular women whose tendency is to be sociable, find themselves disadvantaged—as do sensitive people or those who have made errors in the past but now live exemplary lives. All of these latter categories of people could make a significant contribution to the Parliament, but are prevented as they would be given short shrift and possibly destroyed.

Vigorous debate and even conflict is good, but undermining, lying and sabotaging should play no part in our national Parliament. Perhaps in future this issue will receive the recognition it deserves.

While writing these chapters I have noticed an important organisational difference between the Liberal Party and other political parties in Australia. Unlike members of the Labor Party, The Australian Greens or the Australian Democrats, members of the Liberal Party cannot directly influence the behaviour of their Parliamentary representatives through their National Executive.

This could be seen as a freedom for those representatives to carry out their duties without interference, or it could be a licence for them to behave without the moderating influence of their membership.

From my background in the Australian Democrats I am inclined to organisational methods built on participatory democracy. There needs to be a fine balance between the role of members, the National Executive and the Parliamentarians. I suspect if this balance could be achieved it might lead to better behaviour in campaigns and in the conduct of the Parliament.

Another view of mine concerning the origin of the bad nature of politics is the present system of voting. It seems to me that a 50% plus one, winner take all, electoral system is responsible for some of the problem. A party has to please too wide a range of views and groups to win an election, which in turn leads to falsehood, evasion and political games—as no-one can please everyone all the time.

In Australia, party politics has been travelling on a downhill path for quite a while now, until it seems impossible to win an election in a civil or reasonable manner. It is possible politicians could retain their dignity and principles if they only had to represent the proportion of voters who held similar views to themselves.

This is more or less what independents do and so they can be a voice of reason in an increasingly unreasonable Parliament. Perhaps we need not fewer, but **more**, independents—or at least independent-minded politicians! In essence that is what the Australian Democrats, with their conscience vote, represented in the Senate. Because of the voting system for the Senate, they had only to represent people with similar views.

Changing the system of voting for the House of Representatives to the one used to elect senators would be a way to achieve this. In the proportional representation (PR) system of voting, electoral candidates need only attract a much smaller percentage of the vote and can avoid blatant forms of campaign falsehood and bravura that is presently needed to be elected on the 50% plus one system. This could lead to more diversity of views; perhaps more intelligent discussion and maybe a more co-operative Parliament.

PR is used throughout Australia to elect candidates to the Senate, the upper houses of NSW, Victoria, South Australia and Western Australia, the Lower House of Tasmania, the ACT Legislative Assembly and several local government councils.

Queensland, with no upper house, would benefit greatly from the implementation of proportional representation as a voting method. The elected members would better represent the makeup of the population and the resulting need to negotiate outcomes would compensate for the lack of an upper house, although the size of the electorates might not be acceptable. I would be surprised to see this change in my lifetime, but you never know. After all, the Berlin wall was knocked down.

I have begun to think that another approach to the problem raised by the single house of parliament in Queensland might be possible, and that is a number of robust standing committees to review potential legislation and to allow public comment before the Bills are passed.

Perhaps it is time for even more radical changes to the way democracy is practised. In keeping with the modern spirit, increased public participation and involvement will be necessary. New Democracy is an organisation that researches new political ideas from around the world. It maintains 'We don't need better politicians, we need a better system'. One idea is a 'Citizens' Senate' consisting of people chosen at random from the Australian population. Another is to call people together on 'Policy Panels' much as juries are summoned to decide in cases at law. A long list of respected academics and politicians from all parts of the political spectrum support the organisation.

IS THERE A PROBLEM WITH THE MEDIA?

The Australian public needs and wants responsible reporting and conduct that adheres to reasonable standards of journalism and conduct. Many of the so-called radio 'shock jocks' have already crossed lines of common decency and are making a mockery of the informational role which should be their main reason for existence. Some print media and TV media journalists no longer have as their prime objective the pursuit of 'facts', but have adopted a blatant political bias. That is deplorable. I think their behaviour should be modified by an energetic and democratic press complaints procedure. I liked the idea suggested in the Finkelstein report on the media of a statutory body (similar to the ABC) funded by the Government and at arm's length from both the Government and influential media owners.

The present self-regulating system has little credibility and isn't working satisfactorily. Despite hundreds of highly-skilled and dedicated journalists, there is an unfortunate rise in editorial interference and an increase in biased reporting in some outlets; commentary instead of facts and concentrating on incidentals instead of substance. This is creating social dislocation—a state of confusion and heightened emotions among the public.

Particularly in matters relating to politics, a kind of arrogance has developed in reporting and journalism—a temerity to attack; a desire not simply to report news, but to be part of making it. Interviews resemble gladiatorial contests. News items, instead of focusing on policy or ideas, focus on 'beat-ups' to attract readers. Some of this behaviour may be in response to the rise of 'spin' in the political arena. It is harder to get politicians to speak clearly and without a forked tongue. Other instances relate to the so-called '24 hour' media-cycle and the pressure to attract attention to news outlets. Lindsay Tanner, a former ALP minister in the Rudd and Gillard Governments, in his book *Sideshow* says 'mediathink is taking over politics. .... Genuine outcomes are completely swamped by transient appearances'.[2]

Perhaps the rise of social media such as Facebook and Twitter will lead traditional media to modify some of its flaws. But social media poses another threat—the rise of unmediated information. Well, a blessing, but also potentially a threat, as standards of proof and scrutiny will be lost if the skills of seasoned journalists are not passed on to others.

Social media can have both a positive and negative impact on issues. I am aware of despicable jokes about sexuality, immigrants, Aboriginals, Muslims, homosexuals and a raft of other topics that appear to play on the uncivilised parts of our natures. There was a disgusting underhanded campaign waged against the former Prime Minister, Julia Gillard. Regulation can only do so much about this, and it might be best for other social media users to deal with it themselves by calling it for what it is—low trash!

Traditional employers of journalists are under increasing cost pressures because of lost advertising and are cutting back on investigative reporting. How will young journalists find opportunities to learn and grow and be mentored by the amazing kind of journalists that we have had in the past? Will there be the same kinds of opportunity for reporters like Phil Dickie and Chris Masters to spend weeks and months investigating a story without writing a line? Investigative journalism, in particular, is vital to a healthy social climate, so a solution is needed if we are to keep talented and experienced journalists employed.

We are in a transitional period that is confusing and potentially dangerous. I have a view about the role of elders and veteran journalists in this transitional time. If not already, then they need to make a deliberate attempt to mentor young people entering the profession. In the social climate of 2013 it isn't easy to cross the generational gap—either way, but youth still needs heroes and people to look up to. As elders we must accept this responsibility and pass on the wisdom of the past while being willing to hear what the youth culture is telling us. Eventually there will be a balance we can all live with.

Most enterprises need to be regulated, but media is a tricky business to try to regulate as it deals with information, freedom of speech and the eventual health of our democratic society.

The Finkelstein recommendation of a half-way regulatory mechanism—separate both from government and industry—is not an impossible ask, yet it is difficult to see how this could be implemented by any government if media and conservative opinion is against it. However, it might be achievable with perseverance.*

Radical changes to settled traditions take a long time to gestate, to grow and to take hold. Certainly, we need to begin the process as the present models of both government and media regulation appear to have outworn their usefulness.

Will major changes take place? It's hard to say. There is a lot of practical experience with the proportional representation system in many countries around the world—particularly in Europe. There is also experimentation with innovative changes to political systems and a rising concern about the role of

* See Appendix K: Executive summary from the Report of the Independent Inquiry into the Media and Media Regulation.

the media, but political parties often only pursue changes if there is a chance they could make it work for themselves. That is the nature of political power.

WILL WE SEE THE RISE OF A NEW CENTRIST PARTY?

There is no lack of energy at present to set up alternative political parties, although none appears to have the characteristics or the widespread support that the Australian Democrats enjoyed during their 30 years in the Senate. The times are right for a revival of a centrist party. People are dissatisfied with the way the present Parliament is working. They are sick of the falsity; the pettiness; the lack of focus on reasonable policy discussion and negotiation. They want renewal. They want a humanised form of government. The Australian Greens are not a centrist party. They are a party of the far left that won support through its environmental policies. They have no brief to make the Parliament a better tool of government.*

DID THE AUSTRALIAN DEMOCRATS FULFIL THEIR POTENTIAL?

Apart from actual legislation, the Australian Democrats played a significant role in Australian politics from their inception in 1977 to their final disappearance in 2008/9.**

During the years 1981 to 1984 I paid particular attention to the conduct of the five Australian Democrat Senators. I read speeches from the Parliament, attended National Executive meetings, participated fully in discussions within the Queensland division and from time to time had discussions with the senators themselves. With a small number of senators to cover all the portfolios, the workload was crushing. Each of them carried the responsibility for numerous areas of government business. They came with a huge agenda—as the spearhead of progressive ideas that had been building up in the community for many years and now could be liberated.

The role of a minor party in the Senate (even when holding the balance of power) can be confining. It is not responsible for making major decisions—rather it influences. It is not usually responsible for introducing new legislation, it can only try to amend what the Government puts forward, and if major parties agree on an issue, it hardly has a role at all. However, a minor party can be very influential in affairs—by putting forward new ideas; by insisting on modifications to legislation that is harsh or simply inadequate. It can insist that legislation be sent to a committee and discussed thoroughly.

* Since 2007, some former Australian Democrat members have joined the Greens Party.

** See Appendix D for a list of Democrat achievements.

This is something that the Democrats did with verve—the present diligent scrutiny of issues in the Senate is one of their legacies.

Members of a minor party can be active in the community listening to people's views and making them known in the Parliament. They can also take progressive ideas back to the community—to inform and involve citizens. The Democrats fulfilled these expectations.

IS THERE ANY CHANCE THE AUSTRALIAN DEMOCRATS COULD RE-EMERGE?

They have faded from sight, but could they be revived or a similar party emerge? It would take leadership, some high-profile candidates, a kick-start, publicity and *money*. You never know! Democrat cells are active in most States.

Since the debacle in the years leading up to 2007, membership has dropped to a shadow of its former self, but most States still have a presence and have begun selecting candidates for future elections.

Australian Democrats were honest brokers, forward-thinkers with members prepared to try new ideas in order to solve problems; a centrist party, not linked either to business or to unions. The Greens are not fulfilling this role. With a few exceptions, they do not engage to assist legislation, instead they are inclined to oppose, hoping not for an acceptable compromise, but rather an out-of-reach solution. Their idealism is commendable, but their way of doing politics is disruptive.

Before the Greens, the Democrats were the main defenders of strong conservation and environmental values.* A fair proportion of the senators—Colin Mason, Norm Sanders, John Coulter and others—were active in conservation groups prior to their passage into the Australian Democrats.

However, in time the Australian Democrats environmental message was overtaken by the Greens, whose style was younger and arguably more aggressive. The Greens were further to the left and on occasions rigid in their views. They had an excellent leader in the person of Bob Brown and exposure in Tasmania where many of them were involved in Tasmanian logging protests and the battle for the legal recognition of homosexuality.

The Greens began attracting youth from both major parties. Their policies were clear, adventurous and in line with what young people had been learning in school and from their pop idols. Also, the Green movement was gaining ground overseas.

* See Appendix M: Saving the Franklin

The vigorous opposition by Janine Haines and Cheryl Kernot to the ravages of economic rationalism was overtaken by the extreme vocabulary of One Nation proponents. Emotionally this struck a chord with the people of Australia who were in the frontline of job cuts and anxiety about career security, health, education and their traditional way of life. Who can blame voters, yet, their emotional response sidelined a party that had fought long and hard and intelligently against the extremes of economic rationalism.

DEMOCRAT VALUES AND PRINCIPLES

The Australian Democrats had values and principles that stood them in good stead during their 30 years in the Senate,* although according to a founding member, Fay Lawrence, 'In the beginning Australian Democrats boasted they did not have an ideology.'

Although, in certain cases, budget bills could be returned to the House of Representatives for amendments, Democrats in the Senate *would not block Supply*—would not deny the legitimate government the right to the money they needed to carry on governing.

This was a lesson from the November 11, 1975 dismissal of the Whitlam Government when the Liberal opposition in the Senate 'held up' Supply for several weeks. Their action created fears about the stability of political institutions, the role of the Governor-General and the relationship to the monarchy.

Democrat Parliamentarians were entitled to a 'conscience vote'. Chipp was very clear about this. Chipp himself recounted experiences prior to his time in the Democrats when he had spoken against the nuclear industry and the use of nuclear power and could make no headway even within his own party, the Liberals. His colleagues would come to him after a discussion or a vote and say, 'We agree with you, Chippie, completely, but you know what would happen if we voted with you.' So, to Chipp's exasperation, although the support was there, they felt they couldn't express their own views in case of being pressured. As leader of the Democrats, Chipp would impress upon new Democrat Senators the necessity of voting according to their conscience.

Democrats did not do 'deals'. In other words, a bill was opposed or passed in the Senate on its own merits, not traded for support on another bill. Senator Harradine, a Tasmanian independent, was notorious for this practice. On several occasions when holding the balance of power he gave his support for legislation in exchange for benefits for Tasmania.

* See Appendix E: Democrat Ideology.

When Senator Harradine supported the Telstra sale it is possible he had no strongly-held belief about its merits one way or another and simply took the opportunity to garner benefits for his State. However, Democrats saw this kind of deal-making as having the potential to corrupt policy determination.

Democrats were committed to a careful scrutiny of all legislation. In a larger party with Ministers or shadow Ministers for each policy area this can be achieved without much difficulty, however, with the limited number of senators in the Democrat party-room, it was a herculean task.

They had assistance from community groups and individuals, but the responsibility for what they would accept or oppose was theirs—not just collectively, but individually, as each of them had to consult his or her conscience and could not simply rely on the view of their party.

One way the Democrats dealt with the workload was to send important bills for scrutiny to Senate committees. They worked strenuously to reform the committee system so it worked efficiently to review major legislation, and if a suitable committee didn't exist, then they established it for the purpose.

When Senator Macklin was the Australian Democrat whip he was able to bring about a number of improvements to the way the Parliamentary process worked. He told me how the Democrats managed to change sitting times in the Senate: 'A good example of the pressure of history was the fact that the Senate sat from mid-afternoon to the early hours of the following day. It was difficult to understand just why this was the case, but it may have had something to do with the couple of hours that it took the nobles to ride their horses to the Parliament at Westminster after they had risen at a leisurely hour. Add a later rising from bed followed by a longish meal to a two-hour canter and one gets to mid-afternoon.

Whatever the origin, the insanity of starting the day at a time when everyone else was thinking about the end of work did not seem to have overwhelmed those who had spent their lives in the place. On one occasion, I had to speak for an hour (we managed to reduce this to 20 minutes within two years) from 2 am in the early morning with the Presiding Officer asleep in the chair and the Government and the Opposition with one member apiece left in the House—of course these "Senators-of-the-watch" were also asleep across their respective frontbenches. Since we were not being broadcasted that left me and the Hansard reporter and the Clerk at the table as the only people awake and listening for a whole hour to my splendid intervention on behalf of sanity and progress or whatever it was I was speaking about.

'A short time later, I managed to change this archaic system by the simple expedient of an announcement at one of our Whips meeting which we held each morning to organise the program that all of my Democrat Senators were going home at 10.30pm. The problem with this would have been to create a situation where the Liberal-National Government of the day could pass whatever they liked after we had gone home since they had more senators than the Opposition. This outcome naturally significantly upset the Opposition Labor Whip, but I calmed him down when I also told both Whips that we would be happy to recommit every vote taken in our absence. This upset the Government Liberal Whip who saw his program being thrown out the window every day, with a commensurate intolerable delay in the passage of legislation.

'After some discussion, the Whips agreed that if we started earlier then we could get in even more debating hours than we had had to date. The Government Whip could tell the Leader of the Government in the Senate that more hours should equal quicker legislation and the Opposition Whip could tell the Leader of Opposition in the Senate that the extra hours would mean that they could engage in more tactical attacks on the Government. On this basis both groups bought the idea—actually they had little choice—and so the Senate moved to starting earlier on each sitting day in the week except when the parties had their party-room meetings. Since we already had a Democrat party meeting every morning at nine am to examine every bill the Government was introducing, we didn't have to change our system. Everyone was pleased and some sanity was brought to the Senate's sitting hour which, in a roll-on effect, changed the House of Representative's sitting hours as well. A welcomed side-effect was that the staff of Parliament House thought that we were god's gift to sanity since they were able to get home at a reasonable hour instead of the insanity that had become the norm.'

Democrat Senators understood their role was not to govern, but to moderate, to review, to negotiate, to bring progressive views into the equation and on occasions to oppose bills if they felt the public was sufficiently up in arms.

Participatory democracy was a principle dear to Democrat members. Following each election, a ballot of Democrat members across Australia was conducted to determine the leader of the party in the Senate. During the term, leadership ballots could be called if a petition with 50 names was presented to the National Executive. This was probably a bit extreme, as a list of displaced Democrat leaders would attest.

The other democratic right was to participate in policy formation. Policies were balloted one by one. The national journal carried discussion on policy while State branches conducted policy forums and discussions. The nature of Democrat members was such that senators' decisions were watched intently and they would know sooner rather than later if their actions and behaviours in the Senate displeased people.

INTERNAL DISPUTES

There are many arguments in politics. You might say politics is just a long series of arguments—after all, it is about 'who will get what they want'. I suspect, however, that Democrats in the inner sanctum of their party-rooms made it into an art form. That it did not constantly grab the media's attention was a triumph of good sense, but also a minor miracle. Every senator, branch and State division was at one time or another embroiled in arguments and splits. I suppose this is one of the benefits of a democracy—differences can be sorted out by arguments instead of by wars or coups or poisonings.

Conflict can be valuable, but in reasonable doses. With all that has been learnt about communication, negotiation and behaviour over the past half century, surely we could find a way to moderate conflict.

Party ombudsmen (not always men!) operated at State and national levels. Their role was to bring the 'Wisdom of Solomon' to the resolution of disputes within the party. It's difficult to know how well this worked, but it is possible there may have been even more disputes without them. (Although how there could have been *more* disputes is difficult to imagine!)

Generally speaking, these processes worked well, although when John Woodley acted as national ombudsman for a period of time he noted that the powers given to the ombudsman were so extensive they had the ability to paralyse the party, and had on one occasion done so.

During his time as ombudsman the role was modified to give it more balance and prevent it being used to hold the party to ransom. The individual still had the right and the opportunity to be heard, but the party was given the right to be heard and the ability of the party to operate couldn't simply be denied because some person or persons had a complaint.

The power for 50 members to petition and call a leadership ballot caused the party unnecessary difficulties—particularly during the rise of the Greens party. While Bob Brown held the helm and steadied the Greens, the Australian Democrats went through a period of leadership instability. Some was caused by individual self-interest and some by misguided attempts to change the direction of the party. There were too many leadership changes over a short period of time.

Following Cheryl Kernot until 2008, there were five leaders. Moreover, because the process was relatively simple to instigate, leaders had no certainty about their survival, which limited their authority in the electorate as well as in the party-room. The participatory process was undermined in some of these leadership changes by influential party members—senators and office-bearers—using that influence to sway the mind of the members, sometimes with methods that were not in keeping with Democrat ideals and values.

Was the Democrat philosophy asking their members, officials and leaders to be perfect? If so, clearly it failed. We were all less than perfect. We were often inadequate in our knowledge and in our skills.

We sometimes failed to live up to the high standards of 'honesty, tolerance and compassion' that Chipp had set. Even he failed. The 'shadow' side of our humanity sometimes came to the fore and we forgot our main mission: to lift the standard of politics in Australia.

Sex and the Democrats. I know enough about that to set your ears on fire. But I'm not telling. Why not? For one thing, this is a book about politics—my experience of it. It is my view that the most important aspect of a politician's behaviour is whether he or she represents the electorate faithfully and puts its issues first. If they do, then how they behave in private is not a matter for this book.

There are, however, some instances when sex and politics cross paths. One such issue was Chipp's attitude to women, which could be offensive. Democrat women took a risk in rebuffing Chipp if they wanted his support. It is disappointing to think someone so brilliant politically could have such a huge personal flaw. A person can have great talent and ability, but often with that person any flaws they have can also be big.

Another instance when sex and politics crossed paths was with Cheryl Kernot and Gareth Evans. Clearly, this was an affair that crossed the boundary. It was significant, particularly when Kernot was Democrat leader and Evans was manager of Government business in the Senate, and it could have been reported at that point. Laurie Oakes, the journalist who broke the story after Cheryl left the ALP, waited until the Kernot autobiography came out and there was no reference to the affair in the book. Neither had the 1999 Gareth Evans biography by Keith Scott any reference to it, but by 2002 Laurie Oakes was in possession of evidence of both the affair and also Gareth's denial in the Parliament.

Oakes later said he hadn't known about it until a short time before he wrote the article, although other accounts I have read suggest the information was circulating among members of the press quite some time before then.

Perhaps Oakes knew but had no confirmation. Other journalists developed the story. Once in the public arena it reverberated around the nation. Some in the press gallery thought this behaviour unbecoming. Others thought the opposite. The rights and wrongs of revealing personal affairs were debated heatedly.

It is interesting to note, however, that Cheryl—who told no lies, and behaved to protect loved ones—bore the brunt of the fallout. Gareth went on to further his career and was not hounded by the media. A woman who had contributed greatly to Australian political life was brought to a standstill for doing what many politicians (mostly male) had done before with impunity. The Labor Party hardly noticed her passing. The Australian Democrats picked themselves up and continued.

Sexuality is a powerful instinct and if you are lonely or overwhelmed, or simply need love and approval, resistance can be an unequal battle. What were they to do? They had families and political parties and the media to consider. Gareth lied to the Parliament. Cheryl left it out of her book. Their predicament caused them and others a great deal of pain.

Perhaps leaving the Democrats was the decent thing for Cheryl to do. So much depended on the Australian Democrats leaders as the party structure was fragile. A disproportionate weight fell upon them to be not only the face, but also the substance of the party. From the beginning in 1978 to just prior to 2000, Democrat leaders were exceptional people—Chipp, Haines, Kernot, Lees—moreover, they each led the party for sufficient time to gain the voters' trust.

WHY?

There is no one reason for the demise of the Australian Democrats. The loss of Cheryl Kernot's leadership left a gap, but the party was in good shape and went on to do extremely well in the 1998 election. Some feel, however, that Cheryl's time was the highlight of Democrat history and the decline of the party began after her departure. The decision by Democrats to support the Howard Government's legislation on GST upset the electorate, but the effects began to fade as an issue in the electorate when the new tax bedded down. Among members of the party, however, it continued to cause unhappiness.

The rise of the Greens contributed. They seized their opportunity when Democrat leadership struggles led to upheaval in the party. In the 10 years following Kernot's departure, from December 1997 to 2007, there were five Democrat leaders, an average of two years for each leader, whereas in the previous 20 years from 1977 to 1997 there were five, an average of four years each.

The advent of the Greens was slower than the rise of the Democrats had been. Malcolm Martin, a Democrat active in the Hunter region of NSW observed, 'They built their political party from the ground up and not from the top down',[4] whereas the Democrat branch structure was thrown up willy-nilly and without much support or follow-through. This would certainly have been a destabilising factor.

Tony Walters has a view that much of the Democrat success depended on 'smoke and mirrors'.[3] There was always too little party structure across the nation; membership was low; money in short supply; swinging voters sometimes swung against the party; the media and hence the general public still had to be convinced what a 'third party' was doing in a game that usually just required two main players.

Then again, early Democrat leaders were all seasoned politically. Most of them had been involved in politics for years—the Liberal Party in Chipp's case; the New Liberal Movement in Haines'; the Australia Party for Siddons and Mason. The later waves of Democrats had less exposure to the rigors of politics before they came into the Senate.

Natasha Stott Despoja, a young prodigy, had insufficient experience or maturity to lead the party in difficult times. The Democrat party-room was not united behind her. As a group their age was, on average, 10 years less than the previous sets of senators. They were younger, but also marginally less experienced than their predecessors.

Janine Haines was relatively young when she led the party, but while she was concentrating on policy and publicity she had the good fortune to have a competent deputy in Michael Macklin who, as party Whip, managed the internal working of the party in the Senate. With similar assistance, Natasha Stott Despoja's leadership may have been more successful—her brilliance and someone to work with other senators and hold the team together.

During the critical years, the behaviour of the National Executive appears on occasions to have been a more negative than positive influence. Party elders who should have kept calm heads and been above the fray, instead became involved in the 'causes' and 'feuds'. Emotions were out of control.

And finally there was the issue of 'Work Choices'—the Howard Government's attack on the rights of working people. On this issue the temperature had risen to white-heat. It separated neighbour from neighbour and employer from employee. Even in the case of Peter Costello and his Baptist minister brother, Tim Costello—brother from brother.

The fact that Cheryl Kernot had negotiated with the Coalition to introduce changes to the industrial relations system went against the party. This was not quite fair as, for reasons previously noted, this was to soften some of the more drastic aims of the first round of the Howard Government workplace reforms. Nonetheless, this action was seen as a negative among wage-earners.

It was an agitated and desperate time. Political forces were throwing everything they had into the fight, which concentrated the minds of many to vote for one or other of the major parties. Could the Democrats, essentially idealistic middle-class, academic-minded people, have survived these difficulties? It seems their luck ran out at last when a number of the scenarios coincided and led to their demise. The final blow occurred in 2007 when for the second election in a row no Democrats were elected.

****

My journey of discovery has also come to an end. I am conscious of the rare privilege it was to have been involved in such significant events and able to talk to such worthwhile people.

I am grateful to belong to a country with a multitude of good-hearted people and to have participated alongside some of them over the years to improve public policy and action. We learnt from our failures, but our survival and our successes are a cause for celebration. Each of us, in great ways or small, changed the future.

****

APPENDICES

APPENDIX A

FULL TEXT OF DON CHIPP'S RESIGNATION SPEECH TO THE HOUSE OF REPRESENTATIVES: MARCH 24, 1977

I wish to announce to the House that I have resigned from the Liberal Party of Australia as from today. I believe I have conformed with the courtesies demanded of such a decision. I have informed you, sir, the Leader of my party, the Right Honourable the Prime Minister (Mr. Malcolm Fraser), the Victorian State President of the Liberal Party of Australia and the Chairman of the Hotham Electoral Committee of the Liberal Party. It naturally follows that I shall not be presenting myself as a candidate for the Liberal Party of Australia at the next House of Representatives election.

I shall continue to represent the division of Hotham in this House for the duration of this Parliament or until such earlier time as circumstance may demand. Although I am proud of the high personal vote I receive from the electors of Hotham, I recognise that I am here by virtue of my former membership of the Liberal Party and therefore believe it is proper that I should generally give my vote in support of the Government in the business before the House and in the conduct of the business of the House.

However, I will exercise the right—which is already held by all members of the Liberal Party—to vote against the Government on any issue which a member believes to be not in the best interests of the country or this constituents. I extend my gratitude to the many friends and members of the Liberal Party in Hotham who have loyally supported me over the years and given me the privilege of serving in the House.

I hope that my friends and colleagues in the Parliamentary Liberal Party will understand my reasons in taking this decision and that the personal friendships and relationships that I have made and enjoyed over the years will not be impaired by my action. I note in passing that notwithstanding the tab of 'rebel' that some people have chosen to put upon me, I have never exercised that right of voting against my party in my 16 years in this place. In fact, I think it fair to me to place on record that during the 15-months term of this Government I have been publicly critical of its decisions on only five occasions. These were:

1 The 25% cut in overseas aid;
2 The abolition of the Australian Assistance Plan which I, with the full authority of the Joint Parties, had previously commended in his House as being one of the most exciting and progressive social reforms ever undertaken;

3 The proposed abolition of the financial benefits for pensioners;
4 The original breach of the promise to index pensions; and
5 The decision to devalue the currency, and once that decision was taken, the refusal to lower the tariffs so as to contain the inflationary effects of that move.

When these five public criticisms are put against the dozens of times I have publicly supported the Government, even on occasions when I did not agree with it, I believe the tag of 'rebel' is probably unfair. There have, in fact, been a great number of issues with which I have strongly disagreed and on most of which I have been invited by the media to criticise my party.

I have refrained from that criticism in the interests of party unity and with a view to assisting the Government in overcoming the massive problems it faces, many of which were inherited from the results of the gross maladministration of the Labor Party's terms in office. However, the number of significant Government actions which conflict with my own views are now so many that I feel that my continual membership of the Liberal Party, as it is now led, managed and structured, would be incompatible with my beliefs and would constitute an act of hypocrisy.

Inevitably some people will impugn my action and ascribe to it the motive that I am taking this course because I am not in the Cabinet. To that I simply state without argument that under no circumstances could I, or would I, serve as Minister under the present leadership. Members of the House would know that one reaches a decision such as this—after giving 16 years of one's life to it—not without a great deal of deep thought and troubled deliberation; but as one who at least in latter years has tried to pursue a course of true liberalism I find I can no longer do that within the confines of the party. In these circumstances I believe the only honourable thing to do is to resign.

For the record I simply state my areas of contention without debating them. I cannot agree with the Government's current economic policy. Particularly, I am concerned with its failure to honour the promise to the private sector to give it stable and definite future guidelines to allow it to plan and invest for the future. I believe the private businessman, especially the small businessman, who employs the bulk of the workforce of this country, is more confused, more in the dark about the future, and less confident than he was 15 months ago. This seems to be strange behaviour for a party that champions the cause of free enterprise.

I am very critical of the lack of consultation between the Government and the Trade Union movement. It would be cruel and unfair to ask the worker to be the sole bearer of the cost of reducing inflation; but wages are too high and taxes are too high, provide incentives for increased productivity by both workers and management. Interest rates are devastating, especially to the young, and yet no attempt at real, sensible and sensitive discussions between the Prime Minister and the President of the A.C.T.U. has been made. In fact the Prime Minister has refused to enter such discussions. Instead, while the economy continues to slump, these two leaders seem to be continuing in a public slanging match while the economy continues to deteriorate and the responsible blue and white collar Australian workers and management suffer. I confess to a very deep concern about the intransigence of the Prime Minister in bringing in the Industrial Relations Bureau Legislation at this time—a time of remarkable industrial peace and at a time when it is being vigorously opposed by both employees and employers alike. I have been grossly disappointed with the attitude of the Government on uranium mining. Notwithstanding the repeated requests by the Fox report for a full Parliamentary debate, we have had two hours only on it and it is now off the notice paper. I am grateful to the Leader of the House (Mr. Sinclair) for giving me an understanding this morning that the matter will be restored to the notice paper.

The last straw on this issue was the action of the Deputy Prime Minister (Mr. Anthony) in launching a pro-uranium book simultaneously with a statement by the Ambassador of Japan advocating the mining of Australian uranium.

The breach of our promise to continue the Australian Assistance Plan; wage indexation, the value of the currency, the Social Welfare Commission, increased research on solar energy are matters which have disturbed me greatly.

Further, an incredible attitude towards Timor, an overt and capricious provocation of Russia, an almost pathetic reliance on the non-proliferation treaty which the fox Report describes as giving only 'an illusion of protection'; the absence of strong Cabinet action to overcome the bureaucratic bungling and red tape affecting human beings seeking refuge from Indo-China are some other matters which have left me deeply concerned.

On the other hand I draw no comfort from the current attitudes and policies of the A.L.P., although the state of the world economy contributed in some way to Australia's economic problems during its three years in office, its mismanagement of the economy resulting in the unique situation of causing unemployment to increase simultaneously with inflation was near catastrophic. I would be a little encouraged if I believed that it has learnt some lessons from errors, but that does not seem to be the case. It is still motivated by events of the past, still obsessed with its socialist ideas and a hatred of private enterprise, and dominated by the shadowy faces in the trade union movement. In opposition its performance has been little short of ludicrous in questioning and probing the Government on the real issues that affect the country.

I draw no comfort at all from the public opinion polls which indicate a Labor Government is possible—if not probable—in the near future. I find it almost unbelievable that the leader of the opposition (Mr. E. G. Whitlam), a man who led his party to its most humiliating defeat in history just 15 months ago—now ranks about equally in popularity and respect with the Prime Minister. Does this mean that the people of Australia hold both men and both parties in relatively low esteem?

In conclusion may I say that I have become disenchanted with party politics as they are practised in this country and with the pressure groups which have an undue influence on the major political parties.

The National Country Party properly represents the interests of a small sectional group—some of the rural community—but improperly in my view, and unduly influences national politics quite out of proportion to the small group it represents.

The Labor Party is dominated by the vested interests of trade unions. The Liberal Party, although properly concerned with the vital role of private enterprise, seems too preoccupied with the wants of what is euphemistically known as 'big business' to the sacrifice and detriment of medium and small-size businesses who form the backbone of our industrial and commercial sectors.

The parties seem to polarise on almost every issue, sometimes seemingly just for the sake of it, and I wonder whether the ordinary voter is not becoming sick and tired of the vested interests which unduly influence the present political patterns and yearn for the emergence of a third political force, representing middle of the road policies which would owe allegiance to no outside pressure group.

Perhaps it may be the right time to test that proposition. That move will have to come from those people in Australia who believe in the encouragement of free enterprise, who believe it has not had a 'fair go' from interfering governments who regularly change, without warning, the conditions under which they operate. it must come from people who believe in true justice for the workforce and compassion for those in need, but who believe that actions must be taken to prevent social problems from occurring rather than trying to cure them and hide them once they have arrived. But above all, it must come from those people who are disgusted with those politicians and political parties who indulge mainly in cheap political point scoring in the endless pursuit of votes at any price, and from people who want their Parliament to identify the real and significant problems of the future and to take action now which will make the country a good, safe and sound place for future generations.

APPENDIX B

ELECTORAL RESULTS

Table 1 Results of 1972 Queensland State election

Queensland state election, 27 May 1972 Legislative Assembly << 1969 — 1974 >>					
Enrolled Voters	997,489				
Votes Cast	921,763		Turnout	92.41%	+0.64%
Informal Votes	15,566		Informal	1.61%	-0.18%
Summary of votes by party					
Party	**Primary Votes**	**%**	**Swing**	**Seats**	**Change**
Labor	424,002	46.75%	+1.76%	33	+ 2
Liberal	201,596	22.23%	-1.45%	**21**	+ 2
Country	181,404	20.00%	-1.02%	**26**	± 0
Democratic Labor	69,757	7.69%	+0.46%	0	- 1
Independent	30,187	3.33%	+0.48%	2	+ 1
Total	**906,946**			**82**	

Table 2 Results of 1977 Federal election

Senate (STV) — 1977–80—Turnout 95.08% (CV) — Informal 9.00%

Party	Votes	%	Swing	Seats Won	Seats Held
Australian Labor Party	2,718,876	36.76	−4.15	14	27
Liberal/National (Joint Ticket)	2,533,882	34.26	−5.60	7	
Australian Democrats	823,550	11.13	*	2	2
Liberal Party of Australia	783,878	10.60	−0.48	10	27
National Country Party	36,619	0.50	−0.04	0	6
Country Liberal Party	15,463	0.21	−0.01	1	1
Independents	127,850	1.73	+0.13	0	1
Other	356,089	4.81	+2.75	0	0
Total	7,396,207			34	64

Independent: Brian Harradine

The table below shows Australian Democrat Senators and terms of office from 1978 to 2008.

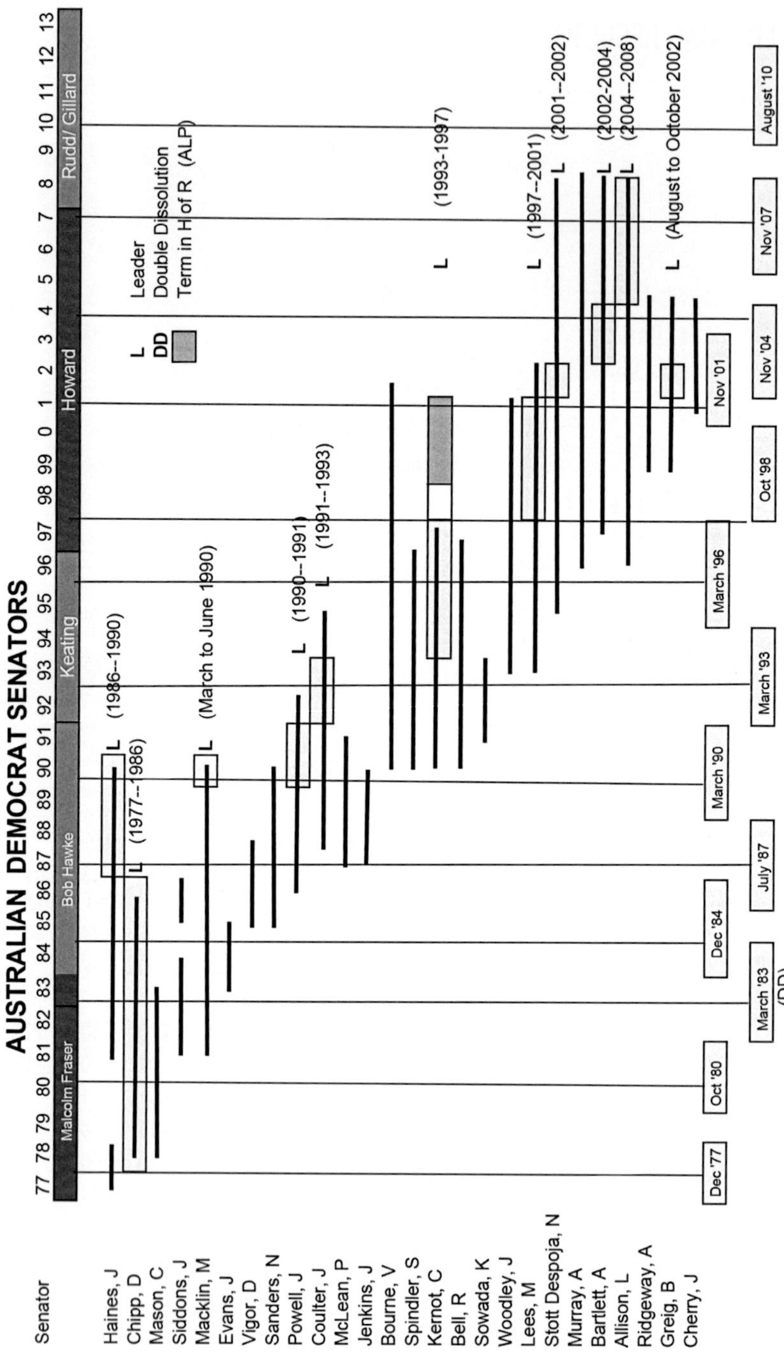

AUSTRALIAN DEMOCRAT SENATORS

Senator

77 78 79 80 81 82 83 84 85 86 87 88 89 90 91 92 93 94 95 96 97 98 99 0 1 2 3 4 5 6 7 8 9 10 11 12 13

Malcolm Fraser
Bob Hawke
Keating
Howard
Rudd/ Gillard

Haines, J — L (1986--1990)
Chipp, D — L (1977--1986)
Mason, C
Siddons, J
Macklin, M — L (March to June 1990)
Evans, J
Vigor, D
Sanders, N
Powell, J — L (1990--1991)
Coulter, J — L (1991--1993)
McLean, P
Jenkins, J
Bourne, V
Spindler, S
Kernot, C — L (1993-1997)
Bell, R
Sowada, K
Woodley, J
Lees, M — L (1997--2001)
Stott Despoja, N — L (2001--2002)
Murray, A
Bartlett, A — L (2002-2004)
Allison, L — L (2004--2008)
Ridgeway, A
Greig, B — L (August to October 2002)
Cherry, J

L Leader
DD Double Dissolution
Term in H of R (ALP)

Dec '77
Oct '80
March '83 (DD)
Dec '84
July '87
March '90
March '93
March '96
Oct '98
Nov '01
Nov '04
Nov '07
August '10

APPENDIX B

Below is a table showing the Senate numbers from 1978 to 2008.

	TOTAL	ALP	LIB/NAT	DEM	GREENS	OTHER	Majority in Senate	Balance in the Senate
1978-1981	64	26	35	2		1	LIB/NAT	No-one
1981-1983	64	27	31	5		1	LIB/NAT	Harradine/Dem
1983-1985	64	30	28	5		1	ALP	Dem
1985-1987	76	34	33	7		2	ALP	Dem
1987-1990	76	32	34	7		3	LIB/NAT	Dem
1990-1993	76	32	34	8	1	1	LIB/NAT	Dem
1993-1996	76	30	36	7	2	1	LIB/NAT	Dem/Harradine/Greens
1996-1999	76	28	37	7	2	2	LIB/NAT	Dem/Greens/Other
1999-2002	76	29	35	9	1	2	LIB/NAT	Dem/Greens/Other
2002-2005	76	29	35	8	2	1	LIB/NAT	Dem/Greens/One Nation
2005-2008	76	28	39	4	4	1	LIB/NAT	Family First

APPENDIX C

CITIZENS FOR DEMOCRACY COMMITTEE

Three Co-ordinators:	Bev Floyd
	Peter Meggitt
	Di Zetlin (then, Brian Hoepper)
Financial Secretary:	Bob Leach
Original committee members	Ian Lowe
	Lorraine Brazel
	Chris Griffith
	Joan Shears
	Tim Grau
	Darryl Grigg
	Ian Maclean
	Georgina Fatseas
	Noel Turner
	Drew Hutton
	Craig Boules
	Gay Pittam
	Alan Bradley

APPENDIX D

DEMOCRAT ACHIEVEMENTS

In 2007 a thin booklet was published by the Australian Democrats which contained potted histories of each successful Democrat or member of a Parliament within Australia. That booklet was '30 years Australian Democrats'. It also listed outcomes that senators thought were their major achievements:

General

- *Maintained the inalienable right of Indigenous Australians to the land*
- *The Rainforests Preservation Agreements Bill 1982 was the first legislative attempt to protect Australia's rainforests.*
- *Amendments to Income Tax Assessment Act (1981) to remove tax deductions for destroying native trees.*
- *Great Barrier Reef Marine Park amendment (Prohibition of Mining or Drilling Activities) Bill 1985 and the Queensland Rainforests Conservation Bill 1984.*
- *Blocked the amalgamation of the ABC and SBS and in 1988 blocked timed local calls by Telecom.*
- *Fought to save the Daintree rainforest through amendments to the World Heritage Properties Conservation Act in 1986, aspects of which were eventually taken up by the ALP in 1988.*
- *In the forefront of the movement against joint American military bases in Australia.*
- *Campaigned for a bill to have both Houses of Parliament approve overseas troop deployments, with the Defence Amendment (Overseas Troops) Bill 1985 coming twice before the Parliament.*

Haines

- *Spoke on the rights of Aboriginal people and the continuing disadvantage that they faced, in her maiden speech to Parliament.*
- *Spoke about the rights of women and strongly criticised the availability of pornography and its impact on attitudes towards women.*
- *Spoke frequently about the importance of education.*
- *Introduced a bill to implement the International Covenant on Civil and Political Rights.*
- *Fought to have childcare facilities in the Parliamentary triangle.*

- *Was a key player in the debate on sales tax and argued against imposing a tax on clothing and footwear, books, newspapers and building materials.*
- *Strengthened the Commonwealth sex discrimination legislation.*

Mason

- *Introduced the World Heritage Properties Conservation Bill in 1983.*
- *Introduced a bill for a referendum to ask the Australian people whether they wanted citizenship-initiated legislation.*
- *Major mover in the Royal Commission that eventually resulted in freeing Lindy Chamberlain.*

Macklin

- *Nuclear disarmament in the midst of the Cold War.*
- *Convinced the Government to protect Moreton Island from sandmining.*
- *Worked to have the Government establish the Vietnam Veteran Counselling Service.*
- *Successfully amended legislation to establish the first oversight body in Australia of ASIO.*
- *Amended legislation to gain tax deductibility for Nursing Mothers of Australia and Amnesty International.*
- *Ensured radical reform of Australia's antiquated electoral laws for the first time in 60 years.*
- *For the first time in Australia's democratic history had donations to political parties disclosed to the public.*
- *Argued for the right of East Timorese to self-determination not to be cast aside so Australia could make money from their oil.*
- *Argued for World Heritage values to be incorporated into domestic law.*
- *Argued for electronic advertising of cigarettes to be banned.*
- *Argued that prisoners be given the right to vote.*

Siddons

- *Negotiated with Paul Keating on the capital gains tax e.g. none on the family home.*
- *Introduced an Industrial democracy bill through the Senate.*
- *Campaigned on the nuclear issue and on nuclear power.*

Evans

- *Initiated High Court actions against Malcolm Fraser and Bob Hawke for misleading advertising in the lead-up to his election campaign.*
- *Involved in the campaign to save the Franklin River.*
- *Initiated the 'Cherry Pickers Bill', which was the first private members bill passed by the Parliament for many years.*

Vigor

- *Established a scheme to provide risk capital to inventors.*
- *Campaigned on effective labelling and packaging of consumer products.*
- *Introduced the Hare-Clark voting system to the Australian Capital Territory.*
- *Highlighted problems with the Australia Card.*
- *Succeeded in having smoking banned on aircraft.*

Sanders

- *Involved in the campaign to block the Franklin Dam in Tasmania.*
- *Made improvements to civil aviation by introducing amendments to aviation legislation.*
- *Democrats manage to set the Civil Aviation Authority up.*

Powell

- *Established in 1987 a Senate inquiry into Agricultural and Veterinary Chemicals and their alternatives—and advocated on an ongoing basis for clean green agriculture.*
- *Successfully amended 1986 Disability Services legislation to include the psychiatrically disabled, who had been excluded.*
- *Forced numerous legislative amendments against poverty traps—and advocated on an ongoing basis for sole parents and their children.*
- *Successfully pressured the Government to remove the ban on gay people in the armed forces in 1992.*
- *Successfully introduced the Smoking and Tobacco Products Advertisements Prohibition Bill in 1989 to ban the print advertising of tobacco products.*

McLean

- *Tabled the Westpac Letters to reveal bank malpractice and corruption.*
- *Prompted the setting up of a banking inquiry.*

Jenkins

- *Raised the issue of child migration.*

- *Put forward humanitarian amendments to the Immigration legislation.*
- *Opposed American bases on Australian soil.*

Bourne

- *Took part in a first Australian delegation to investigate human rights abuses in China and Tibet.*
- *Initiated an inquiry into ways the Senate committee system could be made more responsive to the composition of the Senate.*
- *Proposed a streamlined process to refer tabled treaties to the relevant legislation committees, which led to the formation of the joint treaties committee.*
- *Reformed the committee system such that anyone could participate in any inquiry and chairs were divided between parties.*
- *Split the committee system into references and legislation committees so that any legislation could be referred to a committee.*
- *Convinced the Australian Foreign Minister to ask the Papua New Guinean Prime Minister to allow an Australian Parliamentary delegation to visit his country, and that delegation acted as a catalyst for peace.*
- *Participated as part of the Senate human rights sub-committee in visits to detention centres and writing a critical report.*
- *Was present in the Senate when the Mabo legislation went through and when the East Timor Independence ballot passed.*

Spindler

- *Spearheaded the party's campaign against the 1991 Aidex armaments exhibition.*
- *Led Democrats negotiations over the passage of the Native Title Bill 1993.*
- *Disallowed additional court fees and customs duty on wheelchairs.*
- *Amended Industrial Relations Reform Bill 1993 to prevent discrimination in employment on the basis of sexual preference, age and physical and mental disability.*
- *Tabled a Senate resolution calling on the Government to investigate ways of prohibiting imports tainted by child labour.*
- *Established a fighting fund to finance legal challenges to woodchip licences and to boost the campaign to protect endangered forests*
- *Held an enquiry independent of the Parliament when the Senate Select Committee on Tariffs 1992-3 was established.*

Kernot

- *Blocked legislation that would take the right to protection from unfair dismissal away from small business employees.*
- *Pushed for legislation that has enabled all Victorian workers under common rule awards to be covered by the full Federal award safety net.*
- *Removed tallies from allowable award matters and replaced with incentive payment.*
- *Improved the enforcement capability of the workplace relations by reviewing penalties.*
- *Moved amendments to introduce new whistle-blower provisions in workplace relations law.*
- *Participated in the passing of the Mabo legislation.*
- *Initiated the family/carers'/ leave case.*
- *Prepared a complete alternative budget.*

Coulter

- *Produced the 100-page Getting to Work policy package, with an emphasis on environmental sustainability and new, more meaningful economic indicators.*
- *Introduced the first legislation into Parliament limiting the use of ozone-depleting substances.*
- *Pushed for early action on greenhouse-gas emissions through the Senate committee system.*

Sowada

- *Initiated an inquiry into youth unemployment issues.*
- *Involved in debates on the higher education contribution scheme (HECS).*

Woodley

- *Chaired an inquiry into the deregulation of the dairy industry, but despite the report the deregulation went ahead.*
- *Involved in Mabo legislation.*

Lees

- *Blocked regulations which would have cut pharmacists' incomes from prescriptions.*
- *Forced the Government to agree to improve the Pharmaceutical Benefits Scheme safety net.*
- *Forced the Government to establish a $12 million child nutrition program.*

- *Initiated a Senate inquiry into the Government's proposed GST package.*
- *Ensured that everyday commonly used medicines would be GST free.*
- *Negotiated for specific goods with proven public health benefits such as sunscreen and Folate supplements to be GST free.*
- *Negotiated for first-aid and life-saving courses provided by not for profits to be GST free.*
- *Negotiated for complementary health service to be GST free for three years.*
- *Negotiated $240 million over four years for the Australian publishing industry.*
- *Negotiated for complementary health service to be GST free for three years.*
- *Negotiated to make fresh food GST free.*
- *Won an increase to the buffer for social security allowances, increasing social security benefits by 2 per cent in real terms.*
- *Won a lowering of the qualifying age for the age pension savings bonus to 55 years.*
- *Won an extra $15 million in assistance to the homeless through the supported assistance accommodation program.*

Stott Despoja

- *Negotiated stronger anti-piracy and copyright enforcement measures as part of the parallel importation legislation.*
- *Removed many of the worst aspects of a series of anti-terrorism amendment bills in order to uphold fundamental human rights.*
- *Persuaded the Government to remove taxation from full-time postgraduate scholarships.*
- *On two occasions forced the Government to abandon plan for voluntary student unionism.*
- *Convinced the Government to exempt family farms from the Austudy/ Youth Allowance assets test.*
- *Forced the Government to amend legislation to the Australian Research Council to ensure it had the capacity to initiate its own inquiries.*
- *Successfully lobbied the Government to implement labelling of genetically modified food.*
- *Forced the Government to introduce legislation banning human cloning and regulating therapeutic cloning and stem-cell research.*

- *Won retrospective financial support for foster parents who were denied access to childcare benefits.*
- *Successfully amended the Senate standing orders to allow women to breastfeed in the Senate.*
- *Introduced legislation to extend the Privacy Act to the private sector; after negotiations with the Government the Coalition agreed to introduce legislation if her bill was withdrawn.*
- *Introduced Australia's first and only nationally paid maternity leave legislation.*
- *Introduced a private member's bill which directly led transfer in Australia to successful passage of national stem-cell legislation, allowing somatic cell nuclear transfer in Australia.*

Allison

- *Removal of the Health Minister's veto over RU486—the nonsurgical abortion option.*
- *Forcing State and Federal Governments to adopt a national 'safe schools' framework against bullying.*
- *Negotiated a shift of $3 billion in funding over three years from excise cuts to clean fuels and greenhouse abatement.*
- *Won a national program to address persistent chemicals in the environment and national standards for the use of industrial residues.*
- *Initiated an inquiry leading to significant overhaul of Federal environment powers.*

Murray

- *Required Government Ministers to justify confidential clauses in Government contracts.*
- *Successfully moved a motion enforcing an order for tougher controls on Government advertising.*
- *Strengthened powers and independence of the office of the Inspector General of Taxation.*
- *Initiated Auditor-General's performance audit into politicians' entitlements.*
- *Instigated an inquiry into children in institutional care that produced two unanimous reports.*
- *Successfully argued for greater disclosure of company directors' golden handshakes.*

- *Convinced the Government to establish a charities consultative committee within the tax office.*

Bartlett

- *Personally negotiated the amendment and passage of the act which ensured the permanent protection of a range of important heritage and environmental sites on former Defence lands around Sydney Harbour.*
- *Successfully amended the Taxation Act to allow tax deductibility for land -conservation measures.*
- *Successfully campaigned against the renewal of sand-mining leases at Shelburne Bay in far north Queensland.*
- *Was the only Federal politician to visit the refugees on Nauru, playing a key role in achieving their eventual freedom.*
- *Established a Senate inquiry into the unresolved scandal of the stolen wages of thousands of Aboriginal people.*

Ridgeway

- *Dealt with Indigenous issues in a way that kept the debate alive.*
- *Achieved recognition for midwives under general public funding for Medicare.*
- *Helped to shape discussion on national identity and cultural diversity in this country.*
- *Negotiated with the Prime Minister to acknowledge Indigenous peoples in the new preamble proposed for the Commonwealth constitution.*

Greig

- *Introduced a bill to give effect to the Convention on the Prevention and Punishment of the Crime of Genocide.*
- *Introduced a bill to eliminate discrimination against gay, lesbian and bisexual.*
- *Introduced a bill to promote government use of open-source software above all others.*

Cherry

- *Negotiated $52 million reform to social security breaches to remove unfair treatment of job seekers with minor faults.*
- *Forced the Government to give 40,000 remote-area Telstra-users access to local calls and low-cost Internet connections.*
- *Negotiated with Allison for same-sex couples to be granted equal access to superannuation.*

- *Negotiated $460 million of extra payments for low-income earners' superannuation co-contributions offset by reduced tax cuts for high-income earners.*
- *Negotiated with Allison to deliver choice of super funds to workers and achieved significant further consumer protections.*

APPENDIX E

DEMOCRAT IDEOLOGY[1] BY HIROYA SUGITA

'...careful analysis of the Democrats' party platform ... makes it possible to extract the general thrust of the Democrats' officially endorsed ideological character:

1 distinctive emphasis on social justice and improvement of equality not only by economic, but also by social and cultural means;

2 a robust commitment to improving the quality of life, protecting the environment and achieving an environmentally sustainable economy;

3 firm stand on civil and moral liberties based on their belief in individual conscience and initiative;

4 promotion of community activities by decentralising powerful sectional interests; and

5 belief in participation in various decision-making processes and in a cooperative approach based on maximum consensus.

Judging from these traits of the Democrats' platform, the Democrats' ideological character can be summarised as combining social liberalism with post-materialism.

Social liberalism was well presented in the early 20th century by L.T. Hobhouse in his book *Liberalism* (Hobhouse 1911). While based on the principle of individual initiative rather than on a collectivist idea, social liberalism places greater emphasis on social provision. In essence, Hobhouse argued for:

1 equality of opportunity, including gender equality;

2 importance of achieving the 'common good' such as securing equitable distribution of wealth and guaranteeing 'the right to work and the right to a living wage';

3 state's justifiable, and desirable, function for achieving the 'common good';

4 certain degree of state ownership; and

5 taxation as a means to facilitate achieving the 'common good'. (Hobhouse 1911)

The concept of post-materialism was developed by Inglehart (Inglehart 1977, 1985, 1990). Expanding Maslow's theory of a 'hierarchy of needs', he categorises Maslow's five needs into materialist needs (survival and safety) and post-materialist needs (affection, esteem and self-actualisation) and argues that, in affluent and developed societies, the values of the middle class have undergone a gradual shift from materialist needs to post-materialist needs (Inglehart 1990:11)'.

APPENDIX F

CHIPP WAS INTERVIEWED ON THE ANDREW DENTON SHOW

Andrew Denton: One other leader. Somebody who you supported, Natasha Stott Despoja. Was it a mistake do you think, did you make an error of judgement with her?

Don Chipp: At the time of appointing her, of recommending her be leader. Yes, I think so. I don't think she was ready. She said she was ready, but I don't think she was. Wonderful lady, magnificent human being, great with the one-liner, quick, I think was too young to be thrust into that hell of a position of leading a third party and negotiating with… because a third party balance of power means that you control the bloody Parliament.

Andrew Denton: Mm, did she have the intelligence?

Don Chipp: Oh yes.

Andrew Denton: Do you think [she was ready] for it?

Don Chipp: Yeah. She also fell in love at the same time. I think that might have distracted her.

APPENDIX G

TEN POINT PLAN

1 That the party-room move to establish a constructive working relationship with Senator Lees as a like-minded Independent, and that the Whip make contact with Senator Lees and report to the next party-room meeting on the outcomes of the meeting.

2 That the party-room establish a Working Party to establish a Code of Conduct for staff and also for Senators dealings with staff. This working party shall consist of two senators and two staff (one Leaders, one electorate) elected by the staff. That the Group report back to the party-room by the end of September.

3 That the party-room adopt the following protocol for Leader's staffing:

- That the party-room conduct an annual needs analysis of staffing needs with a view to allocating staff according to party-room agreed priority issues and portfolios;
- That all staff be subject to annual performance appraisals which involve the Leader and the relevant portfolio Senators, or, in the case of senior strategic and media staff, all Senators;
- That a working group of the Leader, the Deputy and two staff representatives develop job descriptions, performance appraisal and professional development procedures;
- That the selection panel for portfolio researchers shall consist of the Leader (or her nominee) and the relevant portfolio Senators;
- That portfolio positions shall be advertised externally unless that selection panel agrees that an exceptional case exists;
- That where there is conflict over the prioritisation of the work of a researcher between senators, the matter shall be referred to the party-room for resolution.

4 That the Leader provide a report to the party-room detailing any role (if any) that her staff played in the activation, prosecution, support or halting of action against Senator Lees by the organisational wing of the party.

5 That following the August sittings Senators agree to the engagement of an independent facilitator (e.g. Di Bretherton) to work through conflicts in the party-room and assist with the development of new protocols.

6 That the Whip contact the National President with a view to developing a draft protocol for interaction between the party-room and National Executive and discussing the National Executive's proposal for a

Parliamentary code of conduct, and report back initially to party-room by the end of August.

7 That the party-room adopt a protocol that no senator, including the Leader, will formally or informally lodge a complaint against another Senator without first raising the matter in the party-room with a view to mediation.

8 That the party-room establish a committee of three headed by the Leader to draft a report to the National Compliance Committee Review Committee that deals with the proper balance between the right of Senators to speak out and their constitutional obligations.

9 That the party-room advise the National President and the National Policy Co-ordinator of concerns with the National Executive motion restricting the right of Senators to speak on policy during election campaigns and invite the National Policy Co-ordinator to meet with the Senators to discuss concerns that portfolio holders have in relation to the formulation of party policy, explore ways of improving the policy process and explore issues of presentation of policy during campaigns.

10 That the party-room advise all members of the National Management Committee and National Compliance Committee that the interests of reconciliation and rebuilding within the party would best be served by a moratorium on any disciplinary action against any member arising out of the issues of the past two months.

APPENDIX H

THE TRANSCRIPT: BJELKE-PETERSEN ON THE DOCTRINE OF THE SEPARATION OF POWERS.

Bryan Palmer's excellent website on Australian politics preserved the interplay between Forde and Bjelke-Petersen at the Fitzgerald Inquiry into the Possible Illegal Activities and Associated Police Misconduct:

> **Michael Forde**: What do you understand by the doctrine of the separation of powers under the Westminster system?
>
> **Sir Joh Bjelke-Petersen**: The Westminster system? The stock?
>
> **Forde**: The doctrine of the separation of powers under the Westminster system?
>
> **Bjelke-Petersen**: No, I don't quite know what you're driving at. The document?
>
> **Forde:** No, I'll say it again. What do you understand by the doctrine of the separation of powers under the Westminster system?
>
> **Bjelke-Petersen**: I don't know which doctrine you refer to.
>
> **Forde**: There is only one doctrine of the separation of powers.
>
> **Bjelke-Petersen**: I believe in it very strongly, and despite what you may say, I believe that we do have a great responsibility to the people who elect us to government. And that's to maintain their freedom and their rights, and I did that—sought to do it—always.
>
> **Forde**: I'm sure you're trying to be responsive to the question, but the question related to the doctrine of the separation of powers or the principles.
>
> **Bjelke-Petersen**: Between the Government and the—Is it?
>
> **Forde**: No, you tell me what you understand.
>
> **Bjelke-Petersen**: Well, the separation of the doctrine that you refer to, in relation to where the Government stands, and the rest of the community stands, or where the rest of the instruments of Government stand. Is that what--?
>
> **Forde:** No.
>
> **Bjelke-Petersen**: Well you tell me. And I'll tell you whether you're right or not. Don't you know?

APPENDIX I

FROM THE FOREWORD TO THE REPORT ON WORKPLACE BULLYING. 2012

In workplaces across the country, tragically there are too many Australians being bullied at work. This problem is not exclusive to one jurisdiction, one industry or one 'type' of worker.

Described as a form of psychological violence, workplace bullying can result in significant damage to an individual's health and wellbeing, and in extreme cases can lead targets of bullying to suicide. Such behaviour can also undercut the productivity of an entire organisation, which incurs financial costs to employers and the national economy. Beyond the enormous personal and organisational costs, the Productivity Commission estimates that workplace bullying costs the Australian economy between $6 billion and $36 billion annually.

The Committee's inquiry was announced against the backdrop of an ongoing, nation-wide harmonisation process of work health and safety legislation, the primary area of regulation of the risks of bullying at work. Since the Committee adopted this report in late October 2012, the South Australian Parliament passed model work health and safety legislation on 1 November 2012. Harmonised work health and safety laws have now been adopted in all jurisdictions, with the exceptions of Victoria and Western Australia.

In addition to harmonisation efforts, governments, unions and industry groups are collaborating to develop a nationally consistent Code of Practice on workplace bullying. The purpose of the Code is to provide practical guidance to workers and employers to tackle immediate concerns, as well as to assist them to achieve the goal of positive, functional and productive workplaces.

The Committee trusts that this report complements the ongoing efforts of the State and Territory governments to harmonise work health and safety laws as well as the finalisation of the Code.

All too frequently the Committee heard about the regulatory 'minefield' that both individual workers and employers face when confronted with bullying at work. These challenges add layers of complexity to already difficult experiences.

Diverse and contrasting regulation complicates broad public understanding of these laws as well as the system which enforces their application. This is the reason why the Committee is calling for a new single national advisory service to help workers and employers to identify what is and what is not bullying behaviour; to clarify the extent to which workplace bullying is dealt with by workplace health and safety legislation versus antidiscrimination law, industrial relations' instruments, workers' compensation schemes and, in some cases, criminal law; and to provide a range of options for resolving the problem. Although the Committee heard that Australia's approach to addressing workplace bullying, through a risk-management rubric, is an example of international bullying, as well as better support those workers who have been bullied, best practice, the Committee believes that there is real momentum in the Australian community to do more to prevent and manage.

APPENDIX J

WHAT CAME BEFORE THE DEMOCRAT PHENOMENON? COMPILED BY THE AUTHOR

To seek an answer, it is necessary to take a trip back in time to South Australia and Victoria where two centrist political parties, the New Liberal Movement and the Australia Party, were the genesis of the Australian Democrats.

In South Australia, during the premiership of Tom Playford, conservatism in the Liberal Country League (LCL) maintained an electoral malapportionment in favour of rural areas. (This was sometimes called a '*Playmander*'.)

Steele Hall, who followed Playford as LCL leader, won the election with 19 of the 39 seats yet only 43.8% of the vote, prompting a public outcry for electoral system reform. Hall was determined to change the LCL culture and initially tried to do so internally.

He and Robin Millhouse were among a group of LCL Parliamentarians committed to electoral reform. The 1970 loss to Don Dunstan's Labor Party split the LCL. Although Hall was re-elected leader, his job was almost impossible as the conservative wing would not give ground on electoral reform. Meanwhile, Premier Dunstan began the reform process.

In 1972 Hall resigned as leader and went on to lead the New Liberal reform group within the LCL. This group, initially a 'faction' in the LCL, was now a 'movement'—essentially a party, with its own pre-selections, branches, publicity and organisation. Labor's 1973 election win resulted in significant gains for The Liberal Movement. The LCL moved against Hall and the LM. In the wash-up, most LM parliamentary members left the movement. Only Hall, Millhouse and Cameron remained.

A new party was formed. It already had significant organisational structure and soon ran well. At the next election, Hall won a Legislative Council seat, and the party also won Hall's previous Legislative Assembly seat in a by-election. However, with the success of Dunstan's electoral reform bill, the Liberal Movement's 'raison d'etre' melted away. Hall and Millhouse tried to turn the LM into a national party but failed, although much later some state branches still existed. By this time, the Australia Party had formed and talks were held to see if a merger could be organised. Nothing came of it. Finally, in 1976, with the LM running out of steam and the character of the LCL significantly changed, a merger was arranged with the LCL. Steele Hall and most LM members returned to the conservative fold.

Millhouse was not of a mind to re-join the LCL and formed a new party, the New Liberal Movement (NLM). He believed in the value of a 'third party' that was neither Liberal nor Labor. This became a major theme in the Australian Democrats' genesis. Hall's personal assistant in the LM was Janine Haines. She remained with the NLM. Early in 1977, Millhouse, Haines and NLM supporters were prominent in the enthusiastic gatherings at the Australian Democrats' formation.

The reforming Liberal Movement in South Australia has been an example of a brave attempt to change political bias and infuse a more egalitarian approach into government. It was, in an indirect way, eventually successful and after the problem had been resolved by a combination of forces its strength ebbed. South Australian electoral reform is a powerful story.

Steele Hall played a part as an honest man who saw that electoral malapportionment was not good for his State. He toiled year after year to bring his party around, failed and went on to co-found another party. Eventually, when his task was done, albeit by another party, he returned to his original political home.

On the other hand, Robin Millhouse had remade himself and saw a future where neither Liberal nor Labor would automatically dominate political agendas in government. They would always have to answer to a third force, a broker for good sense and intelligent change. By his side was an extremely intelligent, far-seeing woman, Janine Haines.

This shows that what it takes to achieve great outcomes is to believe they are possible and *never give up*. You may not be the one to carry them into fruition, but your efforts will lay the foundation for another generation.

THE AUSTRALIA PARTY

The party started in 1966. Gordon Barton placed a full page advertisement in the Sydney Morning Herald—'An open letter to the President of the United States of America.'* Lyndon Baines Johnson was visiting Australia at the time and the Vietnam War was a contentious issue.

Barton was a successful entrepreneur. He was wealthy, clever and well-educated—a hard-to-match combination. But, more than any of that, he cared about what was happening. He was involved and acted on his belief. The letter ended with the words: 'People all over the world are tired of military solutions and power politics. They are tired of anti-communism as a substitute for common-sense. And above all they are tired of the killing. As

* See Appendix K for full text of the advertisement.

one of these people, and as a person having no connection or influence with any political party or organisation whatsoever, I have written this letter as a matter of personal conscience'.

A thousand or more people responded after the letter's publication and, although Barton had written it as a personal statement, the Liberal Reform Group soon formed at a meeting at his home and stood candidates at the 1972 elections with the aim of reforming the Liberal Party. In 1967 the name was changed to ARM (Australian Reform Movement).

A newsletter, *Reform,* soon allowed the exchange of views in the party. It produced lively conversations and debate. Its editor, Laurie Hull, was a fervent supporter of freedom of speech.

In 1969 Reg Turnbull, a senator from Tasmania, agreed to lead the party to the next election. The name was changed to the Australia Party. The election results were disappointing and Turnbull resigned from the party.

However, dedicated people carried on and the 1970s brought a more successful time with some election wins. During this period John Siddons joined. He later became an Australian Democrat senator.

In early 1977 Siddons approached Chipp to sound him out about leading a new party to the next election. The rest is relatively modern history.

WHAT CAN BE LEARNED FROM THESE FORERUNNERS TO THE AUSTRALIAN DEMOCRATS?

In the case of the Australia Party successful business men with resources supported the fledgling organisation. In the case of the Liberal Movement in South Australia, Hall and Millhouse kept the fledgling party in the parliamentary structure so had related resources.

The era from the 1960s to the '80s brought a transition—changes resulted from post-modern thinking. Authority was challenged. Blacks, women, children were liberated from second-class citizenship. The rationale for the Vietnam War (and its carnage) was challenged. Popular music reinforced the changes. Environmental damage was reassessed and people woke up to the need to protect the Earth.

APPENDIX K

AN OPEN LETTER TO THE PRESIDENT OF THE UNITED STATES

Gordon Barton, full-page in the *Sydney Morning Herald* on October 22, 1966

Dear Mr President:

It is unfortunate that your welcome in Australia has been clouded by the deep disagreement in this country as to our part in the Vietnamese War. I am concerned that the thought, comment and actions of our Government have reflected very little of this disagreement, nor indeed much awareness of what is involved.

The fact that out of a population of 11 million we have had to depend on conscripts to make up two battalions to send to Vietnam is a sufficient indication that enthusiasm for this war is very largely confined to our politicians and their military advisers.

These are some of the reasons for this lack of enthusiasm:

The Vietnamese War has become known as a 'dirty' war. This is so partly because of the hardly disguised cynicism and brutality with which it has been conducted over the 20 years it has been going on, partly because it retains much of its original character of a colonial war, and partly because of the suffering of the civilian population.

Our problem is to satisfy ourselves that we have some very good reason to take part in this 'dirty' war.

Since it is clear enough that the only foreign military forces in Vietnam are those of America and her allies it is very difficult for us to accept the fiction that we are merely helping the Vietnamese people to defend themselves against outside aggression.

Most people accept the common-sense view that there is a civil war in Vietnam and we have decided to support one side. Unfortunately, it is equally clear that the side we are supporting seems to command very little respect or affection either inside or outside Vietnam.

The Government in Saigon is unstable, inefficient and corrupt. That it survives because of the support of what is virtually an occupation army of Americans has not enhanced its popularity.

It is our bitter experience, on the other hand, that a very large number of Vietnamese resent and oppose our intervention in their affairs. That we have a military force of some half million Americans, Australians and Koreans trying to pacify some of these Vietnamese opponents is some evidence of their dedication and the strength of their support amongst the population.

The more honest, if less attractive reason for our intervention in Vietnam is that irrespective of the moral issues involved in the Vietnamese civil war, we have intervened to protect our interests.

Just as you Americans feel threatened by world communism, so do we Australians feel threatened by the prospect of the strong, militant and unfriendly

Asia. As one member of our Government put it to me 'We've got to stop these –'s before they get here.'

It is no small thing to be willing to kill people in a remote country which has offered us no provocation merely to safeguard what we conceive to be our political interests. I believe such a policy will fail by its moral bankruptcy alone.

But it is worse than this.

Our immediate objective is to halt the progress of communism in Vietnam. Yet by our own military policies of 'kill and destroy' we are creating the very conditions of social and economic chaos which communists need for their success.

At the same time we have associated the cause of anti-communism with the brutality, repression and corruption of a thoroughly discredited junta of generals.

Whatever your military advisers say, Mr President, the burning of crops, the bombing of villages, the killing of men, women and children are no way to improve a political situation.

On the wider international scene this war is doing the cause of communism very little harm.

Nor is it doing us much good.

People all over the world are tired of military solutions and power politics. They are tired of anti-communism as a substitute for commonsense. And above all they are tired of the killing. As one of these people, and as a person having no connection or influence with any political party or organisation whatsoever, I have written this letter as a matter of personal conscience.

Friday 21 October 1966

Yours sincerely

Gordon Barton

Authorised by Mr G. P. Barton,

22 Morella Place, Castle Cove.

APPENDIX L

NOT JUST A DREAM

Written by the author in 2013 for the re-emerging Australian Democrats

> Masculinity and femininity have nothing to do with being locked into a male or female body. If we are biologically female the ego is feminine and we carry within us our own inner masculinity, what Jung calls the animus. If we are biologically male, the ego is masculine and the man carries within himself his own inner femininity, the anima. Masculinity and femininity are not matters of gender, though historically in our Western culture their long identification with gender still makes it difficult for us to view them in this liberated way.
>
> *Addiction to Perfection by Marion Woodman* [1]

I have a dream that society and Parliaments of the future will step up to the challenge of integrating masculine and feminine roles.

The masculine, testosterone-driven adversarial mode has driven public discourse for thousands of years, and while there has been considerable change in the treatment of women in our society and the subsequent change in male behaviours, the complete evolution to equality and balance has not yet occurred. We are still mired in the idea that men must be 'men' and women must be 'women'. The position we need to attain is one where each event triggers an appropriate response. In some cases that is 'masculine', protective, angry, strong, wild; in others it is 'feminine', nurturing, kindly, compassionate, or even a mixture. While being authentic, we also need to act appropriately, according to the situation and to the people to whom we are relating.

In the Parliament Democrat Senators tried to steer a middle course politically. They modified the adversarial Parliamentary system by the expansion of committee structures where politicians could behave in a rational, compassionate and co-operative manner. They tried to 'play the ball and not the man'. They advocated reasonable and humane policies.

But if you like, they were just the first wave in the battle to change our society. Unfortunately, the party dissolved in a tidal wave of inappropriate interpersonal behaviours.

Part of that was the inability of the people involved to lift their eyes to the higher goal they had in common. Their goal was the one I am trying to describe, not just the words *honest, tolerant and compassionate*, but the living example.

If members and supporters could focus on this goal, and if they had sufficient support to lift their game then the Democrats could become a positive and permanent force in Australia, but the 'new' Democrats will go the way of the 'old' Democrats if they cannot learn from the past.

The 'old' Democrats were only halfway to this idea. *Honesty, tolerance and compassion.* We knew the words and many of us practised the actions on and off; but we were unable to translate it into a new paradigm for the society. We fell short. We saw only dimly what we were really trying to achieve.

There were arguments everywhere. It wasn't just personal failures that caused the arguments, although that certainly was part of the cause. It was often the misguided belief that our values were so much better than others and we had to 'fight' for them; that the end justified the means.

My hope, however, is that the 'new' Democrats will not give up until they have realised the dream of civilised and intelligent discourse in our Parliaments; until they have set the bar high for discourse across the country—in pubs, clubs and various organisations. It is an impossible dream, but the impossible *can* happen.

APPENDIX M

SAVING THE FRANKLIN

20 years on, history is being re-written about the saving of the Franklin River in South West Tasmania and the role played by the Democrats is being written out. Andrew Darby's piece (Perspective 24/12) fails to mention Democrat senators, Don Chipp, Colin Mason and Norm Sanders, without whose work the Franklin dam would have become a reality.

Darby even quotes blockader Chris Harries but fails to mention he was Norm Sanders' staffer or that Don Chipp, Democrats Leader, rafted down the Franklin, much of the journey with a broken arm, accompanied by wife Idun, Norm Sanders and Democrat Senator Jack Evans.

Dr Bob Brown, head of the Tasmanian Wilderness Society, was a committed advocate but his effectiveness was dwarfed by Democrats who took the fight up at the highest level.

Dr Norm Sanders was Brown's mentor and handed over to him his position as director of the Tasmanian Wilderness Society when Sanders won a seat in the Tasmanian parliament in 1979. Sanders took the Franklin into the state house, leaving Brown to run the campaign on the ground.

Two years later Don Chipp initiated a landmark Senate select committee inquiry into 'the natural values of South-West Tasmania to Australia and the world' and 'the federal responsibility in assisting Tasmania to preserve its wilderness areas of national and international importance'.

Graham Richardson, an ALP Opposition member of the Senate committee, was won over when he saw the Franklin firsthand and understood the importance of keeping it from the clutches of the Hydro Electric Commission (HEC). The committee recommended that 'the Franklin River be preserved in its natural state as a matter of national priority'.

Don Chipp also met with the HEC, armed with research by Colin Mason that demolished the arguments that more hydro was needed. Chipp, the consummate politician, and Sanders, the scientist, exposed the Commission's real agenda which was to create massive surpluses of hydro power and drive the price down in the hope of attracting big industry to Tasmania. James McQueen's 1983 account of the Franklin campaign, said of Norm Sanders;

> He's done much more than help to discredit the HEC; he has induced in it a reaction close to paranoia. From the beginning of the blockade until late January, he seemed hardly to be out of the air. When he wasn't spotting oil slicks on the Gordon, he was breaking the illegal

> jamming of blockaders' radio equipment; when he wasn't spotting HEC operations for the greenies on the ground, he was photographing the Cape Martin, a fishing boat under charter to the HEC as it ploughed through a line of greenie rafts; and when he wasn't doing that sort of thing he was being televised or reported.

In December 1982, Sanders resigned from the Tasmanian Parliament to contest a Senate seat. His seat was filled by Brown.

Two months earlier, the Sydney Morning Herald had published a survey showing 75% public opposition to damming the Franklin and Democrats Senator Colin Mason's World Heritage Properties Protection Bill was introduced and debated at length in the Senate. The ALP voted for the bill and Liberal Senators Neville Bonner and Alan Missen crossed the floor – their votes taking it over the line. (Malcolm Fraser called a double dissolution before it could be sent to the Reps.) On the same day the Tasmanian South West was approved for World Heritage Listing.

The ALP won that 1983 election, as least partly on the strength of promising to protect the Franklin and World Heritage sites. Prime Minister Hawke introduced legislation soon after taking office that was a re-write of the Democrat's bill. Automatic listing of World Heritage sites was missing but the bill was strengthened to provide standing to World Heritage area users.

That legislation was a significant turning point for environmental law in Australia and preceded legislation in 1999 that gave greater powers to the Commonwealth. In this the Democrats again played a constructive role, firstly initiating an inquiry in 1997 into Federal environment powers and then negotiating over 500 amendments to strengthen the 1999 legislation.

Our work in the Parliament continues. From 1 January 2003, the sulphur content in diesel will be halved. Sulphur is the main cause of the black smoke from trucks and buses that triggers asthma and other illnesses. This was another win for the environment and for public health … negotiated by the Democrats.

I'm getting fed up with our history being ignored or hijacked by the Greens Party acolytes who capitalise on and plagiarise the work of genuine parliamentary reformists.

The Democrats were at the Franklin in the 80's and, with seven Senators still effectively holding the balance of power and four MPs in state parliaments, we are still chalking up wins on the environment, in case anyone should think otherwise from the current spate of revisionism.

Lyn Allison
Deputy Leader & Senator for Victoria
2005

BIBLIOGRAPHY

Australian Democrats, *30 years Australian Democrats*
Published by Australian Democrats, PO Box 135, East Melbourne, Vic. 2007.

Baird, Julia, *Media Tarts*
Published by Scribe Publications, Melbourne. 2004.

Chipp, Donald and Larkin, J (ED.), *Chipp*
Published by Methuen Haynes, North Ryde, NSW. 1987.

Coaldrake, Peter, *Working the System*
Published by University of Queensland Press, St. Lucia. Queensland. 1989.

Cox, Eva, *A Truly civil society—1995 Boyer Lectures*
Published by ABC books. Sydney. 1995.

Dickie, Phil, *The road to Fitzgerald*
Published by University of Queensland Press, St. Lucia, Queensland. 1988.

Everingham, Sam, *Gordon Barton—Australia's maverick entrepreneur.*
Published by Allen & Unwin, 83 Alexander Street, Crows Nest, NSW. 2065. 2009.

Haines, Janine, *Suffrage to Sufferance—100 years of women in politics*
Published by Allen and Unwin, St. Leonards, NSW. 1992.

Hawthorne, Susan, *Wild Politics*
Published by Spinifex Press. Melbourne. 2002.

Hewatt, Tim and Wilson, David *Don Chipp*
Published by Widescope International Publishers, Camberwell, Vic. 1978.

Hutton, Will, *The World we're in*
Published by Abacus (an imprint of Time Warner Books UK), London. 2003.

Hutton, Will, *The State To Come*
Published by Vintage. Random House, London. 1997.

Hutton, Will, *The State We're In*
Published by Johnathan Cape, London. 1995.

Katter, Bob, *A Passionate history of Australia*
Published by Pier 9, an imprint of Murdoch Books Pty. Ltd. 2012.

Kelsey, Jane, *The New Zealand experiment*
Published by Auckland University Press, Auckland. 1995.

Kernot, Cheryl, *Speaking for myself again*
Published by Harper Collins, Sydney. 2002.

Koch, T A, *Prescription for change—the Terry White Story*
Published by University of Queensland Press, Brisbane. 2010.

McKeering, Brian, *History of South Brisbane College of Technical and Further Education*
Published by Boolarong Publications, Brookes Street, Bowen Hills, Brisbane. 1988.

Megalogenis, G, *The Australian moment*
Published by Viking, an imprint of Penguin Books, 250 Camberwell Road, Camberwell, Victoria. 3124. Australia. 2012.

O'Reilly, David, *The woman most likely—Cheryl Kernot*
Published by Random House Australia Pty. Ltd., Sydney. 1998.

Pusey, Michael, *Economic Rationalism in Canberra*
Published by Cambridge University Press, Cambridge. 1991.

Reynolds, Paul, *Lock, Stock and Barrel*
Published by University of Queensland Press, St. Lucia, Queensland. 2002.

Rogers, Alison, *The Natasha Factor*
Published by Thomas C. Lothian Pty Ltd, 132 Albert Road, South Melbourne, 3205. 2004.

Schaef, Anne Wilson, *Women's Reality*
Published by Winston Press. Minneapolis. 1981.

Warhurst, John (ED.), *Keeping the Bastards Honest*
Published by Allen and Unwin Pty. Ltd., Sydney. 1997.

Woodman, Marion, *Addiction to Perfection—the Still Unravished Bride*
A psychological study. Published by Inner City Books, Toronto, Canada. 1982.

I have occasionally made use of Wikipedia to check information. This is acknowledged where necessary within the text.

REFERENCES

Chapter 1 Joh's Queensland

1 Lamont, Colin.

2 Rumney, John. As told to the author

3 Katter, Bob. *A passionate history of Australia*

4 Gygar, Terry.

Chapter 2 Emergence of the Australian Democrats

1 Don Chipp's resignation speech. 1977. [See Appendix A]

2 Bowles, Peter. *Courier-Mail*

Chapter 3 Carrying on the fight

1 Journal of the Australian Democrats. 1977. Page 32. paper Dec. 5, 1977

2 Journal of the Australian Democrats. 1977. Page h2.

Chapter 4 We finally have a party!

1 Shaef, Anne. *'Women's Reality—an emerging female system in the white male society:'* Foreword

Chapter 5 President of the Queensland division

1 Kernot, Cheryl. Interview with the author. 2013

2 O'Reilly, David. *The woman most likely, Cheryl Kernot.* p. 124

3 O'Reilly, David. *The woman most likely, Cheryl Kernot.* p. 124-5

Chapter 6 The Queensland gerrymander

1 *Courier-Mail.* December 5, 1985

2 *Telegraph.* November 5, 1985

3 Mike Willesee interviews John Moore, Queensland Liberal Party President, November 6, 1985

4 *Courier-Mail.* December 10, 1985

5 *Courier-Mail.* December 11, 1985

6 *Courier-Mail.* March 25, 1986

7 *Courier-Mail*, March 27, 1986

8 *The Australian.* April 26, 1986

9 Citizens for Democracy files

10 *Courier-Mail.* March 21, 1986

11 On The Nation, March 15, 1986

12 *Stateline:* Paul Reynolds Profile. Broadcast: July 4, 2008. Reporter: John Taylor

13 *The Bulletin.* May 13, 1986

14 Wikipedia. Legislative Assembly of Queensland

Chapter 7 Democrats in the Senate 1978—1990

1 Senate Hansard, 19 November 1982

2 O'Reilly, David. The woman most likely—Cheryl Kernot, p.216

3 Haines, Janine. Suffrage to Sufferance—100 years of women in politics. p.1

4 Macklin, Michael. from *30 years Australian Democrats*

5 Evans, Jack. from *30 years Australian Democrats*

6 Lee, Meg. from *30 years Australian Democrats*

7 Sanders, Norm. from *30 years Australian Democrats*

8 Sanders, Norm. from *30 years Australian Democrats*

9 Powell, Janet. from *30 years Australian Democrats*

10 Kernot, Cheryl. interview with author, 2013

11 McLean, Paul. from *30 years Australian Democrats*

12 Jenkins, Jean. from *30 years Australian Democrats*

Chapter 8 Democrats in the Senate 1990-1995

1 Kernot, Cheryl. interview with author. 2013

2 Lees, Meg. interview with author. 2013

3 Stott Despoja, Natasha. from *30 years Australian Democrats*

4 Bourne, Vicki. from *30 years Australian Democrats*

5 Sowada, Karen. from *30 years Australian Democrats*

6 Spindler from *30 Years Australian Democrats*

7 Woodley, John. interview with author. 2013

Chapter 9 Democrats in the Senate 1995—1997

1 Stott Despoja, Natasha. from *30 years Australian Democrats*

2 *The Australian Financial Review.* Jan 20, 1997.

3 Allison, Lyn. from *30 years Australian Democrats*

4 Murray, Andrew. from *30 years Australian Democrats*

5 Woodley, John. Interview with author. 2013

Chapter 10 Democrats in the Senate 1997—2008

1 Bartlett, Andrew. from 30 years Australian Democrats

2 Cherry, John. from *30 years Australian Democrats*

3 Ridgeway, Aden. from *30 years Australian De*mocrats

4 Greig, Brian. from *30 years Australian Democrats*

5 Lees, Meg. Interview with author. 2013

Chapter 11 The beginning of the end

1 Oss-Emer, Liz. Interview with author. 2014

2 Oss-Emer, Liz. Interview with author. 2014

3 Rogers, Alison. The Natasha Factor, p. 100.

4 Oss-Emer, Liz. Interview with author. 2014

5 Oss-Emer, Liz. Interview with author. 2014

6 Oss-Emer, Liz. Interview with author. 2014

Chapter 12 Work can be hell

1 O'Reilly, David. *The woman most likely, Cheryl Kernot.* pp. 124-5

2 Hawthorne, Susan. *Wild Politics.* p.175

3 Wikipedia. November 13, 2012

Chapter 13 Conversations with Democrats

1 Megalogenis, George. *The Australian Moment*, p. 289

2 *30 Years Australian Democrats*, p.43

3 Baird, Julia. *Media Tarts*, p. 154

Chapter 14 Back to shaping the future

1 Bleich, Jeff. *QnA* ABC-TV February 25, 2-13

2 Tanner, Lindsay. *Sideshow*, p.3

3 Martin, Malcolm. As told to the author, 2013

4 Walters, Tony. Interview with author, 2013

Appendix E

1 Warhurst, John. *Keeping the Bastards Honest—The Australian Democrats' first twenty years* pp. 136-7

Appendix L

1 Woodman, Marion. *Addiction to Perfection* p. 14

INDEX